Crashproof
Your Life

Crashproof
Your Life

A Comprehensive, Three-Part Plan
for **Protecting Yourself**
from **Financial Disasters**

Thomas A. Schweich

Contemporary Books

Chicago   New York   San Francisco   Lisbon   London   Madrid   Mexico City
Milan   New Delhi   San Juan   Seoul   Singapore   Sydney   Toronto

Library of Congress Cataloging-in-Publication Data

Schweich, Thomas A., 1960–
    Crashproof your life : a comprehensive, three-part plan for protecting yourself from financial disasters / Thomas A. Schweich.
        p.   cm.
    Includes index.
    ISBN 0-8092-2226-4
    1. Finance, Personal.   I.   II. Title.

HG179.S339   2002
332.024—dc21   2001037145

Contemporary Books

A Division of The McGraw·Hill Companies

1 2 3 4 5 6 7 8 9 0   VBA/VBA   0 9 8 7 6 5 4 3 2 1

ISBN 0-8092-2226-4

This book was set in Adobe Garamond
Printed and bound by Maple-Vail

Interior design by Jeanette Wojtyla

McGraw-Hill books are available at special quantity discounts to use as premiums and sales promotions, or for use in corporate training programs. For more information, please write to the Director of Special Sales, Professional Publishing, McGraw-Hill, Two Penn Plaza, New York, NY 10121-2298. Or contact your local bookstore.

This book is printed on acid-free paper.

To my wife, Kathy, and my children, Emilie and Thomas Jr.

Contents

Acknowledgments

I would like to acknowledge the efforts of the many people who made this book possible. First, I would like to thank my editor, Judith McCarthy, who has shown energy and enthusiasm for the project from the beginning and who even took the time to review a draft of the book while she was on maternity leave. Second, I would like to thank my agent, Wendy Sherman, whose attentive guidance has been indispensable to my career as a writer. I have never met a harder-working person. Third, I would like to express appreciation to my friends and colleagues who assisted me as I wrote the book. They reviewed sections of the book and provided me with their valuable comments. They include many of my colleagues at Bryan Cave LLP, including Lawrence Brody, Lucinda A. Althauser, former Senator John C. Danforth, and former United States Attorney Edward L. Dowd Jr. I would also like to thank former United States Attorney Joe D. Whitley; H. Chandler Taylor of the Moneta Group; Fielding Childress of the Charles L. Crane Agency; Eric P. Newman of the Eric P. Newman Numismatic Education Society; James C. Palmer of the Beekman Estate; John W. Walbran of The Boeing Company; my Wall Street cousin, Robert J. Schweich; and my wife, Kathy Schweich, who served as my initial copyeditor. (I, of course, made the final decisions concerning what to include in the book.) Thanks also to LEXIS/NEXIS for making my research so much easier. Finally, I would like to thank my assistants, Colleen Kashif and Kathy Morganstern, who have put in many hours helping me edit the book and planning my media and speaking engagements.

Acknowledgments

Introduction

Are your finances crashproof? Do you have the professional stability, solid investments, and protection from personal liability that can weather the economic challenges of the chaotic world around you—challenges that could range from a global financial jolt to a natural disaster, from a corporate downsizing to a nasty lawsuit brought against you by a business adversary? If you think, as many people do, that you lack such security, you need this book.

On the other hand, you may not worry about risks to your job, investments, and personal dealings. After all, you survived the turn of the millennium without so much as a hangover. In addition, despite the recent jitters in our economy, you probably made some money in the stock market during the period of booming corporate growth of the late 1990s. Further still, your professional services may be in high demand. So why worry?

Let's get something straight at the outset. If you are not worried about professional, financial, and personal risk, *you really need this book*. In an era of diminishing privacy and instant communication, and a time when a tabloid mentality is pervading the public consciousness, everything you do wrong is likely to become known by more people more quickly than at any time in the past. Worse still, everything you do *right* is more susceptible to being distorted and contorted by those who do not have your well-being at heart. As a result, regardless of whether the economy does well or poorly, more lives will suffer economic crashes in the coming years than ever before. And the most severe crashes will happen to the people who do not expect them—people who have not taken the most basic steps to prepare for the serious financial risks that could materialize in their lives at any time. If you do not believe you could crash, consider the following stories, all of which occurred during the booming economic years of the past decade.

- A star executive at a major oil company reads a joke titled "25 Reasons Why Beer Is Better than Women." He thinks the joke is hysterical. When he gets to work the next day, he E-mails the joke to a couple of friends. They forward it on to others at the company. Soon it is all over the company's E-mail system. Several women hear the joke and are extremely offended by its vulgar and sexist tone. They complain to management and file a lawsuit alleging a "hostile work environment." The company has to pay the women $2.2 million. The executive who initiated the E-mail finds that his career ends then and there.

- Executives monitoring employee Internet and E-mail use at Xerox, Dow Chemical, and the *New York Times* find that dozens of their employees use E-mail and the Internet for purposes not related to their jobs. Some forward gruesome pictures of car accidents to coworkers. Others do their gift shopping on-line during work hours. Without giving these employees a second chance, Xerox fires forty people, Dow fires ninety people, and the *New York Times* sends pink slips to twenty-two people. The fired employees all suffer major career crashes.

- A thirty-five-year-old woman puts everything she has into an Internet start-up venture in 1999, giving the company's creditors her personal guarantee that she will pay the debts that the company incurs. She has no trouble raising money for the first year, but then, after she fails to turn a profit, the sources of funding dry up. She closes up shop and finds herself sued by twelve suppliers of goods or services for more than $5 million. Like more than one million other people that year, she declares bankruptcy and loses everything.

- A family patriarch is diagnosed with Alzheimer's disease at the age of fifty-seven. He has a lifetime limit on his health insurance coverage and the policy does not cover nursing-home care. By the time he dies, the family members have spent $1.5 million of their own money to care for him, and they have virtually nothing left financially.

• A group of retirees buys an investment security from a bank. The retirees believe the investment to be an insured certificate of deposit. Bank officials represent the purchase to them as extremely safe. But the retirees do not read the prospectus, which states that the investments are uninsured and have moderate-to-high risk. The bank goes bust and the securities become worthless. Dozens of retirees find themselves wiped out financially and are forced back into the job market just at the time they planned to enjoy their golden years.

• A successful female entrepreneur is involved in a serious car accident in which she accidentally kills a twenty-one-year-old engineering student. Her legal liability runs as high as $1 million, but her automobile liability insurance covers only $300,000. She, too, suffers a total financial crash.

• A thirty-year-old man is an engineering executive at a major aerospace company. He has seven years of top performance evaluations. One day he learns that the company has decided to outsource the purchasing of the supplies that his group designs. He loses his job instantly. He joins the almost 500,000 others who had their jobs downsized or outsourced during a booming economic year. He finds a new job, but at 30 percent less money, and he has to start the process of proving himself all over again.

The stories go on and on. It is a simple truth that there are crash risks all around you, more now than ever before. To avoid them you need to be extremely well prepared, and I have the experience to prepare you. As a trial lawyer, risk-avoidance lecturer, and former prosecutor, every day I see and hear of people who have suffered economic crashes—employees who have lost their jobs, investors who have been defrauded out of their savings, families who did not understand their insurance policies. You name it and I have seen it. And in almost every single case, I say to myself, "They could have avoided it if only they had . . ."

This book will show you how to minimize and, in many cases, avoid these crash risks entirely. When you are done reading, you will be ready to contain and conquer risk in your professional, financial, and personal dealings. Indeed, once you have mastered the art of crashproofing, you will feel a sense of security that will resonate throughout your life.

The Faith and Focus Fallacies and the Theory of Crashproofing

Crashproofing is the process of identifying and avoiding potential problems in your professional, financial, and personal life. You learn the risks that face you on the job, with your investments, and at home; then you plan systematically to reduce or eliminate them. While the crashproofing process covers the essential aspects of your professional, financial, and personal life, this book covers crashproofing the only *economic* risks that might confront you—risks to the income you generate from your job, risks to the savings and investments that constitute your financial base, and risks posed by potential economic liability in your personal life. This book does not cover risks in other areas of your life, such as your physical or mental health. It also does not cover problems in your interpersonal relationships, except to the extent that these relationships endanger your professional well-being or finances, or expose you to personal financial liability. This book has a very specific purpose: making sure you get the money you need and you keep the money you have.

To begin, a simple premise will tie the entire book together: crashproofing works because it is consistent with the way everything works. It is a social and scientific fact that everything tends to crash. When I was taking high school physics and college astronomy, I remember being somewhat alarmed when I learned about the "expanding universe"—the widely accepted belief that a big bang created a universe that is moving from an initial state of total order to an eventual state of total disorder. The universe started as a dense, condensed, ordered little ball; then it exploded and expanded into a diverse, obtuse, chaotic mess. "Everything tends toward disorder," said the professors.

This fact should disturb you. To think, the whole universe is moving in the wrong direction! In fact, it is universally accepted that the universe moves to disorder—that everything is a little less ordered now than it was just a minute ago. You see the universal tendency toward disorder all around you. Civilizations struggle to survive, and then they crumble. Visit the Parthenon in Athens or the Colosseum in Rome—each a crumbling remnant of greatness; each a symbol of civilization ruined by the tendency of all things to crumble. Or, on a more basic level, look at a vase of flowers. It may fall off the table and shatter into a mess of wilted roses, glass shards, and a puddle of water, but the pieces will never pick themselves up and put themselves back together again. Your desk at work and your basement at home probably follow this same trend. Everything does.

So if the natural direction of the world, and your life, is toward disorder, it becomes an inescapable fact that everything around you will eventually crash unless you intervene to stop it from doing so. Moreover, with E-mail, the Internet, and satellite media all available to instantaneously transmit gossip, bad news, and the efforts of backstabbers, the speed at which disorder can take over your life is ever increasing. Therefore, the best way to ensure your security is to understand and plan for the risks that *will* materialize around you.

Keeping this basic principle of crashproofing in mind, you will find that this book differs from other personal finance or self-help books you may have read. This book teaches you how to work *with* the universal forces that govern us all, not against them. You watch the risks unfold, and then you take careful steps to thwart them. Other personal finance and self-help books and seminars adopt a very different approach that, in my mind, actually invites a crash. For example, many such books (and even more seminars) promote the theory that you can overcome adversity if you keep a positive attitude and have faith in the future. It all started decades ago with a children's book and the slogan "I think I can, I think I can," and it continues today with a parade of authors and motivational speakers who tell you that "with enough time, faith, and hope, things will get better."

I call this the faith fallacy. It does not work. This "I'm a winner" approach might deceive you into feeling good for a while, but it cannot work consistently for a prolonged period of time. In fact, if you rely upon faith in the future to solve your problems, your life will almost certainly crash. Why? Because when you depend on the passage of time to resolve your problems, you turn yourself over to the forces of a universe that by definition tends toward disorder and chaos. If your strategy is simply to hope for a better tomorrow, you are inviting disorder to come in and make a mess of your life. Eventually disorder will do just that, no matter how positive your attitude is. It is failure with a smile. Indeed, unless you take the time to study the *negative* possibilities around you and then build the specific structures you need to resist the universal trek toward turmoil, you are asking for a hard fall.

At the other end of the spectrum, books and gurus tell you that if you work hard enough and focus on your goals, you will achieve greatness and success. I call this the focus fallacy. Turn on the TV. You see a lot of famous actors and business tycoons telling Barbara Walters that you can achieve anything you want if you just work hard enough. Well, this is not true either. For every person who makes it big in any field of endeavor, thousands squander their money, their self-esteem, and maybe even their lives by banking on a solitary dream—one very focused goal—that they ultimately do not achieve. Remember, no one interviews the losers. Indeed, the more specific your goal is, the harder the forces of disorder that lurk around you will work to prevent you from achieving it.

In fact, if you study the lives of many successful businesspeople, politicians, or entertainers, you'll often find that they initially set out to do something totally different than what they ended up doing so successfully. Just recently, I read about a great diplomat who confessed she had set out to become a concert pianist and about a famous lawyer who had at first set out to become a rock star. As such stories indicate, you need to maintain flexibility in your goals so that you can maximize the number of opportunities you have to achieve real security and real success—maybe in a place or profession that you cannot even imagine right now.

So forget open-ended faith and closed-minded focus. The former is a quick fix and the latter is a long shot. The lesson for successfully navigating the new century is crashproofing. Rather than expending all of your valuable, limited time and energy trying to feel good about yourself or striving for that elusive, focused goal, devote your attention to understanding and eliminating potentially adverse outcomes in your life. When you eliminate the negative, you then leave open an infinite number of positive possibilities for your future. I can assure you that if you follow the nine laws of crashproofing discussed in the coming chapters, your life will be an open book of unlimited potential. So cut away the negatives in your life, and then watch yourself take off and glide smoothly to success.

A Three-Pronged Approach to Crashproofing

The crash risks we are about to attack are everywhere around us. In order to attack them successfully, we need to break them down into understandable and manageable categories.

In your professional life, you run the risk of losing your job because of "single-event crashes" such as a poorly written E-mail or letter, or a problem in your relationship with someone else (a nasty boss or a harassing coworker), and "major-event crashes" such as mergers and downsizing. In your financial life, you run a gamut of risks from global crashes like market downturns to individual financial crashes caused by such things as excessive personal debt or becoming the victim of a dishonest broker or shady financial planner. In your personal life, you risk crashes resulting from situations as diverse as becoming a victim of a natural disaster not covered by your insurance or having to pay for the care of a sick parent. We are going to deliver a knockout punch to all of these risks.

Developing comprehensive crashproofing structures will eliminate these diverse risks. As a matter of pure science, you contain disorder through structure. Such structure can be physical in nature. For example, your home is a structure that resists heat, cold, and bad weather. This book will discuss how to protect your home and belongings, and generally how to use physical structure to prevent crashes. But physical structure is just a small piece of the puzzle. You need much more than just physical structure to crashproof your life. Crashproofing structures can be legal in nature. The trust or will that you sign to dispose of your assets is a legal structure that resists the haphazard, contentious, or disorderly disposition of your estate. When properly set up and used, insurance policies, employment contracts, and retirement accounts all represent legal structures that will resist the economically destructive forces around you.

However, even physical and legal structures are not enough to make you crashproof. Some of the structures discussed in this book are structures you must build in your mind. They are mental or intellectual structures. Organizing your writing effectively, for example, represents an intellectual structure that allows you to communicate with clarity and prevents you from allowing dangerous misinterpretations by your friends, relatives, bosses, subordinates, suppliers, and customers. You need to know the dangers of sloppy writing, emotional voice mail, and ineffective spoken presentations, and how you can structure your thoughts to avoid these threats to your economic future.

Every suggestion in this book represents some form of crash-resistant structure. Structure alone, however, is not enough. You need *comprehensive* structure. I could have written a book that covered only professional crashproofing, for example. But it would have had two gaping holes in it. You may have excellent job security, but that security means nothing if you lose all your money in a stock market scam. You may have both a great job and sound investments, but your life still could crash if you have to spend a million dollars taking care of a sick relative who lost his or her health insurance. In order to be effective, therefore, the crashproofing structures you set up must be comprehensive. These structures must reduce your professional risks, financial risks, and personal liabilities.

With these principles in mind, *Crashproof Your Life* effectively structures itself. The book is divided into three parts: professional, financial, and personal crashproofing. Each part in turn contains three risk-reducing structural principles, which I call the laws of crashproofing.

Part One deals with professional crashproofing. In an age of E-mail, lawsuits, downsizing, mergers, and dangerously ephemeral corporate careers, you need to have a well-anchored professional life before you even think about how to invest your money or organize your life to reduce personal liability. Part One will, therefore, ensure that you avoid the mistakes that cost people their careers every day.

Once you have crashproofed your career, you need to structure your finances to reduce the economic risks that could confront you at any time. Part Two will help you create low-risk, high-yield financial structures that will leave your money safe and growing. Then you will be two-thirds of the way to being crashproof.

Finally, once your job and finances are structured to reduce and eliminate risk, Part Three will cover the most difficult and often the most contentious area of crashproofing—personal liability. As callous as it may seem, your parents, your children, and your neighbors pose serious financial risks to you. Many people with good jobs and a lot of well-invested money have seen their financial lives crash when their personal lives took an unexpected turn for the worse. Part Three will help you set up the personal structures that can dramatically reduce your potential liability in this sensitive, but critical, area of your life.

At the end of each part, you will find a checklist of actions you can take to reduce risk in your life. At the end of the book, you will find a list of recommended reading on many of the subjects covered. I also have a website, www.crashproofyourlife.com, which I update regularly with additional tips taken from real-world experiences and events of the preceding few weeks. Risk is like a chameleon; it always changes color. The website will help keep you up-to-date on the latest crash risks and how you can avoid these ever-changing problems. If you read the book, work on the checklists, follow up with some of the recommended reading, and visit the website from time to time, you will be as crashproof as a person can be.

Crashproof Your Life

PROFESSIONAL CRASHPROOFING

Your job is the engine of wealth generation in your life. Having a stable means to create wealth is the first and most important part of achieving total security. Indeed, as long as you have a good job, you can probably weather some personal or financial misfortune outside the workplace. Because your job generates wealth in your life, you need to protect your job before you take any other crashproofing precautions. That is why professional crashproofing is Part One of the book.

There are three threats to your professional security: yourself, your coworkers, and other companies—including competitors, customers, and suppliers. To combat each of these threats, I have developed a law of crashproofing. Each of the three chapters that constitute Part One of the book starts with one such law. The laws themselves provide general guidance, which will then be fleshed out with more specific examples of what to do and what not to do on the job.

Crashproofing Law #1 is geared toward making you more careful about your professional communications and your own on-the-job actions. Crashproofing Law #2 provides you with guidance on how to deal with bosses, coworkers, and subordinates whose actions could adversely affect you. Crashproofing Law #3 will assist you in handling potentially adverse corporate events, including mergers, downsizing, outsourcing, bankruptcy, and the ending of a product or service line in which you work. Once you have learned these three laws and put them into practice, you will have as much professional security as an employee or business owner can ever have.

1

Protecting Yourself from Your Own Actions on the Job

Act as if Your Worst Enemy Is Perched on Your Shoulder

A successful vice president of a major U.S. financial institution entered her office building on a cool, sunny Monday morning. She got on a crowded elevator with a coworker who was not happy working at the company and was actively seeking another job. The coworker looked at her and said, "Another miserable week at this place." "Yeah, I know what you mean," the executive politely replied.

Her cell phone rang. She answered it in the elevator and proceeded to discuss the pricing for a financial software program that she was trying to sell to her clients. She agreed to cut the price by 10 percent because of the potential for working with the client's parent company in the future.

Once in her office, she dumped some papers from her briefcase into a pile on one of her chairs, turned on her computer, and logged on to the Internet. She spent just under ten minutes finding a birthday present for her mother, ordered the gift, and then checked her E-mail. An E-mail from a coworker discussed a newspaper article about a competitor who was reducing commissions on its financial services. Angry about the competitor's tactics, she needed to let off some steam. "We ought to cut our commissions so low that we put those SOBs out of business. We could afford it for a while, they could not," she quickly typed, and clicked "Send" without thinking about it too much.

Then it was time to get to work. She had a lot to get done that week and was tired of clients showing up without appointments—which had happened three times the previous week. She told her secretary to tell her boss that she was on a teleconference, and she taped a handwritten sign on the outside of her door: No Walk-ins Today. Now she could really accomplish something.

Not an atypical morning for many workers, but in just twenty minutes, this employee made eight mistakes that could cost her the job that she loves so much and does so well.

1. She made a statement in public that could be twisted to imply she thinks her company is a "miserable" place to work.
2. She discussed company proprietary data in a crowded elevator.
3. She put important papers in a place that she is likely to forget.
4. She did personal shopping on a company computer without permission to do so.
5. She made an anticompetitive statement about another company.
6. She used profanity in a written communication that could be forwarded to anyone.
7. She countenanced a subordinate to lie on her behalf.
8. She made herself inaccessible to her clients.

While this executive is fictitious, real workers have made these mistakes thousands of times, and I have in my own law practice seen at least one person (and in some cases several people) lose his or her job by making just one of the mistakes just listed. Moreover, a stunning percentage of employees admit that they have made these or similar career-jeopardizing mistakes, but they have not yet gotten caught or otherwise suffered adverse consequences from making them.

I recently conducted a survey of corporate employees and business executives who attended the risk-avoidance programs I give to companies and trade organizations around the country. I asked the attendees to jot down anonymously either "yes" or "no" to a series of simple questions. They did not have to write their names down and I did not share the answers with anyone else at their companies, so they had guaranteed confidentiality. I did, however, promise to report the results in this book. Here are the questions and their rather disturbing answers:

1. Have you ever sent an E-mail that would probably cost you your job if it got into the hands of the wrong person?

   Yes: 45 percent   No: 55 percent

2. Have you ever used your work computer for personal purposes without company permission or authority?

   Yes: 91 percent   No: 9 percent

3. Have you ever discussed confidential company information in a public place?

   Yes: 45 percent   No: 55 percent

4. Have you ever lost an important company document or computer file that you were never able to retrieve?

   Yes: 91 percent   No: 9 percent

5. Have you ever used profanity in an E-mail or written document that you generated at work?

   Yes: 20 percent   No: 80 percent

6. Have you ever made a statement or told a joke on the job that a woman or minority, ethnic, or religious group would likely find offensive?

   Yes: 84 percent   No: 16 percent

7. Have you ever asked someone to lie for you on the job?

   Yes: 35 percent   No: 65 percent

8. Have you ever lied on your resume?

   Yes: 31 percent   No: 69 percent

9. Have you ever known anyone who committed a sexual act on the job during work hours?

   Yes: 20 percent   No: 80 percent

10. Have you ever known anyone who committed a criminal act on the job (falsification of records, misreporting of income, kickbacks, and so on)?

    Yes: 15 percent   No: 85 percent

Statistical extrapolation indicates that the percentage of people who would answer yes to at least one of these questions is over 99 percent. Yet, as we shall learn, committing even one of the missteps referenced in these questions could instantaneously cost you your job. These mistakes and many others end bright and successful careers across the country every day.

Why do so many people make such serious errors in judgment on the job? I got a clue recently when I was watching a cartoon on TV with my eight-year-old daughter. One of the main characters had a sidekick—a parrot perched on his shoulder at all times. The parrot would overhear conversations between the main character and other characters, and the parrot would then blurt out the contents of these conversations at various inappropriate times, causing great embarrassment to the main character.

The problem was that the main character never got wise to the parrot on his shoulder. He never became more careful about what he said, so the cycle of statement followed by embarrassment continued throughout the show. It made for funny TV.

You may not realize it, but you, too, have a parrot on your shoulder at work. But it is not so funny. In this new professional era, 73 percent of large companies monitor the E-mail and other on-line activity of their employees. Nearly half of all employers reserve the right to listen in on your phone calls (although some localities require advance notice to the employee). Every E-mail that you send may be immediately forwarded to anyone else without your permission, and most information systems do not permit you to delete your E-mail permanently. It may be there forever. You have no privacy for your on-line activities.

Moreover, companies now have video cameras monitoring the halls, the garage, and sometimes even the main office area, and I'll soon tell you some stories about the workplace conduct these little cameras have picked up. Then there is the devastating effect that litigation has had on corporate privacy. The average Fortune 500 company has over four hundred lawsuits or investigations going on at any given time—all of which involve the production of internal corporate documents, notes, and computer files. The current corporate environment of business-by-subpoena means that your corporate competition may get hold of even the most obscure notes and documents you generate, and these documents may be filed publicly as part of a court pleading.

It gets worse. No state in the union gives you any privacy protection for voice mail that you leave on someone else's machine. By voluntarily leaving a voice mail, you have consented to being recorded and have therefore waived any privacy rights you might otherwise have had. If you say something on a voice mail, the recipient can do anything with it—the person may play it for a boss, coworker, customer, supplier, or lawyer. There are even documented cases of foreign governments using listening devices in airplanes to monitor the business conversations of executives whose products or services threaten their competitive edge.

The bottom line here is that you have to assume that anything you write, say, or do at the workplace will become known to people who want to embarrass, fire, replace, or otherwise hurt your professional future. There is virtually no privacy in the workplace, and you must conduct yourself accordingly. Crashproofing Law #1 is based on the premise that we all have parrots on our shoulders, poised to hurt us at the worst possible times.

To combat the risks associated with this loss of confidentiality in the workplace, we shall discuss four basic areas where you can badly hurt yourself on the job: what you write, what you say, what you do, and what you don't do.

In each area, you must conduct yourself with the same level of care you would adopt if your worst adversary were perched on your shoulder watching everything that goes on in your professional life. In order to defeat this adversarial apparition, you must always *exercise care* and *exude confidence*. Your adversaries will seize upon any lapse in care that occurs on the job, and they will circle like vultures if they detect you are unsure of yourself. In fact, you will see that you can attribute each crash in the following examples to a lack of care, a lack of confidence, or both.

Write or Wrong?

Effective writing is the greatest strength you can have on the job. Keeping your written words well-structured, succinct, and to the point can make you an invaluable asset at the office. Too often, however, people who have good writing skills let their guards down and write something that devastates their careers. Writing-related career crashes have become extremely common and usually result from either excessive informality (most common in E-mail), inappropriate embellishment (most common in resumes and marketing materials), or excessive aggression (most common in the case of letters written during business disputes). If you can learn to remove the informality, dishonesty, and aggression from your professional communications, you will have taken a strong first step toward crashproofing your job. Let's discuss some particularly dangerous written communications.

E-Mail

In early 2000, a landmark legal decision held that Microsoft had engaged in anti-competitive practices that violated federal antitrust laws. While Microsoft appealed the antitrust findings of the lower court and obtained a partial reversal of the decision, the lasting legacy of the Microsoft trial may be, however, less in the application of antitrust laws to computer software and more in the ramifications of the first major "E-mail lawsuit."

Twenty years ago, federal regulators often proved antitrust conspiracies by looking at internal corporate documents such as strategic plans, marketing projections, minutes of meetings, and competitive analyses performed by company executives and accountants. The Microsoft case represented a major change in the way federal agencies conduct investigations and litigation. Instead of focusing their proof on traditional corporate documents, they made E-mail the centerpiece of their case. Think about it. Two of the largest entities on earth—Microsoft and the United States government—fighting over hundreds of billions of dollars, and the critical evidence is a collection of E-mail snippets.

For example, the government introduced the E-mails of Microsoft executives who discussed "clubbing" one competitor into submission and cutting off the "air supply" of another competitor. Many of these E-mails proved more than embarrassing for the executives who wrote them. They resulted in a devastating lower-court judgment against the company, and they seriously damaged some stellar careers. However, Microsoft fought back, introducing into evidence, for example, an E-mail written by an allegedly neutral court expert in which the expert said he had "sold his soul" by installing a Microsoft product on his computer. How neutral can this expert be, asked Microsoft's counsel, if he considers Microsoft to be the equivalent of the devil?

The Microsoft case, as well as many other recent high-profile cases involving both public and private entities, have proven that E-mail is the most dangerous form of written communication in the workplace. You have to learn to structure your E-mails with the same degree of care that you would structure even the most formal corporate documents such as proposals, memoranda, legal pleadings, and contracts.

It is ironic and dangerous that people are so informal with their E-mails. It would seem that people would be more careful about writing something that can be forwarded to anyone instantly and, in many cases, can never be deleted permanently; yet people almost universally let their professional guards down when they write an E-mail. They do not spend time organizing what they say or con-

sidering the ramifications of their words, and they do not proofread their statements or write second drafts. If you want to crashproof your job, you must write
each E-mail as if your boss, coworkers, competitors, suppliers, and customers
are going to read every one of them because they may do just that. Anyone can
forward your E-mail to any of those people, and anyone can subpoena your
E-mail if you ever get into a business dispute.

Several categories of E-mail tend to cost people their jobs. Many such E-mails
have cost companies a million dollars or more as well, so if you are a small business owner, you need to ensure that your employees are as careful as you are.
Their mistakes might well cost you your business. Here are some guidelines.

Never Write an E-Mail That Could Offend an Insular Group of People

In this context, *insular* means identifiable by a particular physical, religious, sexual, or nationality characteristic. The most dangerous E-mails in existence now
are those that are offensive to female employees. The Supreme Court has held
that women (among other groups) can sue employers for allowing a "hostile work
environment." That means you can violate federal law by making generally offensive remarks, even if they are not directed at particular employees. For example,
as mentioned in the Introduction, a major oil company was recently sued for
harassment because an employee circulated an E-mail titled "25 Reasons Why
Beer Is Better than Women." What followed in the E-mail was a series of unflat-
tering (indeed, downright vulgar) comparisons between the female gender and
beer. The guy who circulated the E-mail thought it was funny; the women did
not. They got $2.2 million, and he saw his career ruined.

The same rules apply to insensitive E-mail about minorities or people of particular religions, although it is encouraging that examples of such overt racism
or religious intolerance are becoming less and less common these days. Even the
most prejudiced employees tend to have enough common sense to avoid overtly
racial slurs. For some reason, however, men still remain very insensitive to the
feelings of women, and they continue to write E-mails that offend women, without thinking twice about it.

Women, however, are not off the hook. There are documented cases of
women getting into trouble by writing sexually aggressive E-mails about men.
Moreover, there are many other insular groups whose feelings tend to be for-
gotten by people of both genders. For example, a female executive at a drug company recently saw her career crash when she lamented to a coworker that she did

not look forward to handling claims of respiratory problems made by users of their latest diet pill. She sent an E-mail complaining that she might spend her career paying off "fat people who are a little afraid of some silly lung problem." The "fat people" got hold of the E-mail and had it printed in newspapers across the country, forcing the drug company to issue an embarrassing apology, devastating the career of the person who said it, and contributing to settlements totaling billions of dollars to the group of overweight customers who had suffered ill effects from the drug.

So keep this fact at the forefront of your mind: your duty to write carefully goes beyond avoiding statements that offend minorities or persons of a different gender. You need to be sensitive to the feelings of any insular group—including people who are elderly, young, overweight, German, New York natives, stutterers, gay, bald, or just downright ugly. Any time your E-mail makes comments that sweep in a group of people based upon general characteristics rather than particular qualities, you run the risk of a career crash. If you do it you risk losing everything you have worked for in your career.

Never Use Profanity in an E-Mail or Other Written Communication

Corporate E-mail is riddled with profanity. I once had the displeasure of having to defend a company in a contract dispute in which the program manager employed by my client had written approximately eighteen E-mails that used aggressive profanity in describing the competitor that had sued my client. The program manager did not even use the standard "abbreviations" like f*** or sh&%!!!. No, he just wrote everything out in pica typeface with the offending words in boldface. The competitor got the E-mail as part of the litigation process and amended its claim to ask for additional damages. The basis for the amended claim was that the profanity in the E-mail indicated malicious intent and therefore permitted the award of massive punitive damages. Fortunately, an executive at the opposing company used similar language, so we got out of the mess. But the program manager at my client's company ended his career then and there.

While I am not a proponent of professional profanity in any context, it is most dangerous in written communications and most common in E-mail. Keep profanity out of your E-mail. It is a simple yet valuable rule that many corporate employees and business owners forget. Think of what that adversary sitting on your shoulder could do with your aggressive language and you will naturally clean up your act.

Avoid Images of Violence and Explicit or Implicit Sexuality in E-Mail

E-mail (and its attachments) tends to be littered with images of death, violence, pornography, and sexual innuendos. I have seen dozens of E-mails (and in some cases informal memos) in which employees of one company said they wanted to "murder," "destroy," "mutilate," "snuff out," or "club" competitors, coworkers, or customers. These images of violence offend coworkers and provide ammunition to ruthless competitors and rivals.

Sexual allusions, even if inexplicit, can also cause problems for corporate employees and executives. I witnessed an employee get demoted simply for saying in an E-mail that he wanted to "slip it to" a nonpaying customer. The trouble arose because the phrase "slip it to" implied sexual violation. An employee of the customer company had the E-mail forwarded to her and raised enough hell to get the offending employee demoted.

Similarly, I know of a situation where an employee of a medium-sized company received a reprimand and was put on probation for writing an E-mail stating that his new marketing program would be so effective that he would have the competition "screaming like a hooker." You may think that you would never write such an E-mail, but go through your sent E-mails sometime and you may be surprised at some of the things you have said.

Some companies take even more drastic action than reprimands and demotions when dealing with E-mail that contains images of sexuality or violence. During 2000, the Dow Chemical Company fired some ninety people (and suspended at least two hundred more) for sending offensive E-mail at work. Many of the individual E-mails that resulted in the firings were either sexually explicit or violent, including E-mails that attached photographs of gruesome automobile accident scenes. Most of these E-mails did not indicate workplace discrimination, nor did they evidence hostile intentions toward coworkers or customers. The company just deemed gruesome pictures and sexual images sent via E-mail to be offensive and inappropriate at the workplace. As a result, many careers crashed. It is a fact of the contemporary workplace. Any time you include an image of violence or gratuitous sexuality in your E-mail, you allow others to pose serious and legitimate questions about your professionalism. It is not worth the risk.

Never Acknowledge Legal Liability in an E-Mail

As much as corporate employees say they do not like lawyers, they all seem to act as if they want to be lawyers. Many careers crash because a good executive becomes a bad lawyer.

You have company lawyers for a reason. They assess legal liability. Unless you are the company lawyer or are communicating to the company lawyer under the umbrella of the attorney-client privilege, you should never speculate about legal liability in your E-mail. I recently saw a career crash when a procurement manager at an aerospace company received a $3 million claim letter from a supplier. Instead of telling the company lawyer about it, he jetted off an E-mail to his boss that stated, "I think that if they sued us, they would win the entire amount." Even though the company had valid legal defenses to the claim, I advised company executives that they should consider writing a settlement check. Because if the case went to court, the E-mail admitting liability might be admissible evidence, and no juror in the world would listen to the corporate defenses—however valid they might be—after they read an E-mail that so completely and explicitly acknowledged responsibility.

Corporate employees, especially engineers and accountants, tend to speculate a lot about legal liability, and many lose their careers as a result of such speculations. I have seen engineers speculate that their companies "breached the contract" because the company had failed to meet the requirements of a contract specification. It sounds logical that failing to meet a specification is a breach of contract, but there are in fact many legal excuses for missing design or performance specifications. So even if you fail to meet the requirements of a specification, you still may not have breached the contract. Consequently, an employee who speculates that the failure to meet a specification is a breach of contract has done both the company and his or her career a great disservice.

I have seen accountants send E-mails recommending the company take a multimillion-dollar financial reserve on its books because "we have obvious legal exposure here." Again, the accountant is qualified to write that the company should take a financial reserve, but he or she should not acknowledge legal exposure. Leave such assessments to the company counsel, who evaluates the facts with a solid knowledge of the law and the protection of the attorney-client privilege.

Respond Decisively to Offensive E-Mail That You Receive

Another downside of E-mail is that you cannot control what you receive. Once you receive an E-mail that contains inappropriate language, the moment you open it, you may become part of the problem in the eyes of the people whom it offends. If, for example, the E-mail is offensive to women or minorities and a harassment or discrimination lawsuit ensues, just by reading the E-mail you have become a witness in the case. Sure, you can defend yourself on the grounds that you did not have any control over what people chose to send you, but you won't get the chance to explain the situation until after everyone hears that you were subpoenaed to testify in a nasty harassment or discrimination proceeding. Not the kind of backpedaling I would like to have to do.

Often people receive offensive E-mail because they are on a lengthy address list. For example, in the ten days prior to writing this section of the book, I received two highly offensive, sexually explicit E-mails that remote acquaintances simply sent to everyone on their E-mail address lists.

When it comes to sexually explicit or otherwise insensitive E-mail sent to my place of work, I adopt a zero-tolerance policy. I immediately respond with the following words: "Please do not ever send me another E-mail like that again. If I am on a mailing list for such E-mail, please take me off. Thank you." When you respond with such blunt simplicity, you are doing more than protecting yourself from allegations of complicity. You are helping the sender of the E-mail as well. When the sender realizes that you, a friend, are concerned about the contents of the E-mail, the sender will probably be more careful about sending such E-mail in the future.

I might add that there is software that can screen for certain words and block your receipt of offensive E-mail. It is worth considering. Of course, sometimes employers will not allow one employee to install software that would block the receipt of a particular kind of E-mail; moreover, many offices rely upon E-mail to communicate with their employees, and from time to time an offensive or explicit word does need to be in an E-mail. If, for example, you had been working at the *New York Times* when the independent counsel released his report on the Clinton-Lewinsky scandal, you may have had a legitimate need to send an E-mail that contained a word normally considered offensive but which was part of a significant news story. The best approach, therefore, is to open all your E-mail, but respond forcefully against any E-mail others could use to suggest that you are part of a workplace problem.

To sum it up, E-mail causes career-ending trouble when it is offensive to insular groups, profane, violent, gratuitously sexual, or legally speculative. Every time you write an E-mail, read it carefully before you send it. Think about your potential adversaries getting hold of it and how they might use it against you. Ask yourself who might find it offensive, and then edit it accordingly before you click the mouse. Do not forget, of course, that many of the same rules that apply to E-mail also apply to memos, personal notes, marketing materials, and meeting minutes; so you should exercise similar care in putting together these documents as well. In my experience, however, people are naturally more careful when they write memos and other more formal written communications. The greatest danger is the informality, accessibility, and permanence of E-mail.

Resumes and Other Havens for the Little Lie

Once you have ensured that you are careful not to generate offensive or careless documents, you have to ensure that everything you write is scrupulously honest. I will assume you are not a pathological liar. What is surprising, however, is the number of basically honest people who convince themselves that a little professional lie here or there is OK. The prime example of a document in which otherwise good people include overt misrepresentations or "little white lies" is the resume. Recent studies indicate that 30 percent of resumes contain misrepresentations, and companies are getting wise to the practice of resume fraud. Law firms have been burned by hiring "lawyers" who never passed the bar. Residents of major cities have elected officials to public office who claimed college degrees they never actually obtained. Companies have hired self-proclaimed Vietnam War veterans who have never left the United States. In fact, dozens of people out there, including a former Illinois circuit judge, have claimed on their resumes that they won the Congressional Medal of Honor, when the closest they ever came to combat was watching *Saving Private Ryan* after it came out on video.

Because so many companies have in the past trusted the truth of job applicants' resumes only to end up embarrassed, there is a growing movement within the business community to engage in much more thorough investigation of the claimed credentials of potential or actual employees. Employers are screening employees carefully—conducting criminal background checks and drug tests and sometimes even hiring private investigators to track down the accuracy of every detail contained on a resume.

You cannot afford even minimal embellishment on your resume. Typical white lies that have cost people their current or a potential future job include ratcheting up a previous job title (an intern calling herself a "communications consultant"), lying about a degree (an accountant saying she "graduated" from a university that she attended for only a few months), and misrepresenting the importance of an award (a college graduate calling himself a champion pole vaulter when he was only the "champion" at a second-rate high school).

Employers are right to ferret out even the most benign misrepresentations on resumes of prospective employees. If you lie in a description of yourself, you are saying something about both your professional confidence and professional morality: you do not think you are good enough to succeed just by your own accomplishments and abilities, and you cannot be trusted to tell the truth. Resume fraud can bring short-term gain, but more often it brings long-term disaster. Even small lies can cost you your career.

The same rules hold true for other documents you generate. For example, another area where employees commonly get into trouble for stretching the truth is in the writing of marketing materials. Employees frequently overstate the quality of their products or services, or lie about the amount of time in which they can finish a job. There is no quicker way to lose your job than to lie about the amount of time a project will take and then have to answer to an irate boss, whom the customer contacted to complain about your inability to meet the promised schedule. Always be careful and realistic in assessing the amount of time a job will take and the quality you can deliver.

Letters

Just as E-mail provides the best example of written materials that tend to contain careless statements and resumes are the best example of documents that tend to contain damaging misrepresentations, letters provide the most common example of written communications that contain overly emotional phrases. This section will discuss how to handle correspondence in situations where emotions run high.

There is very little room for emotion in the workplace. While a corporation is in some respects a legal person—it can make contracts, be sued, grow, and die—a corporation's ability to make a profit depends upon the smooth, machine-like operation of its components. There is no place for unbridled hostility, anger, hatred, and revenge in a well-run company. Your job is in jeopardy every time you let your emotions get the better of your reason. Indeed, overly emotional written communications have cost thousands of people their careers over the years.

Responding to nasty letters is the perfect example. If an unhappy customer or supplier sends a letter to your company complaining about something or someone, the letter will probably use threatening phrases like "outrageous," "ludicrous," "ridiculous," and "offensive." If you are directly involved in the matter the letter concerned, you will be tempted to respond with an even more

aggressive letter. You become too close to the situation. Indeed, responsive letters tend to be riddled with as many or more of these overwrought phrases
and superlative adjectives, as well as snide personal swipes and sarcastic comments—all of which may seem perfect at the time because they allow you to
let off some steam.

Unfortunately, after an exchange of nasty-grams, the other company usually
escalates the dispute and your boss or sometimes even the CEO gets involved.
The boss views the situation more objectively than you do and learns of the dispute after the heat of the moment has passed. When the boss reads your overly
emotional letter, you look unprofessional and combative. If the other side is a
valuable customer or supplier and is mad enough about your letter, your company may decide to appease the other side by sacrificing your career. I have been
involved in many disputes where one side capitulated after getting the satisfac-
tion of having an employee for the other side fired. Do not become a pawn in
larger corporate disputes by becoming overly emotional in your written
communications.

In fact, you must learn to wring the emotion out of your professional correspondence or your career could well crash in an instant. The proper way to
respond to excessive emotion is with well-structured reason. For example, when
you receive an unfocused, angry letter that is full of untrue allegations, always
respond with a well-organized fact-intensive piece of correspondence. Also, make
your response self-contained so that an outsider could fully understand the problem and your defense without reading any document other than your letter. Start
a responsive letter, therefore, by restating your adversary's claim or complaint in
simple and unimpressive terms. To use a real-life example, if you sell specialized
computer hardware and an unhappy customer sends an aggressive letter complaining about the processing speed of the hardware, consider a reply that opens
as follows: "Our company received your May 19 letter in which you claim that
we failed to provide to you hardware that met your processing speed
requirements."

Then immediately disagree in objective terms and cite three or four reasons
why the other side is incorrect: "We respectfully disagree with your claims for
the following reasons: (1) all acceptance testing indicated that the hardware
exceeded the processing speed requirements, (2) our field representative spoke
with several of your users during the first weeks after installation and they were
to a person pleased with all aspects of the product, and (3) your marketing manager indicated that your information technology department altered the hardware in a manner that could affect the processing speed."

Follow this devastatingly unemotional paragraph with three paragraphs, each one fleshing out in simple terms the facts that support the three reasons for your disagreement with their letter. Give dates, times, and the specific contents of conversations (verified by the people who participated in them) that support your position. Then conclude with an olive branch: "We hope that this letter satisfactorily explains the situation. As always, we are willing to discuss the matter with you at any time." This type of unemotional, well-structured response will protect both your company and your career.

A final word about letters and other formal business documents: pay careful attention to grammar and spelling, and learn the proper technical jargon if you become involved in a new field of expertise. Even the most beautifully constructed professional correspondence looks inept if it contains glaring typos, errors in grammar, or incorrect terminology. Everyone needs to know the difference between simple words like *there* and *their*. Moreover, if you are writing on a specialized topic, you may need to understand more complex terminology. For example, I recently handled a case involving military munitions. One lawyer in the case prepared a brief that consistently and mistakenly used the word *ordinance* for *ordnance*. The former word refers to a law, the latter to munitions. This lawyer looked like an idiot to the judge hearing the case, who in fact had a military background. Worse yet, the lawyer also repeatedly referred to "troupes" when describing our men and women in uniform (who are, for the record, "troops").

I generally have others proofread my correspondence and other professional documents that are longer than two pages. I tend to get too close to the written product and lose my ability to spot errors. I then agree to proofread their work to return the favor.

In sum, if you can learn to keep emotion out of your professional correspondence and other written communications and write with precision, structure, and accuracy, you will have taken the next big step toward crashproofing your job.

Spoken, Not Stirred

Written communications pose the greatest risk to your professional life because your adversaries can confront you directly with what you write. There is no ambiguity, no issue of memory, and little room for interpretation—it is all there in black and white. On the other hand, you have more inherent protection from the consequences of most of your oral communications because people tend to forget exactly what words other people use in a conversation, and if there is a disagreement, it is their word against yours. Nonetheless, many careers still crash because of oral statements made on the job. This section will discuss a few high-risk areas: voice mail, "elevator talk," meetings, and oral presentations or speeches. Again, the first law of crashproofing applies: speak as if your worst adversary is listening to everything that you say, and structure your words carefully to avoid mistakes and misimpressions.

Voice Mail

What you say in voice mail can in some circumstances be more dangerous than what you write in E-mail. Like E-mail, voice mail constitutes a transcription of your words that anyone can forward to anyone else. Also like E-mail, voice mail does not require interaction with the recipient, which tends to make people less careful and sometimes more aggressive in voice mail than they otherwise would be with their oral statements. Unlike E-mail, however, and even more danger-ous, voice mail allows the recipient to hear your tone, inflection, and demeanor, and you do not get the opportunity to edit your words.

There is a widespread misconception among corporate employees that they have privacy rights concerning the voice recordings they leave on someone else's phone or answering machine. You have no privacy protection for voice mail. A careless or aggressive voice mail may be used by the recipient (or anyone to whom the recipient forwards it) for any purpose. The reason is simple. The very act of leaving a voice mail indicates that you consent to be recorded. Once you con-sent to being recorded, you lose, as a matter of law, the privacy rights you have for the words you use. So if you leave a voice mail that contains offensive humor, aggressive language, or anything else that could embarrass you, a recipient who does not have your interests at heart can record that voice mail on a cassette and play it for anyone at any time.

In my law practice, I have had the opportunity to use the contents of pro-fane voice mail against witnesses in business disputes. In one case, the witness used at least eight words of profanity in a single voice mail. In another case, the offending individual left a threatening and almost incoherent voice mail for a client of mine at 2:00 A.M. after waking up angry about a business dispute. Indeed, just the timing of that voice mail—left in the creepy hours of the night—made the person who left the voice mail look emotionally unstable. Nothing can jeopardize your career more than having a boss, customer, judge, or jury hear a transcription of your voice spewing out unprofessional statements at strange hours of the day or night.

Although much more benign, rambling and ill-conceived voice mails—even pleasant ones—can also have adverse career consequences. As in other aspects of crashproofing, you must constantly combat the universal tendency toward disorder with carefully imposed structure. Many people leave voice mails before they have clearly thought out what they want to convey. Consequently, people frequently leave long-winded and often pointless voice mails. A four-minute voice mail is inherently irritating. It is a one-way conversation in which you impose your words on someone else without giving them the chance to short-circuit irrelevant issues, correct wrong statements, or ask questions. Most long voice mails could get the same message across in twenty seconds or less, and most contain statements the recipient would, in a normal conversation, interrupt to exchange ideas with you.

I have heard many customers and bosses complain about the voice-mail habits of individual employees, and even though they are so seemingly small, such habits can adversely affect a career. Before you leave a voice mail of any substance, therefore, plot in your mind exactly what you want to say. Consider even jotting down a couple of points. Call the person, and leave a short voice mail—thirty seconds or less—that lays out the basic issue that you want to discuss. Then hang up the phone!

A final point on voice mail: some systems allow you to delete a voice mail you have just sent and start over, as long as you have not hung up the phone yet. In such a case you do have a fleeting second chance if you decide the voice mail you have left contains inappropriate or imprecise language. Learn how to use the delete feature on the various voice-mail systems that you use, and always spend a couple of seconds after leaving a voice mail of any substance evaluating whether to delete the voice mail and take a second crack at it.

Elevator Talk

My grandfather used to use the World War II catch phrase "loose lips sink ships," which referred to the belief that you never knew when an enemy spy might be listening to what you were saying. Today, loose lips sink companies and careers. In recent years, corporate espionage has become a serious problem for many companies, especially in the high-tech industry, where it is already difficult to protect intellectual property rights. Recently, several countries accused a European government of bugging the headrests in the business- and first-class sections of transatlantic flights to learn trade secrets from top executives who were traveling overseas. There are proven cases of companies planting "spies" in other companies to learn trade secrets and other proprietary information. You need to be extra careful these days not to let your company secrets into the public domain because, five minutes later, they could be on the Internet and everyone will know them.

People make two mistakes that cause them to talk to the wrong people—or talk to the right people in the wrong place—about company business. First, they think no one is listening when they talk to coworkers in public areas. A Midwest gossip columnist once got wind of a corporate merger when he overheard two employees discussing the pending merger on an elevator. It was not a good day in the two employees' careers when news of the pending merger appeared in the morning paper and a third employee, who had been on the elevator, reported the source of the leak to company management.

I once made a startlingly bizarre mistake along those lines. I was traveling with a coworker on an airplane. He was seated across the aisle from me. During the course of our conversation, I made some negative remarks about a lawyer whom I knew and did not particularly admire. As it turned out, that very lawyer's spouse was sitting directly behind me, heard the whole conversation, and really let me have it as I was exiting the plane. The odds of that happening had to be a million to one or worse, but it is a true story. I learned a lot that day. It happened to me, and it can happen to you.

Running a Meeting

If you are to succeed professionally in the era of pagers, cell phones, and Palm Pilots, you must not take up too much time with meetings, or you will lose the interest of those around you. Consequently, the ability to run a well-structured, time-efficient meeting is now an essential job skill. Many careers have been sent on a downward spiral by as little as one unsuccessful meeting. If your meetings are consistently poorly run and fail to produce results, your bosses, coworkers and even subordinates will lose respect for you, and then it is just a matter of time before you are shown the door.

The average professional now spends over three hours per day in meetings. Surveys find that people consider meetings to be too long, unfocused, and often irrelevant to their job responsibilities. As a result, over 90 percent skip meetings they are supposed to attend. Naturally, they judge whether they will attend by their perception of the meeting convener's effectiveness. Even if you get someone to attend, if you do not run the meeting well, nothing good will come out of it. Approximately 90 percent of employees admit to daydreaming in meetings, 73 percent admit they do other work while attending meetings, 30 to 40 percent doze off from time to time, and 6 percent pretend to be taking notes when they are not. One clever employee admitted he gets out of boring meetings by using his cell phone under the table to dial his own pager. The pager goes off in the middle of the meeting, he looks at the number on the pager as if it is quite important, and he sheepishly excuses himself from the meeting. If the meeting is bad enough, people will do anything to get out of it; and if your meetings get that reputation, your career is at risk.

Take the case of the manager of a manufacturing client of mine who had a staff meeting every Friday afternoon. He had fourteen people reporting to him. He asked me to give a briefing to his people on a rather mundane legal issue that had come up within his group, pertaining to the termination of subcontracts. I had never attended his staff meetings before, so I brought fifteen copies of my presentation handout with me. Four people showed up. Soon I learned why.

The manager spent the first twenty minutes of the meeting explaining where the other ten people were. It was obvious from the discussion that most of them had invented a reason to not be there—a doctor's appointment, a sick child, an unexpected rush project, you name it. The manager then proceeded to ramble for ten minutes about the pros and cons of moving the department's Christmas party from the week of Christmas to two weeks before Christmas. He then discussed a funny article he had read about the author of the Dilbert books (five irrelevant minutes), the location of the annual executive conference (five irritating minutes), how all of his subordinates were not really missing anything by not being invited to the annual executive conference (ten insufferable minutes), a "potty" break (fifteen wasted minutes), and a discussion of Viagra (ten offensive minutes). After that, he asked the four people in attendance whether they had anything interesting to report. They each said no. He asked me to give my legal presentation on subcontract terminations (ten minutes of near-Einsteinian brilliance). He proceeded to follow up my presentation with a twenty-minute description of a legal problem he once had with his neighbor. It had something to do with a sewer line. Finally, the four attendees just started to get up and leave, whereupon the manager pronounced: "Good meeting, guys. Let's go home." Two hours had passed, and the meeting had accomplished nothing other than my ten minutes of fascinating insight into subcontract termination clauses. Six months later, this manager was in the first wave of people let go in a corporate downsizing initiative. It was no surprise to me.

Not only are bad meetings a risk to your career, but many meetings are so poorly run that companies place great value on people who can run a meeting effectively. Here are some basic rules on running meetings that could both save and enhance your career. They are based upon the universal principle that you defeat the tendency toward disorder in your life through the effective use of structure. According to the most basic rules of science, the components of effective structure are space, matter, and time. Interestingly, you will find that our discussions of workplace structure are susceptible to being broken down into these components. We'll start the discussion of meeting structure with the component of space, then move to matter, and then to time.

Control the Location of the Meeting

Space is a major component of effective structure. In the case of meetings, space means location. Having a meeting in the right location will help you structure it to be efficient and productive. The location of the meeting should be related to its purpose. If you are meeting to discuss the purchase of new books for a corporate library, have the meeting in the library. In addition, if the meeting is an important one, you should underscore the importance of the meeting by having it in a room that is not used for day-to-day activity. If you hold an important meeting in a room everyone uses for everything all the time, people attending the meeting will come with the mundane expectations they associate with that space. People do not put their minds to best use when they are sitting next to two boxes of documents a coworker left in there yesterday. So, if you convene a meeting for a group of contracts managers, have the meeting in the nice conference room near the office of the divisional manager of contracts. If you are raising money for a charity, have the meeting in a room that is plastered with posters of the people whom your charity helps.

Finally, arrange the table or tables in the meeting so that people face each other. If the meeting will have twenty or more people, arrange the table in a U shape to create an open feeling, a sense that you are encouraging constructive dialogue.

Control the Subject Matter of the Meeting

Once you have organized the meeting space, you have to rigidly control the subject matter of the meeting. Nothing makes you look worse than losing control of the subject matter, with the result that the meeting lasts too long and accomplishes nothing. First, distribute a detailed agenda. Divide the meeting into a few general topics, and place under each heading more specific subtopics. Distribute the agenda a day or two before the meeting, and tell people you expect them to come prepared. Here is an excerpt of an agenda I came across recently that effectively categorizes the subjects of the meeting:

AGENDA
Software Development Strategy Meeting

I. Customer needs and concerns
  A. Icons that are easier to read
  B. Compatibility with related software
  C. Susceptibility to viruses

II. Cost-benefit analysis of potential upgrades
  A. Profitability of current product
  B. Cost to upgrade
  C. Market projection for new product

III. Recommendations

While this agenda represents a good start, it is not yet crashproof. If you want to maintain true control over the meeting, you need to take a couple of additional steps. First, you need to put the names of the people whom you expect to give the initial report next to the topic. That way, they will focus their preparation and thought on their areas of expertise and will be less inclined to ramble on during other parts of the meeting. Too worried about what you expect them to discuss, they won't spend much time on areas you do not expect them to discuss. Second, I recommend that on the agenda you always have a final category that says "Roundtable Discussion" or "Other Issues." That lets people know they will eventually have an opportunity to voice any concerns they have, and it gives you the opportunity to defer any off-point comments to the end of the meeting.

Control the Length of the Meeting

The most important element of crashproofing your meetings is to control time. I have never been to a meeting that really had to last longer than an hour. Meetings go too long because people try to sound impressive or important rather than resolve the issue that necessitated the meeting. Here is how to maintain control. When you send out the notice of the meeting, tell the attendees how long it will last: "There will be a one-hour meeting to discuss software development strategy on March 1 at 2:00 P.M." When you get to the meeting, remind people that it will only last one hour. You may even wish to schedule another appointment or meeting for yourself at 3:15 P.M. so that you can announce that the meeting *has to end* within an hour because you have to leave. You will not believe the kind of momentum and efficiency that develops in a meeting if you set an artificial (albeit reasonable) amount of time for the meeting. It is absolutely amazing.

Start the meeting on time. If people arrive late, ignore them until it is their turn to speak. They will not be late to the next meeting. Then run the meeting according to the schedule. If people veer off point or take too much time, remind them that the meeting has only a certain number of minutes left. Tell people you will address marginally relevant issues at the end of the meeting during the roundtable discussion, but keep the meeting at a pace that leaves only five or so minutes at the end for such discussion.

Once people learn your style of running a meeting, you will find that your meetings become very well paced and no one feels shortchanged. You will earn the respect of your coworkers and clients and take a major step toward crash-proofing your career.

Speeches, Presentations, and Oral Reports

Reliable surveys indicate that 45 percent of Americans fear public speaking, while 30 percent fear death. I guess that means millions of people would rather die than give a speech. Indeed, some of the brightest and most competent people I know completely freeze up when it comes time to make a presentation. They appear nervous and lacking in confidence right when they are the true center of attention. This is not a good result if you want to crashproof your career. Adversaries and rivals snicker at and criticize people who make a bad impression in oral presentations. When you speak, you are up there all alone, and consequently you are the biggest, easiest target you can be professionally. This section will discuss how to ensure your oral presentations enhance your professional reputation rather than limit or even destroy it. You have to be able to deliver a speech that will even win the grudging acceptance of that adversary perched on your shoulder.

Many books and seminars purport that they can make you a great speaker. I am skeptical of them. The ability to deliver Darrow-like oratory requires a certain type of personality many people simply do not have. You can, however, crashproof your speaking style by following a few simple steps.

The same rules of organization and timing that apply to letters and meetings also apply to speeches and other oral presentations, but there is a unique twist. When you give a speech or presentation, all eyes are on you. The audience will make judgments concerning not only your competence but also your personality and your conviction to the course of action you are advocating. You have to do more than present the audience with organization and quality. When you give an oral presentation, whether it is an issue summary at a small meeting or a formal speech at a large convention, you need to draw the audience into your words to the point that they forget where they are. When you achieve this connection, you will know it. You will feel energy coming to you from the audience, and words will flow easily, almost as if you were on automatic pilot. It is a wonderful feeling, a feeling of being crashproofed, and here is how to achieve it.

Develop a Flexible Structure and Rehearse the Speech at Least Two Times

A small number of people feel that they can wing it and do not prepare at all for their presentations. As I am sure you know, these speeches are rarely successful. At the other extreme, however, many conscientious people feel that writing out a presentation and then reading it is the proper way to present to a large group. It seems safe, but it is not. People tend to stumble through scripted speeches. Moreover, audiences generally hate these canned presentations, and they lose interest within the first few minutes.

You should never read a speech verbatim; nor should you simply recite the contents of viewgraphs that you may have prepared as visual aids. That sort of structure is too rigid and is easily cracked by the forces of disorder. Flexibility needs to be built into any structure. That's why in Los Angeles they build skyscrapers on movable metal plates to avoid earthquake damage—it is a flexible structure. When it comes to speaking, you need to adopt a flexible structure by using notes as guideposts and filling in the rest of the speech with rehearsed, but not precisely planned, remarks.

That said, just outlining your speech and rehearsing it in your head or mumbling it to yourself at your desk is not enough. You need to stand up, pretend that there are people in the room, and deliver the speech or presentation (complete with graphics if you intend to use them) two times in its entirety out loud, exactly as you hope to deliver it when the real time comes. Once you have been through it two times, the presentation becomes intuitive, and you will find that the third time through, when you have the real audience, will be your best.

Start the Presentation with a Smile and a Statement of How Long You Will Speak

The first thing a good speaker does is to show quiet confidence. You can demonstrate this confidence with a simple smile. It sure beats the look of nervousness, terror, or confusion with which so many speakers greet their audiences. After that, find a way to work into the first few minutes of your presentation a statement of how long you intend to speak. One of the main reasons why people lose interest in a speaker is the uncertainty of how long the speech is going to last. They look at their watches, they worry they might miss a meeting, or they fear the speaker is winging it and might overstay his or her welcome. Also tell people you will stick around for a few minutes after the talk to answer questions on an individual basis. That limits the number of interruptions you will get during the speech, and it lets the audience members know they will not have to squirm around in their chairs after the talk listening to all sorts of questions that are not relevant to them. Just these initial gestures of courtesy and respect to the audience will prime them to like you and to listen more carefully to your presentation.

Adopt "Roller Coaster" Intonation

Start by outlining your entire speech. Tell them what topics you are going to cover. As you proceed, let them know when you have completed one topic and are starting another, and consider using visual aids to reinforce the structure and progress of your presentation. Within that structure, however, you keep the interest of the audience by taking them through a series of peaks and valleys, or what I call "roller coaster" presentation style. When it comes to intonation, many great speakers start very quietly and then build to a crescendo of nearly yelling, after which they go back to a quiet period, and then build again. This may be a good approach for you, but you should experiment with others. When it comes to the seriousness of your speech, you must also judge just how much humor is appropriate. If any humor is in fact within the realm of possibility, your speech must punctuate the serious stretches at regular intervals with humorous anecdotes and unexpected surprises. I even give out a couple of gag gifts to attendees of my legal risk-reduction seminars who answer my questions to the audience correctly—usually magic tricks and Venus flytraps for those who think most like tricky, treacherous trial lawyers. To stay interesting, therefore, you should break up your talk wherever possible with modulating volume, scattered humor, and unexpected turns of events.

Conclude with Your Original Agenda and a Great Story

Finish your talk by proving to the audience that you fully covered every topic on the agenda you showed them at the beginning of the presentation and referred to along the way. Briefly summarize the points you made on each topic. Then sum up the theme of your presentation and illustrate it with an excellent two- or three-minute story. It can be a humorous story or a very touching one, but it should be based upon something that really happened recently or even in the distant past. For example, politicians often end speeches on legislative matters with a story about an individual citizen whose life turned around as a result of a program similar to the one the politician is advocating. I recently heard a good political orator promoting a welfare-to-work program. He ended his speech with a story about a lady who had been a drug addict. She had three children under the age of six. They were surrounded by filth and crime. As the result of a welfare-to-work program in his state, the lady was off drugs and had a job as a receptionist at a large accounting firm. Her kids were doing well at school, and she had just purchased her first car. The story provided an effective ending to a speech that may otherwise have seemed dry and sterile.

When it comes to what you say at work, therefore, you must always assume that your worst enemy is listening to you, and you must conduct yourself accordingly. You must be careful about what you put on voice mail, refrain from loose talk outside the office, keep control of your meetings, and learn to earn the respect of those who listen to your oral presentations. Once you have mastered the art of crashproofing your written and oral communication, it is then time to turn your attention to the potential ramifications of your actions at work and, more dangerously still, your inactions.

How What You Do Can Undo You

Words often speak louder than actions in the workplace. Many good people lose their jobs because of how they said something, not because of some underlying evil act they committed. That is why we covered bad writing and bad speaking first. Up until now, I have assumed that you usually intend to do the right thing at work and that the way you are most likely to get into trouble is by accidentally writing or saying something with a less-than-ideal choice of words (or maybe by telling a little white lie). In fact, most people who find their careers have crashed can trace the crash to a mistake of expression rather than a seriously bad act.

There remains, however, a sizable group of people who lose their jobs every year because they really screwed up. By that I mean, *they done wrong*. In fact, three of four employees report that they witnessed some form of unethical conduct while at work during the past year—with 56 percent reporting deceptive practices, 39 percent reporting false or misleading promises to customers, 37 percent observing the shipment of substandard product, and in the area of research and development, 32 percent witnessing the altering of safety or quality test results. Even basically good people sometimes get sucked into evil acts and wrongdoing on the job. This section will cover the most insidious temptations on the job and get them out of your system right away.

Some of this professional wrongdoing—such as discrimination— involves your relationships with others. That will be covered in the next chapter, which deals with your interaction with others on the job. In this section, we focus instead on potential bad acts that do not directly involve your relationships with coworkers. Again, Crashproofing Law #1 holds true: act as if your worst enemy is watching everything you do.

Misuse of Company Property

The most common act people commit that costs them their jobs is theft or its equivalent. You probably think you can skip over this section because you are not a thief. Keep reading. I know you are not a kleptomaniac. For that matter, the issue is not whether you bring home a couple of company pens either (although theft of office supplies does cost companies over a billion dollars annually, so I am not condoning it). I have never seen a career crash because someone took home a pad of paper or other small piece of tangible property, and instances of major theft of corporate property by employees are relatively rare.

But here is why you need to be concerned about office theft. In an age and economy where information is the most important commodity, *theft* has a new meaning. Many people who would never steal a physical object have no trouble at all justifying the theft of information or intellectual property. Yet I would bet that, in some new-economy businesses, more people are fired for the misuse of intellectual property than for the misuse of tangible property. Consequently, you need to upgrade your brain to apply the same rules of corporate morality to intellectual property that you apply to tangible office property. Here are some basic rules.

Do Not Use the Internet or Other On-Line Services for Personal Purposes Without Permission

Your company owns and pays for access to the Internet and other means of computerized data exchange from terminals at your place of work. In the case of specialized on-line services, like LEXIS-NEXIS, pricing for the service may be based upon the volume of usage. Consequently, you may be increasing the cost of the service to your company if you use it for nonbusiness purposes. Even if your company pays a flat fee for on-line services, every minute you spend doing personal work on your office computer is a minute when you are not making money for the company. As a result, you must realize that using on-line services for personal work without permission is no better than stealing money from the company petty cash fund.

Knowing this type of activity costs companies a lot of money, most corporations now have a policy on Internet use for personal purposes. Frequently, such use is forbidden entirely, and usually the company reserves the right to monitor your on-line activity. Yet employees still feel they can get away with misusing their company's on-line services. You may have read how Xerox fired dozens of employees and the *New York Times* fired twenty-two employees who made excessive personal use of the Internet at work. My research reveals that over 90 percent of the workforce has done exactly what got those people fired. Resist the temptation.

You also have to ensure that others do not misuse your computer. I recently saw someone lose his job because he sneaked into the office at night, found computers that employees had failed to log off of properly, and then accessed Internet porn sites, charging the costs to a company account. By losing his job, he got what he deserved. However, the worst part of the story is that the people whose computers this person used remained under a cloud of suspicion for weeks before a hidden camera caught the real culprit. They were dragged into a scandal just because they failed to log off their computers at night. This means not only do you have to ensure you do not misuse company cyberspace, but you also have to take the steps needed to prevent others from misusing the cyberspace the company has entrusted to you.

Finally, do not think it is OK to use company on-line services just because your boss told you it was fine—a common defense that is usually unsuccessful. Your boss might just be getting both of you into trouble. Make sure your actions are in accordance with company policy, and if you do feel a need to do personal work using office computerized services, be sure to get permission from someone who has the authority to grant it.

Do Not Misuse Software Licenses

I am astonished at the number of people who copy licensed software from their workplace and bring it home or give it to their friends—my research reveals that it is between 10 and 15 percent of all workers. Your company probably buys a lot of software—financial software, marketing software, presentation and desktop publishing software, and so on. When the company "buys" software, this does not usually constitute a purchase in the traditional sense of the word. Usually, what your company buys is a license: a right to use the software, not ownership of the software. When you copy that software onto your own computer or give it to someone else for free, you are not only misappropriating your company's licensed property, but you are also misappropriating the ownership interest of the company that licensed the software to your company. Once you give it to someone else illegally, there is nothing to prevent him or her from passing it on to millions of people via the Internet.

As a corporate employee, your actions can often be legally attributed to your company as a whole. Consequently, if a company that licensed software to your company finds out you have misused the software, your company may be liable for damages that could total millions of dollars—depending on how far the misuse has spread. While companies may occasionally give misguided employees a second chance when they misuse a tangible piece of company property, they will not give employees a second chance when an act of corporate theft results in major companywide liability. The misappropriation of licensed, patented, or copyrighted material is a guaranteed crash, and you must make every effort to avoid it.

In fact, companies that license a lot of software have now formed trade groups that hire private investigators who track down people who are misappropriating their software. Consequently, if you use software or other protected property illegally, the chances are higher than ever before that you will be caught. Indeed, you never know what office rival of yours might report you to one of these organizations. It is not worth the risk.

Insider Trading

Another cause of major career flameouts (jail time, to be more specific) is the misuse of corporate inside information—i.e., nonpublic, material information on the plans of publicly traded companies. Some of the world's greatest fortunes have been made on inside information. The great steel tycoon Andrew Carnegie made many of his early millions by learning the intentions of important nineteenth-century companies before such information became public. For example, during the 1870s, Carnegie learned from his work with railroad companies that the railroads intended to move from iron rails to steel rails, and he invested heavily in steel before the intentions of the railroads became widely known. Ultimately, as the result of his successful exploitation of this and other inside information, Carnegie became the richest man in the world.

To most people, it seems absolutely intuitive that they should be able to use information that they gain at work to their financial benefit. Therein lies the problem. It may not seem wrong, but it is. Carnegie used inside information to his benefit at a time when there was no law against it. Today, however, many of his actions would have been illegal. After the stock market crash of 1929, federal regulators realized that a few individuals could badly manipulate the market by operating with information the average investor lacked. They concluded that it is inherently unfair, for example, for a well-connected tycoon to dump a stock knowing the company is about to announce bankruptcy, while the average investor bought the stock thinking the company remained viable.

Consequently, starting in the early 1930s and continuing into the 1990s, Congress passed a series of laws that made it illegal to trade the securities of public companies based upon material inside information. States passed similar laws. As a general rule, you may not use information you get on the job to profit in the purchase or sale of corporate securities of publicly held companies if the information is not available to the public at large. Since the time that these laws were passed, the Supreme Court has applied the insider-trading laws not only to employees of companies but in some cases even to outsiders who *receive* the information from an insider.

You have probably heard of the big-time investment bankers who went to jail during the late 1980s—Ivan Boesky was among the most notorious—for trading hundreds of millions of dollars in stock based upon insider tips they received from corporate executives. Many powerful businesspeople have been done in by such greed. Therein lies another problem. Most employees have heard of these high-profile cases and consequently believe that insider trading is a problem only for the wealthy and powerful. In fact, however, while the big cases get more press, most insider-trading cases involve middle management or lower-level employees and small sums of money. For example, one of the biggest insider-trading scandals of the past several years occurred at IBM. It started when a secretary obtained some inside information about an upcoming acquisition and passed the information on to her husband, who in turn passed it on to others— including his brother, the owner of a pizza parlor, a schoolteacher, a doctor, an engineer, and a grocery store owner. They all made stock trades based upon the information, with most of them making a few thousand dollars in profits. The government learned of the improper use of the inside information and pursued some twenty-five people in the case, which resulted in many guilty pleas, fines, and the abrupt end to several modest careers. The IBM case makes clear that every corporate employee (and friend or neighbor of corporate employees) must be careful in how he or she uses valuable nonpublic information.

Anticompetitive Actions

Your goal on the job is to make your company's product or service of the highest quality at the lowest possible price. Once you turn your attention to hurting the competition rather than helping yourself, you run the risk of a career crash for your anticompetitive actions. Here are a few rules for avoiding the types of anticompetitive activity that frequently cost employees their jobs in companies of all sizes.

Do Not Conspire to Drive the Competition out of Business

Trying to drive the competition out of business used to be the objective of business. However, the situation has changed dramatically in the past century, and now employees at all levels need to avoid overt actions designed to destroy the competition. In the early part of the twentieth century, Congress became concerned about the tactics that tycoon John D. Rockefeller used to wipe out competitors to his Standard Oil Company. He and other monopolists would cut prices to drive others out of the market and then raise prices when they had a stranglehold on competition. They would create artificial shortages of supplies and materials that smaller companies could not withstand. In short, they engaged in overt acts to monopolize their industries, and they conspired with other companies to eliminate competition.

Congress did not like these activities—known as antitrust conspiracies—any more than it liked insider trading (although Congress outlawed insider trading after it outlawed antitrust conspiracies). Consequently, it passed the Sherman Antitrust Act and the Clayton Act, among others, which effectively prohibited dominant companies in a particular industry from conspiring with other companies in a manner that could substantially decrease competition. The tactics prohibited by these laws include certain forms of exclusive sales contracts, as well as secret rebates, predatory pricing, bid rigging, tied or bundled sales, and anticompetitive acquisitions. Since then, state legislatures and courts have allowed civil actions against companies that engage in "lesser" anticompetitive acts, including interfering with contractual relationships and defaming the business reputation of a company by spreading false information.

As with insider trading, you do not have to be a tycoon to be found liable for interfering with competition. If your company has a large market share and you work with another company to hurt a third company, you may have just engaged in a conspiracy that violates federal antitrust laws. If you call up a customer and lie about a competitor to get the customer to drop its contracts with that competitor, you may have just violated state tort law. Whether you violate a federal criminal law or a state civil law concerning anticompetitive actions, you will come out of it with career opportunities ranging from cotton candy vendor to license plate maker. Remember, while business owners and top executives get the most publicity for their allegedly anticompetitive actions, most cases resulting in this type of liability involve entry-level or midlevel salespeople and marketing managers who feel they are just going the extra mile for their companies by trashing the competition. They do not realize they are violating the law and ruining their futures by engaging in these tactics.

You need to keep your eyes trained on improving your own company and its products rather than tearing down the competition. As long as you keep yourself working on competitive improvement rather than competitive disparagement, your career can move forward.

Do Not Circumvent Procedures for the Competitive Bidding of Supply and Services Contracts

Every company engages in procurement activity. Your company probably has procedures for acquiring materials, supplies, and services from outside vendors and subcontractors—things that range from staplers to information services. If you do business with federal, state, or local government organizations—from a small municipality to the Department of Defense—you are probably subject to a thick set of regulations when you procure outside services. In many cases, if you supply to a private company that in turn sells to a government entity, you are still subject to various procurement integrity laws.

Company procurement policies, as well as federal, state, and local procurement laws, are designed to ensure that the customer gets proper quality at the best price. The overriding purpose of such laws is to prevent undue favoritism toward a potential supplier that might not be offering the best product or that might not be charging a reasonable price. Procurement rules level the playing field.

Anything you do to interfere with that competitive process could end your career. The most overt examples of subversion of the procurement process involve bribes and kickbacks. Employees of a potential supplier competing for your business may offer you money, a vacation, or tickets to the Super Bowl if you steer a procurement toward their company. In many cases, such activity may be contrary to company policy or downright illegal. It all depends upon the applicable policy or law, but as a general matter, you should check with the appropriate company official before you accept anything of value from an actual or potential supplier seeking business from your company. I know of a successful aerospace executive who lost his job because he accepted a single bottle of expensive wine from a subcontractor. In that case, it was not illegal for the employee to accept the gift, but it was against a clear company "procurement integrity charter" that allowed for no exceptions to a rule banning the acceptance of gifts from suppliers. Know the rules and follow them scrupulously.

Do Not Appropriate Your Company's Trade Secrets

One of the biggest risks to your career may come at a time when you feel the best about your professional future. A competitor calls you up and offers you big money to quit your current job and come work for it. When you get such an offer, remember that competitors steal employees like you for two reasons. First, the competitor wants you for your skills and expertise; it is very cost-effective for a company to hire an employee that another company spent the money training and developing. Second, the competitor wants you for your inside expertise on how your company works.

If you defect to a competitor, you have to be aware of two risks. First, you may have signed a "noncompete" agreement as part of your employment arrangement with your previous employer. These agreements often preclude employees from accepting a similar job with a competitor in the same geographic location for a specified period of time. If a restriction on competition is too broad, a court will not enforce it, but the fact is that you do not want to get into a lawsuit over a noncompete agreement the moment you walk into your new job. The best advice is not to sign noncompete agreements if there is any way out of them, but many employers will insist on them. If you have signed such an agreement, make sure your prospective new employer knows about it and has had a chance to evaluate whether you can legally work at the new company. Then, even if a dispute arises, you will be able to say the new employer was fully aware of the risks.

The second risk you face is an allegation of the theft of trade secrets. Companies consider a lot of information about their operations to be proprietary. In the past, protected proprietary information generally included customer lists or secret formulas—like the Colonel's eleven herbs and spices or the formula for Chanel #5 perfume. Now companies consider many other types of business and technical information to be proprietary, including processes for manufacturing microchips, plans for future advertising campaigns, and any other information that would be valuable in the hands of a competitor. With respect to inventions or processes, the company may obtain patents, which prevent you from appropriating the property for your use or the use of another company. With respect to business strategies such as advertising plans, there may be slightly less legal protection, but companies will often have employees sign broad statements promising not to disclose confidential company plans to people outside the company, and such statements are usually enforceable.

Know exactly what your company considers proprietary or you risk serious consequences. There have been many situations where the old employer sued the defecting employee and new employer before the defecting employee had even started working. Generally, it is OK to tell your new boss how you think your former employer would handle a particular business dilemma or would react to your new company's marketing strategy; these issues involve questions of judgment, not specific secret information from the former employer. However, former employers will not tolerate the clear misuse of their confidential intellectual property because the monetary risk is too high.

Companies place a high priority on protecting their proprietary data because losing it can cost the company significant earnings. According to a survey conducted by the American Society for Industrial Security, during 1999, Fortune 1000 corporations reported $45 billion in losses from thefts of their proprietary information. The average Fortune 1000 company reported two to three incidents of theft, with the average value of loss exceeding $500,000. High-tech companies reported 54 percent of the losses.

As a result of these startling statistics, companies are hiring ex–FBI agents and former Department of Justice attorneys to investigate people whom they suspect disclosed their trade secrets to outsiders, generally new employers. The practice of using such investigators began to gain popularity back in the 1980s, when private investigators helped prove that Hitachi Ltd. had stolen computer designs from IBM.

In the new century, the practice of using investigators to track down the theft of secrets is as common as using them for tracking down people who pirate software, which was discussed earlier. These investigators are good at what they do, and they will pursue you relentlessly if they suspect you have committed such wrongdoing.

Lying or Having Someone Else Lie for You

Overt dishonesty in the workplace is making a comeback, at least in some professional contexts. With so much wealth bloating the business world, the temptation to take a little for yourself may be greater than ever. Competent, productive people justify their dishonesty on the grounds that no one will know or care, or that they deserve something extra because they are otherwise doing a good job. Employers, clients, customers, and the other victims of your dishonesty do not see it that way, however. There are several ways in which successful people feebly justify dishonesty in the workplace and ruin their lives in the process. Here are a few of the most common temptations and what has actually happened to people who succumbed to them.

Do Not Think You Can Get Away with Padding the Hours It Takes to Do a Job

Many people bill for their services by the hour—including accountants, lawyers, plumbers, computer technicians, engineers, and advertising executives. If there is no maximum price on their work, some people become tempted to add hours to the actual time they have worked in order to get a little more money out of their customers. They do it because they feel they can get away with it; they think no one can verify the exact amount of time that they worked. They also find ridiculous ways to delude themselves into concluding that what they are doing is an acceptable practice. To borrow a few excuses I have heard, some conclude that they can do it because "everyone else does it"; others purportedly conclude that they are doing a good job, so they deserve a bonus. Once a lawyer in a successful law firm justified the practice of adding hours to his bills on the grounds that he allegedly worked more efficiently than most lawyers and therefore should not be penalized financially for his better work habits.

First, know that people do get caught. Some cheaters are just downright stupid, such as the Missouri lawyer who was indicted after he sent bills to clients indicating that he had worked thirty-one hours on each of five consecutive days. However, even more discreet bill padders get caught. A few years ago, a major New York consulting firm received terrible press after a few clients compared the "diversity hiring and practices reports" they had commissioned and received from the consulting firm. Each company had expected a detailed report individually tailored to the practices and needs of the company. When the different companies compared their reports, they found that the reports they had received were virtually identical, and, worse yet, each client had been charged the full development price for what was basically the same product.

Moreover, companies are now hiring billing auditors. These auditing companies look at bills and have well-trained experts who compare your company's bills with information contained in a broad database of pricing information for comparable services. While the science is far from perfect, some of these consultants are pretty good at spotting bill padding and excessive inefficiency.

Second, many coworkers who do not engage in bill padding will begin to resent someone who shows up late to work every day and leaves early but still manages to lead the department in number of billable hours. There are numerous documented instances of workers with fraudulent billing practices being turned in by resentful coworkers.

However, the most important reason for avoiding the practice has nothing to do with being caught. The practice is dishonest. If you engage in it, you have no right to expect anyone to treat you fairly in the workplace. I am a firm believer that bad practices catch up to you one way or another. If, for example, you are defrauding your customers and clients by overbilling them, you are likely to develop a careless and patronizing attitude toward them, and it will come across to them in other areas of your work. You will not get away with such professional dishonesty and disrespect for any prolonged period of time. You may not pay for it right away, but eventually you will pay for it nonetheless.

Do Not Understate or Reallocate the Hours You Charge to a Job

Interestingly, I have seen as many cases of employees understating or reallocating the amount of time they or their subordinates work as I have seen cases of workers overstating their time. You may ask why people would understate their time. In many businesses, the ability to get future work from a customer is based upon meeting budgets in prior jobs. Consequently, bosses will try to convince workers not to charge all of their time to a job that is overrunning. Workers resent this practice, and the offending boss often gets reported to upper management.

A more common problem is the reallocation of hours among projects. Consider this situation, roughly based on a true story. A construction company bids $3 million to build a small office complex. It is a fixed-price contract on which the company expects to make a $500,000 profit. That means the costs cannot exceed $2.5 million or the owner of the company will be very unhappy. In order to ensure that the contract is profitable, the company sets up internal budgets for each part of the task: $300,000 for design, $700,000 for materials, and $1.5 million for construction. The chief design engineer has a team working on the design aspects of the building. He soon realizes he is going to expend $350,000 on design and is worried he will not get the promotion he is seeking. So he tells a couple of his workers to charge their work to a new account number, which, unknown to the workers, is one of the construction account numbers.

When the project is done, the accountants show that the design work cost only $280,000, but the construction cost $1.6 million. The construction manager is worried about his job and taken aback that he overran his budget. He goes to the accounting office and finds that the design engineer had some of his people charging to construction accounts. He reports the practice to the boss, and the boss promptly fires the design engineer.

Reallocation of costs and fees is also a potentially criminal practice. Take this example. A manager for a computer software company manages three fixed-price contracts for the Department of Defense. The manager realizes he is overrunning two contracts but underrunning the third. So he directs his engineers to charge all of their time to the third contract even if they are working on the other two. The Defense Contract Audit Agency performs an audit and finds out about the scheme. The Defense Contract Audit Agency then refers the matter to the inspector general of the Department of Defense, who launches an investigation into possible criminal fraud due to the deliberate mischarging of the government. A year later, the manager pleads guilty to filing false claims against the government. He spends two years in jail. As you can see, you cannot afford to become part of a cost reallocation scheme.

Do Not Convince Yourself It Is OK to Inflate Expenses or Entertainment Costs

Once again, I find it strange that people who would not shoplift or rob someone will vastly inflate expense and entertainment accounts and pocket the difference. While there are no hard statistics on this issue, a simple perusal of media stories on such activity suggests that cases of this sort are mushrooming. The St. Louis legal community is still reeling from the news that one of its most prominent attorneys pleaded guilty to fraud for inflating expense and entertainment charges to his clients to the tune of hundreds of thousands of dollars. He was a pleasant, well-respected, and very well-paid lawyer who really did not need the extra cash. Yet he inflated his entertainment expenses over and over, as do others every day. It is wrong and not worth the risk.

Do Not Lie About Illness or Lateness

The billing and expense padding cases usually involve employees who are in management or who are partners at their firms. However, nonmanagement employees also do a lot of lying and cheating on the job, too, and it costs them their careers as well. For example, an acquaintance of mine who works at a Los Angeles consulting firm recently fired his assistant. The assistant had called in sick but then promptly ran into the boss's wife at the mall. The assistant had lied about being sick because she wanted to go shopping with some friends. Having already used up all of her allocated paid leave for the year, she feigned illness just to get the day off with pay. This practice—which is extremely common among both management and nonmanagement employees in companies across the country—is just as dishonest as padding an expense account or overbilling a client. People also lie frequently about the reasons why they arrive late and leave early. These practices cost respectable companies and their honest employees money that they should not have to pay. Consequently, if the right company customers or executives find out you are engaging in such activities, you will lose your job.

Worse still, employees often enlist other employees to lie for them. In the case just mentioned, the assistant actually got a secretary in the office to tell the boss that the assistant had called in sick and "really sounded terrible." The secretary almost lost her job as well. You have to realize that the only thing worse than your dishonesty on the job is luring others into your plots. On the flip side, you have to be sure you do not let others lure you into their intrigue—however minor it may seem. I have seen many corporate employees get into trouble for lying to a caller by saying that the boss was out of the office when the boss just did not want to take the call. There is nothing wrong with just telling the truth—the boss is busy and has not been taking calls. If you make up a lie, you may well get caught. Clever clients call different employees on different lines, and they get inconsistent stories. Your little white lie may have just cost the company a good customer and resulted in a career crash for you.

Do Not Falsify Records

When a company is designing a product, the customer often has a rigorous set of performance requirements, such as the pressure a tire must be able to withstand or the minimum landing approach speed of an aircraft. If the product does not quite pass a test of its performance characteristics and a project is behind schedule or over budget, you may find yourself pressured to falsify test or evaluation records. People justify the falsification of records in such circumstances on the grounds that the product is basically suitable for the purpose for which it has been manufactured and therefore the test failure is inconsequential. Other common situations where people falsify records include the falsification of accounting records to understate losses or overstate profits and the falsification of the contents of cargo to avoid weight and environmental hazard regulations.

There is never an excuse to falsify a record at work. In many circumstances, to do so is a criminal act that can have severe safety or financial repercussions for innocent people. No matter what pressures you may be under to get a job done, you must avoid the falsification temptation. Moreover, where the safety of your customer is involved, you have more than a duty not to falsify records. You have an affirmative duty to ensure that records are accurate. For example, after the tragic ValuJet crash several years ago, the government indicted a group of employees of a cargo company, alleging they had deliberately falsified records to indicate that the dangerous, incendiary oxygen canisters put into the airplane were empty. While the defendants were acquitted on the charges of intentionally falsifying documents, the company was still held liable for "reckless" conduct in failing to ensure that its shipping documents were accurate. The lesson of this story is clear. You must go the extra mile to ensure the accuracy of documents for which you are responsible.

What You Do Not Do

We have now covered professional risks posed by what you write, what you say, and what you do. However, the most subtle and, therefore, in some respects, the most dangerous cause of career crashes is what you *do not do*. This section will start with the innocent career omissions that can cost you your livelihood, such as the failure to keep your office and computer organized in a manner that allows you quick access to key documents and files. Then the discussion will move to more culpable professional omissions, such as the failure to report or the covering up of professional errors or wrongdoings that you or others may have committed on the job.

Office and Physical Files

Many people keep offices that look like they were just hit by a tornado. Often people joke about the piles of paper in their offices or the assortment of dusty

documents in the offices of their coworkers. To many people, office disorganization seems somewhat amusing and only mildly inconvenient. In fact, it is a
real problem for many professionals. Indeed, the failure to organize effectively
the information received or generated on the job has cost many good executives
their jobs and damaged the careers of many others. You cannot afford to take
the risk.

Consider these true stories. A prominent attorney filed a lawsuit against the
U.S. Department of Defense on behalf of a client who felt he was entitled to
more money under a Defense Department contract. The case involved some classified military information. The attorney's firm set up procedures for the maintenance, use, and storage of the classified materials. The lead attorney, however,
kept documents in disorganized piles all over his office. As he prepared a pleading, he found in one of his piles of materials a document that supported a point
he was making in the pleading. As usual, due to his disorganization, he was scur-
rying about to get the pleading filed on time. He attached the document to the
pleading and filed it publicly in federal court. Then he sent copies of the pleading and the attached document to four other attorneys representing parties in
the case.

Unfortunately, when the other attorneys read the attachment, they immediately noticed a marking on the top indicating the document was classified at a
high level and contained sensitive national security information. The lawyer who
filed the pleading not only had failed to notice the small classified marking at
the top of the document, but, more important, he also had failed to fill out a
form required for the viewing of classified documents; failed to keep the document in a secured area of his firm, specially designed for the storage of classified
information; failed to keep the required bright-red "classified" cover sheet on the
document, which would have tipped anyone off to the document's sensitive
nature; and failed to run the pleading by authorized security monitors whom the
court had appointed to review all pleadings before they were filed. As a result,
a federal investigation ensued, and while the lawyer did not go to jail, he was
given a security reprimand that effectively ended his ability to represent clients
who used classified information.

Other less dramatic, but nonetheless serious, examples of the adverse consequences of office disorganization abound. As a person whose career depends
greatly on documents, I hear examples of the adverse effects of office disorganization all the time. For example, one legal assistant almost got fired recently
when she could not keep track of the various piles of documents on her desk.
Instead of sending the opposing counsel a settlement offer as she had been

instructed to do, she accidentally sent the opposing counsel all of the trial strategy memos that her firm had developed internally.

A young accountant suffered a major career setback when he could not locate his copy of an important document relating to a client audit. He knew it was somewhere in the thousands of pages of materials piled up all over his office, but he could not find it, and he needed it for a meeting that was starting in a few minutes. As a result, the accountant had to call his boss on a cruise ship to ask where the boss's copy of the document was. The accountant forgot that the boss was cruising off the coast of Turkey and that it was 3:00 A.M. on the ship. The boss's cell phone was off, so the accountant called the cruise company and placed a ship-to-shore call. The bleary-eyed boss (who thought that the only reason he would be summoned for a call at that hour was for a family emergency) had to climb five decks to get the ship-to-shore call on the bridge of the ship. Worried and tired, the boss picked up the phone and heard his subordinate ask in a chipper tone, "Hey, Mr. Jones, do you know where your copy of that audit letter is?" The boss was less than amused. The boss continued to tell the story long after the young accountant had moved on to another job.

While many people get into trouble because they have too much junk in their offices, occasionally people get into trouble for not having enough. For example, a couple of years ago, a senior marketing executive at a manufacturing company received a subpoena from the Federal Trade Commission for documents relating to some business transactions he had brokered. He invited his company lawyers into his office to look through his files. Every drawer was empty. The executive smiled and said that he stays out of trouble by keeping nothing. Unfortunately, his failure to have any documentation of his negotiations and transactions made it look like he was hiding something and actually made it harder for the company to prove compliance with federal law. The executive left the company six months later.

As a litigator, I have worked with corporate executives, from CEOs to frontline supervisors, in dozens of companies of all sizes, selling all manner of products or services. I have had the opportunity to rifle through the files of hundreds of executives, and I have seen it all. I have seen file folders in which documents from 2001 were mixed in with documents from 1969. One executive's files had professional correspondence intermingled with letters from his ex-wife's divorce attorney, in which the attorney accused the executive of spousal abuse. Some executives keep years' worth of credit-card offers and seminar solicitations littered around their offices for no apparent reason.

As mundane as it may seem, simple and effective office and file maintenance is an important part of crashproofing your career. Such organization will prevent the sort of unfortunate incidents previously related in this section. Equally important, a well-organized office gives the impression of a well-organized person. In an era where rivals will do anything to knock one another down a notch at the office, you cannot afford to even be the subject of "disastrous office" jokes. In order to achieve a workable system, you need to follow four basic rules:

1. Control what you receive.
2. Control what you retain.
3. Organize what you retain.
4. Do not overorganize what you retain.

Once you have such a system in place, you will do your work more effectively, and you will feel an enhanced sense of control and confidence in the office.

The following rules and ideas apply to you even if you do not work in a traditional office. If, for example, you are a salesperson who calls on clients all day long, you need to organize your car as if it were an office. If you deliver packages for a living, your truck will need the same kind of organization that a traditional desk would, and your pager and inventory tracker run the same crash risks that office computers do. So take the following basic principles and apply them to your "office," whatever that may be.

Stop the Flow of Unnecessary Paper Before It Even Gets to You

Until a few years ago, I felt helpless to stop the flow of paper I received from both within and outside the office. From outside the office, I received magazines, seminar leaflet solicitations, faxed solicitations from insurance brokers, and all sorts of other documents that were not necessary to the performance of my job. Now I have a form letter I use to tell companies and organizations to stop sending me stuff. I just punch in the address and send it; I do it a couple of times a year.

You even have some legal protection. There are federal and state laws prohibiting the sending of unwanted faxes or other unwelcome solicitations, and in some circumstances you can sue the organizations that send them to you for violating these laws. Other localities allow you to collect a fine if someone continues to solicit your business after you have written them telling them to stop. I have never done it, but I recently heard of a lady who has made several thousand dollars doing exactly this. She writes the companies telling them to stop soliciting her, and if they do it anyway, she files a form in small claims court. The companies, many of which are from other cities, are not going to hire an attorney to defend against a $500 lawsuit, so they just write her checks—one after the other. The bottom line here is that you can get people to stop sending you unwanted mail and you should do so.

When it comes to unwanted documents that you receive from within your company, you should politely tell the source to stop sending you materials that deal with matters not relating to office business—dogs for sale, yard sales, and so on. Even some business-related materials may just be clutter in your office if they have no bearing on your work. If it is something you never read anyway, tell people to take you off the distribution list. I recently took myself off the distribution list for a newsletter I received on a weekly basis. It came from a lawyer who practices in an area of law that I do not. I never used the newsletter for anything except as a coaster for my soda. If you are fortunate enough to have a secretary or assistant whom you can really trust, sit down with him or her and discuss a process by which that person can screen your mail and take out the junk before you even have to look at it. That way it never even gets into your office.

Discard Immediately What You Do Not Need and Have Regular File-Purging Days

You receive many letters and other documents you do not need to read. *Throw them away immediately*. As to the documents you do read, you will probably never have to read them again. In the case of such materials, read them and throw them away immediately. Spend the first three minutes of each day pitching documents you just finished reading or you do not need to read at all. It feels great. It will get rid of almost two-thirds of the clutter that would otherwise accumulate in your office.

With respect to the materials you need to keep, most of them become obsolete in a matter of a few weeks, and a small percentage remain important for a few months. To arrive at an effective disposition for these documents, you need to have file-purging days. I put file purging on my calendar four times per year. You will be amazed at how many documents become completely obsolete with the passage of short periods of time. When you prepare to purge your files, keep in mind that you may be required as a matter of law to keep some documents. For example, records relative to federal contracts have to be maintained for three years after the contract, and company policy may require that you keep certain accounting and personnel records for a stated period of time. Depending on the law of your state, you may be required to keep documents that relate to actual or even threatened litigation. Know the rules of your company, your industry, and your state. However, the vast majority of your documents may be and should be pitched the moment you do not need them.

Use a Simple Organizational Structure for Your Office and for the Files You Retain

As is the case with all your efforts to reduce the likelihood of a career crash, you combat the forces of disorder around you with simple, flexible structure. The structure needs to flow naturally from your job responsibilities. Start with the basics: your office already has a structure. A floor is a floor. It is there for people to walk on to get from one place to another. It is not a storage facility, and it is not an obstacle course. You will work inefficiently and look bad to coworkers if piles of paper litter the floor of your office. By the same token, a chair is for someone to sit on. Never make a boss, coworker, customer, or subordinate lift piles of stuff off of your office chairs just to have the honor of sitting down and talking to you in your office.

This means you keep no files on the floor, chairs, or windowsills. Tell people with whom you work that they are not to leave anything they deliver to your office on the floor, chairs, or anywhere else but your in-box.

Once you have your office in some sort of preliminary order, you must develop a simple filing system that will resist the forces of disorder, which work hard to make your office a mess again. There are many possibilities, and you must choose the one that is best for you. Here is a baseline structure from which you can develop your own system.

If you need to keep a document, put it in one of three places. First, if you believe you will want to refer to it when somebody calls you or when you write a memo or prepare for a meeting, put it in one of a few small stacks on your desk, which are reserved for a very limited number of documents you may truly need on a moment's notice. At the top of each stack, put a piece of typing paper with the name of the client, customer, or transaction in extra-large letters—for example, STEVENS CASE. Keep the Stevens case documents that you may need right away in that stack for easy reference, and go through the stack once a week to weed out documents that are no longer immediate-need documents. You should never have more than four or five of these immediate-need stacks on your desk at one time. To keep the number of stacks to a minimum, one stack should be labeled Everything Else. Put in that stack the isolated immediate-need documents that do not warrant their own stack. This everything-else stack gives you the flexibility that all effective structures require. Always organize and maintain your immediate-need documents yourself—do not use secretaries and assistants—and always know where everything is located. Also, instruct subordinates never to remove anything from one of the marked stacks on your desk without your express permission.

When a document fails to make or falls off the immediate-need list but you think you should still retain it, put it into a matter file in your file cabinet. Keep a matter file for each transaction or customer you have. A stockbroker needs a matter file for each client. A software engineer needs a matter file for each program on which he or she is working. A lawyer needs a matter file for each active case or deal. Put the correspondence chronologically (newest at the front) in the front of the file and the memos and related documentation in labeled folders behind the correspondence. If you have a secretary or assistant, put him or her in charge of maintaining these files.

Finally, have an area of your cabinet space devoted to subject files. These files are of general interest to what you do but are not related to a particular matter. In my business, subject files would contain legal research on issues that might be relevant to multiple cases. A stockbroker would have subject files for market forecasts or industry analyses. A software engineer would use subject files for articles, industry standard specifications, or other documents that by their nature apply to many different design projects. Arrange the subjects alphabetically. As with your other documents, go through the matter and subject files every few months and throw out documents you no longer need, or send them to storage if there is a remote possibility you will need them in the future. Avoiding a crash due to office disorganization is that simple.

Do Not Overorganize Your Files

Some people—often the ones who used to be the least organized—get on an organization kick and go overboard. If you become too complex or rigid in your structure, you will not keep it current for any useful period of time. It will become too difficult to stay organized, and you will revert to your previous bad habits. For example, while researching this book, I read an article that said you must have nine principal types of files and hundreds of subfiles in order to be efficient at the office. According to the "expert" about whom this article was written, you need the following: a sort tray, a priority tray, a delegation tray, a works-in-progress tray, an office-reference file, a professional-reference file, a "tickler" or reminder file, a planning file, and a personal-items file. Moreover, the tickler file, which you "absolutely have to use" to remind you of due dates, needs to have 31 tabs in each of twelve folders so that you have a tab for each day of the year. This type of file apparently was invented during World War II to ensure that allied troops received their supplies on time.

The last time I checked, I was not in the business of saving the free world. I have no need for such a complicated filing system. You can put a system like this into place, but how long do you think it will take before you scrap it? Whereas flexible, simple structure gives you professional strength, rigid overorganization is actually a catalyst for disorder and failure because it takes too much work to keep it in place. Adopt a structure that makes your life easier, not one that takes on a life of its own.

Computer Files

One of the greatest benefits of computers is that they create no physical clutter—other than all of those cables and wires, which you can hide behind your office furniture. Because of the lack of physical clutter, people tend to believe that computers only add to efficiency and healthy structure at work. Not true. While computers inherently reduce physical clutter, an unstructured approach to the storage of data on your computer can also contribute to a career crash because computers create two other kinds of clutter: mental clutter and legal clutter. For example, if you keep all of your computer-generated documents in a single file folder or in a huge, complex array of folders, you may not find it any easier to locate something you need than if you had a floor full of documents or that previously discussed World War II filing system. To avoid mental clutter, you need to develop a system of immediate-need, subject, and matter files for your computer, or some other structure similar to what you use for hard-copy documents, or you will face the same organizational problems that you face with a messy office.

Computers also create a unique problem—legal clutter. Computer-caused legal clutter arises in two diametrically opposed situations: when you find that you cannot access a computerized document that you want and when you learn that you cannot discard a computerized document that you do not want.

How Computer Crashes Cause Career Crashes

Employees are often unwilling to discuss the unreliability of their company's computer network for fear of making customers or clients nervous. However, having had the opportunity to work within dozens of companies, I can tell you that all of them have significant problems with system malfunctions that sub-

stantially and negatively affect productivity. Often these system crashes are nothing more than an inconvenience or an opportunity to take an unscheduled coffee break. However, sometimes the consequences are much more serious. Take
the case of the lawyer who had to file a brief before 5:00 P.M. on a Thursday for
an important case before a federal judge. On Thursday morning, he had a near-
final draft of the document on the firm's computer system. It was about thirty-
five pages long. At 2:30 P.M. the firm's computer system went down. It was down
for six hours. The lawyer could not access or print the document. He called the
judge—a crusty man who had never used a computer in his life—and told the
judge the document was finished but the firm's computer system had just gone
down. He asked for an extension. The judge said, "Just type it up from your last
draft." The lawyer had not printed the last draft, or any draft for that matter,
and told the judge that unfortunate fact. "That isn't very smart, is it?" asked the
judge and told the lawyer to come in and argue the case without a brief on file.
The lawyer lost the motion, and even though the loss probably had little to do
with the lawyer's failure to file a pleading, the client blamed the lawyer's loss on
the failure to file. The lawyer lost a good client.

Part of your file structure at work must include the following:

1. Repeatedly "save" your work to the hard drive so you do not lose completed sections of your documents when the system goes down.
2. Keep hard copies of important drafts until the final document is done.
3. Back up important documents to disks or local networks.
4. Maintain your ability to type a document the old-fashioned way on an
   electric typewriter.

When I write books, I save my work to the hard drive every time I finish one
page, I print out a hard copy of my work every other day, and I save what I have
to disk one time per week. Even if I never experience a fatal computer crash, this
process gives me a very comforting sense of security as I work. That is valuable
in and of itself.

Legal Clutter Created by Computers Extends to Drafts and Deleted Documents

The more dangerous problem with computer files is their permanence. This issue
was briefly touched on in the section discussing E-mail. Even when you delete
a document from your computer, it frequently remains retrievable. The perma-

nence of the imprint of computerized documents extends beyond E-mail to drafts of letters that were never sent and early versions of memos that you edited heavily before you issued them. These draft and deleted documents often contain information you never intended to let see the light of day—aggressive strategies you ultimately decided not to pursue, emotional outbursts you ultimately toned down, or factual statements you eventually determined were not true and therefore deleted from the document or left on the hard drive but never forwarded to anyone.

Drafts that are left unguarded on your company's computer system are the most dangerous types of computerized documents because they are often accessible to anyone at work—including rivals and enemies. If you are writing a controversial document, you need to make use of special passwords and other security mechanisms that prevent others from accessing the documents while you are writing them. Then you must delete old versions of the document after you have developed the final version. That will provide you a basic level of protection against finding your draft work product used against you by coworkers and outside adversaries. Indeed, there are numerous documented cases of disgruntled employees searching the files of other employees before leaving the company and then later using the documents against the other employees in employment-related litigation.

Using passwords to protect documents and deleting outdated versions of documents can give you some protection, but there remain risks. If an outsider truly wants to get at your drafts and deleted documents, there are forensic computer experts who can often reconstruct the documents from hard drives and backup tapes. There are two ways around this risk. First, as always, be careful what you write, even at the outset. Jot down notes and ideas on a piece of paper that you can really throw away so your early drafts on the computer do not contain the kinds of errors and mistakes that have been discussed throughout this chapter. Second, learn from your company information technology person how easy it is to reconstruct deleted documents from your system, and, if possible, work closely with your technology experts to purchase system encryption and overwriting mechanisms that give you the capacity to restrict access to and wipe out drafts.

Of course, the forensic experts (who reconstruct the deleted items) and the overwriting experts (who try to prevent the reconstruction of deleted documents) are in a battle right now—each one trying to stay ahead of the other—so you can never be sure that you will be able to keep adversaries armed with subpoenas and experts from reading early drafts of your documents. Taking care is always better than trusting the erasure capabilities of your company computer experts.

The Cover-Up

Not taking the time to organize your office, physical files, and computer files can contribute extensively to a career crash. Usually, however, it takes a while for your office situation to get into such disarray that you start to see adverse effects upon your career. Other omissions result in quicker crashes. Indeed, the quickest way to see your career crash is not to come clean with your professional mistakes.

I have seen dozens of careers suffer huge setbacks when people would not admit, or took affirmative steps to cover up, their misdeeds. Ironically, the misdeeds in and of themselves usually would not have ended the careers of the guilty persons. Rather, it was the act of covering up the misdeeds that caused the career crashes.

Let's start at the top. While President Clinton's affair with an intern a few years back was a major lapse in judgment, the reason he got impeached and almost lost his job was that he lied about it under oath—he tried to cover it up. Most people agree that if he just would have admitted the affair and moved on, his legacy would not have been so badly damaged. In the 1970s, President Nixon had to resign not because he ordered the now infamous Watergate break-in (which had not been proven when he resigned) but rather because he covered up information about the break-in when he learned about it, rather than coming clean.

If a crash due to a cover-up can happen to the president on the job, it can happen to you on the job as well. I have seen many people lose their jobs because they tried to hide their mistakes or the mistakes of others—and often when the mistakes they were hiding were not really that bad. For example, I recently handled a case where a midlevel contracts manager for a manufacturing company agreed in a memorandum to a supplier that a certain contract provision relating to replacement of defective parts would not apply to the supplier. The signed contract said that the supplier would have to replace certain parts under certain conditions, but the contracts manager sent the supplier the memorandum just prior to signing the contract, which told the supplier that the company would not enforce that particular provision against the supplier. Several months later, the company found problems with the parts provided by the supplier and told the contracts manager to send a letter demanding that the parts be replaced in accordance with the contract. The manager knew he had waived (i.e., agreed not to enforce) the relevant contract provision but did not tell anyone. He even signed the demand letter.

Of course, the supplier responded with a pithy letter that attached the contracts manager's earlier memorandum waiving the relevant contract provision. The contracts manager had to know that this letter was coming, but he still failed to come clean with his error. As a result of the stinging letter sent by the supplier, the management of the company was embarrassed and fired the manager. I am convinced that the manager would still have his job today had he just admitted he waived the contract provision at the outset.

Often, ignoring or covering up a problem results in criminal liability. While the general rule in the United States is that you cannot be criminally liable for failure to act, there are enough exceptions and loopholes to that rule that you should never rely upon it. For example, failure to report instances of toxic waste dumping can be a crime. Knowingly allowing the government to pay an inaccurate invoice—even if the original billing problem was an innocent mistake—can result in jail time for the people who knew about it and failed to correct it. Lying to a court or government investigator, even about legal conduct, can in some circumstances result in criminal penalties—fines and jail time.

Crashproofing Law #1 applies here as well as it has in all of the preceding discussions. You must act (or fail to act) on the assumption that your worst adversary is perched on your shoulder. Every time you think about concealing or covering up your own errors or those of others, also think about how those who might want to hurt you could seize upon your inaction and cause your career to crash. You will find it is almost always the better course of action to fess up and move on with your career. The consequences of covering up are far worse than a humble approach of candor and openness.

2

Managing Your Relationships with Others on the Job

Professional Emotion Is Like a Wet Rag: Wring It Out

Once you have structured your own actions and inactions on the job to avoid a career crash, it is time to turn your attention to your interaction with others on the job. The overriding objective in dealing with others is to maintain respectful, *unemotional* professional relationships. Chapter 1 touched on the dangers of emotion when it discussed writing letters. However, when it comes to interaction with others on the job, learning to deal effectively with professional emotion is the most important skill you can have. Many executives, employees, and business owners who are honest in their professional conduct and who are careful not to make career-ending mistakes in their memos and meetings, still wind up seeing their careers crash because they allowed their emotions to cloud their professional reasoning as they interacted with others on the job. Interestingly, positive emotion causes crashes as often as negative emotion does.

As you interact with others on the job, your objective should be to wring the emotion out of your professional life to the extent possible. This section will discuss how to develop healthy, mutual professional respect between you and those with whom you work—and how to prevent those balanced relationships from degenerating into emotional disasters.

This skill is essential in today's workplace because employers in our country are legally entitled to fire people for virtually any reason—even if they are doing a good job. Forty-nine states have adopted what is known as the "employment-at-will" doctrine: an employer can fire you for any reason or no reason at all. The only exceptions are that an employer cannot fire an employee for refusing to succumb to sexual advances, refusing to commit a crime or fraud, or refusing to engage in other illegal conduct such as discrimination.

Yet an underlying misconception remains in the minds of many workers that they can be fired only if they do something wrong—like stealing trade secrets, writing a profane E-mail, or committing any of the other misdeeds discussed in Chapter 1. The truth is the boss can fire you because he or she does not like your hair color, does not like your smile, does not like you at all, or just feels like firing you for the hell of it.

The same rule, of course, holds true for your customers and clients. You may do a great job for them, but they have an absolute right to go to someone else the next time. There is no legal obligation for one company to do business with another company. Many careers have crashed when employees who did good work for a client just assumed they would get the next job for that client but did not.

Given this very precarious situation, you cannot rely solely upon your care, confidence, and competence on the job to prevent a career crash. Other people need to *like* working with you. Bosses have to want you on the job. Coworkers have to feel you are a person with whom they want to associate. Subordinates must respect you. Clients and customers have to smile when they think about giving you more of their money. In short, you must supplement your stellar professional conduct with well-balanced professional relationships.

At the same time, you have to be careful not to have others with whom you work like you *too much*. If you become a boss's pet, you will engender resentment among coworkers. If you associate with one group at work to the exclusion of another, you will make enemies. If you develop too chummy of a relationship with a supplier, you may not always act in your company's best interests when it comes time to get the best product or service at the best price for your company. Professional relationships pose complex questions of balance.

The answer is Crashproofing Rule #2: wring the emotion out of your professional relationships so that you treat everyone with the same level of respect and professional distance. This entails developing a sense of equilibrium in your dealings with bosses, coworkers, subordinates, suppliers, and customers. Equilibrium is evenly balanced structure. When you develop strong animosities toward others at work, you upset the workplace equilibrium and invite career trouble. By the same token, when you develop workplace bonds that are too strong, you tend to value those bonds over the interests of your company, and you risk a career crash due to the disturbance of workplace equilibrium.

Crashproofing Law #2 requires that you work to achieve balanced relationships among the people with whom you work. You start with the basic rule that you must learn to treat everyone at work in the same manner. You learn both to be nicer to people whom you do not like and to put a little more distance between yourself and those whom you do like. Of course, there are some narrowly defined exceptions to the rule of equal treatment. But if you follow the advice provided in this section, then even when you single someone out for different treatment, that person will never know it and you will still maintain the professional equilibrium essential to a crashproofed career.

Once you develop solid professional relationships on the job, you have to move to the next phase in developing your workplace equilibrium. You must balance the interests of subordinates, superiors, customers, and suppliers as they make competing demands upon your time. You have to give people the proper amount of access to you, always leaving each person with the impression that he or she is as important to you as anyone else is. Again, the general rule is you should treat everyone the same. We will, however, discuss some exceptions, such as how to give your top clients and customers special access to you without offending people and organizations of lower priority.

In view of these considerations, the following discussion of workplace relationships divides into three easy parts: dealing with people whom you like, dealing with people whom you do not like, and balancing the needs of your subordinates, superiors, customers, and suppliers. When you are done implementing Crashproofing Rule #2, you will have the professional security that comes with solid, stable workplace relationships.

People You Like—Keeping Your Attractions in Check

There can be no doubt that your emotional attraction toward someone with whom you work can adversely affect your job performance, and it is an inescapable fact that some such attractions have resulted in what could only be termed "spectacular" career crashes. This section will start with the most high-risk conduct—namely workplace sex—and then move into the dangers involving less salacious, but often equally dangerous, workplace emotions, including overly informal relationships with subordinates and misplaced loyalty to coworkers and outsiders who do not have company interests in mind.

Mutual Attraction

Approximately 59 percent of the American workforce admit to having had a relationship with someone they met at work. Many of them were married to someone else at the time. Approximately 31 percent of the workforce admit to having "known of someone" who actually had sex at work either during office hours or after the office had closed.

Having worked closely with employees of hundreds of companies and organizations, I know more stories of workplace romance gone awry than could be related in an entire book. As a result, I start with a simple premise. The best rule is to avoid sexual relationships with coworkers entirely. This is especially true if you are married—for reasons that far transcend the purpose of this book—but the recommendation that you abstain from workplace relationships holds true for single people as well. Too many people have been badly burned professionally by office romance. Try avoiding it. Companies do not like office romance, and about 27 percent now have some sort of policy restricting it.

I am, however, a realist. No one can change human nature and the chemistry of physical attraction, and neither I nor anyone else is going to convince a substantial percentage of people to avoid entirely sexual relationships with coworkers. So let me also provide you some information and advice on how to handle office romance based upon real-world examples of sexual relationships in the workplace.

If you are not willing or able to look elsewhere for romance, remember that work relationships that become sexual relationships almost invariably cloud professional judgment, so you must put some restrictions on how you handle such relationships or your career may crash. Here are a few guidelines even the most lustful should be able to follow.

Do Not Flaunt Your Physical Relationships on Company Premises

I should not even need to make this point, but many very intelligent people have ruined their entire lives by egregious displays of affection at the office. Making out in a cubicle in front of others does not sit well with your coworkers. Yet employees do much worse. Consider this true example, to which I have made minor alterations to protect what is left of the reputation of the person who did what follows.

A very successful, Harvard-educated senior manager at a Fortune 100 company carried on a sexual relationship with a secretary whose work area was near his. Many people in the department knew that the two would sneak out for trysts on a regular basis. The manager was already on thin ice because his superiors had come looking for him a couple of times when he had just slid out with the secretary, and they had been unable to find him.

One day, an executive vice president came looking for the man in question. Someone told him that the man said he was going to his car. The executive took the elevator down to the parking garage to try to find the guy before he left. The executive could not find the man, but, on his way back to his office, he walked by two security guards sitting in a booth containing the monitors connected to the garage security cameras. The security guards were laughing uncontrollably. "They're at it again," they said to the executive as he walked by. He stopped and asked what they were talking about. One of the guards told him that two people had been having sex in a car in the garage on a regular basis for several weeks, but they did not know that their every move was being captured on closed-circuit television for the viewing pleasure of the guards. Although the picture was not too clear, it took no more than a minute for the executive vice president to determine that the man in the car was the guy he had been searching for. Ten minutes after this Harvard man's final moment of workplace bliss, he returned to his office, and the security guards escorted him out of the building for good— a common scenario in professional crashes. Career over.

Having sex at work may seem daring and inventive, but it is absolutely not worth the risk under any circumstances. And, by the way, it is not that original anyway. Even a former president has done it. There are much more exciting opportunities elsewhere where you will not risk a career crash. Rent a hot-air balloon or a unicycle instead—I don't care. Just don't do it at the office.

Maintain Physical Distance from Your Romantic Interest While on the Job

If you find yourself attracted to a subordinate or a superior, you are running a big risk. Many companies have clearly stated policies prohibiting superior-subordinate relationships because the companies recognize that, when the breakups occur, these relationships often become sexual harassment lawsuits. It is illegal to use a position of power to gain sexual favors, and while all might be fine while the relationship is good, the situation might deteriorate into legal harassment if the subordinate wants to break up and the superior does not. This is a very common occurrence in companies. Based upon my experience, it seems the average Fortune 500 company has twenty or more such lawsuits going on at any given time.

For that reason, I highly recommend you avoid a relationship with someone who has lines connecting to yours, directly or through someone else, on the organization chart. Even if the romance thrives and there is never any sort of harassment suit, you still run the risk of disgruntled coworkers complaining that you are showing or receiving favoritism by virtue of the on-the-job romance. If you find such a romance developing, do what I recently saw a couple do. Have one of you put in for a transfer to another job in the company that does not involve a direct reporting relationship. Also, if possible, have that person transferred to a different floor or even a different building. Then you have done your best to prevent later allegations of harassment or favoritism.

Unilateral Attraction

Even more dangerous than a consensual sexual relationship at work is a situation where one person wants the relationship and the other does not. As a matter of statistical fact, most often this situation involves an older, more senior male harassing a younger, more junior female. However, there are reported cases of senior female executives harassing males and senior male executives harassing other males. I recently learned of a lawsuit filed by a junior female executive against a senior female executive, so these problems come in all shapes and sizes.

These attractions are, indeed, fatal attractions when it comes to careers. In almost every case where I have heard such allegations, the more senior executive lost his or her job. In most cases, even the junior executive left because he or she felt uncomfortable in light of the departure of the senior executive. In one case, the situation deteriorated so badly that the senior executive ended up in a psychological care facility for several weeks.

If you have an attraction to someone junior to you on the job and feel a need to pursue it, stop immediately if the other person does not seem interested. If you do not stop, you run two risks. First, the junior employee may succumb to the pressure and agree to a nearly forced relationship with you. Eventually that person will tire of the situation and will have an open-and-shut sexual harassment suit. Generally, an employee pressured into a sexual relationship will recover damages well into the six figures. If you are the supervisor, your career is over as soon as the suit is filed.

Second, the junior employee may continue to resist you. What often happens in these situations is the senior executive becomes resentful and starts to make derogatory and insulting remarks about the subordinate. If the anger is great enough, the senior executive may take ridiculous actions to hinder the progress of the subordinate. Some very successful, high-level executives have done this. For example, a thirty-five-year-old executive at a major corporation relayed this story to me. He and I were trying to locate a former employee who had worked for his company long ago so that the former employee could testify for us at a trial. The executive told me the former employee probably would not testify voluntarily because he had been fired for the following reason. Years earlier, the former employee had developed an attraction to a secretary. The secretary rebuffed him. One day when she bent over to pick up some papers, she felt a quick but minor pain on her back. When she turned around, the man was laughing. "What did you do?" she asked him. He just kept laughing and walked away. The secretary found out later that day from someone else that the man was bragging to others how he had "bounced a quarter off her butt to see how firm it was." He was fired the next week. When we tracked him down, we learned that he had not been able to get a steady job anywhere else during the ensuing fifteen years. This was a smart man who let his frustrations get the better of him, and he ruined his life in the process.

Stunningly, about six months later, the young executive who had relayed this story to me was escorted out of the company by security guards. Why? Because he, too, had made suggestive remarks to a secretary who was not interested in him, and she eventually complained to senior management. So even an executive who had witnessed firsthand the destruction of someone else's career for making unwanted advances to a subordinate did exactly the same thing. This is the best example I know (but only one of many) of how overpowering sexual attraction can be at work, how it can consume reasonable and competent people, and how it can destroy careers. You must exercise extreme personal discipline and *leave the person alone* if you ever find yourself rejected by a subordinate on the job. You will get over it, and you will be glad that you did not pursue it.

Dealing with People You Do Not Like

Careers also crash because of overt conflicts between employees. You need to know how to handle the most common situations: what to do if you are the vic-

tim of harassment or discrimination, what to do if you just do not like someone, and how to handle incompetent coworkers.

How to Handle Being a Harassment Victim

Sadly, even the victims of harassment and discrimination often suffer career setbacks. Federal laws protect victims of harassment and discrimination by pre-
venting retaliatory discharge of the victim and by requiring reinstatement of the
victim with back pay if he or she is fired. However, all the legal protection in
the world does not make for a healthy, productive work environment for the victim of harassment or discrimination. Too often, the victim of harassment suffers terribly on the job even after the harassment incident is resolved legally.

If you are the victim of harassment or discrimination, I recommend you make
one and only one attempt to resolve the problem in a calm, professional manner
with the person committing the harassment before you report it or retain a
lawyer. It may be the best meeting you ever had. Meet with the person in a place
where you are not totally isolated but where others cannot hear you—a conference room with glass partitions, for example. Tell the person politely that you
will under no circumstances enter into a relationship with him or her and that
the advances are "unwelcome"—an important term from a legal standpoint. Tell
the person you still intend to work with him or her professionally. Then say in
no uncertain terms that if that person commits even one more harassing act,
makes one more harassing statement, or spreads one more rude rumor about you,
you will report the matter to the appropriate company official and retain a
lawyer. Tell that person his or her career will be over and you are not kidding.
Smile and ask if you have been understood. Agree not to tell others about the
meeting so long as the person behaves. This approach works like a charm most
of the time, and it prevents your needing to take any further action that could
ultimately cause your career as much disruption as it will cause the other person's. If, of course, the harassment does not stop, go right to the appropriate company official, or if your company does not have such an official, retain an
employment lawyer.

Just Not Liking Someone

Throughout your career you will develop a long list of people whom you do not
like. When you find a person who falls into that category, you need to make it
a high-priority professional goal to find a way to work effectively with that per-

son—even a competitor or adversary. Corporations place great value on people who get along with difficult coworkers, suppliers, and customers. You can find yourself an indispensable part of your company if you are the person who makes relationships work.

More important, not getting along with someone can lead to having devastating charges leveled against you. When someone accuses a supervisor of harassment or discrimination, often the supervisor's defense is that he or she just did not get along with the accuser. An employer—or worse yet, a judge or jury—has little ability to distinguish between a personality conflict and an act of harassment or discrimination. So you are risking everything if you rely upon the "we just did not get along" defense. You may find yourself wrongfully liable for an illegal act.

Also, jilted or disgruntled employees often become so angry that they will simply invent claims that bosses or coworkers have behaved illegally or unethically. They will do anything to destroy the people with whom they are having a personality conflict. Vengeful coworkers commonly level charges against other employees that range from violating company policy to cheating customers to violating federal laws or regulations applicable to the workplace. It is a common tactic, and even if you end up proving your innocence, your reputation suffers merely by virtue of the accusation.

Consequently, you must consider working well with others as much a part of your job as competent technical performance of your job duties. You do not have to like everyone; rather, you need to find a way to work with people you do not like. If you think of developing a good working relationship with someone you do not like as a standard job responsibility similar to writing a good memo, it becomes a lot easier to do. Working well with others is simply not optional any more.

Dealing with Incompetent Subordinates

The people whom I dislike the most at the office are those who simply do not have the technical skills or commitment necessary to do the job. Unfortunately, even with the employment-at-will doctrine, sometimes it can be hard to get rid of them. I recently heard of a case of an ex-employee who threatened to sue his employer for discrimination under the Americans with Disabilities Act. The worker came in at least forty-five minutes late every day; as a result, he was fired. He claimed (through his lawyer) that he had "compulsive lateness disorder" and could not be fired for his disability. Stunningly, because the company had not carefully documented the real reasons why he was late (late night partying, dislike of his boss), lawyers for the company were worried enough about the claim that they reinstated him and provided him counseling.

Incompetence is a very legitimate reason to fire someone. However, if you have an incompetent employee working for you, you are opening yourself up to major career problems if you do not document the incompetence thoroughly before taking adverse action. For example, in many harassment or discrimination cases, supervisors try to defend their decisions to terminate an employee on the grounds of incompetence. Incompetence can be, of course, a valid defense to a claim of unlawful discharge. In most of these cases, however, the accuser asks for and gets copies of his or her annual employment evaluations. Often, the supervisor claiming that the employee was incompetent had given the employee good evaluations for many years preceding the firing—usually because the supervisor did not have the guts to put the truth on the evaluation form. As a result, the supervisor's defense that the employee was incompetent looks fabricated, the judge or jury believes that the supervisor did in fact discriminate, the accuser wins the legal battle, and the career of the supervisor is over.

If you have an incompetent employee, you must do the following:

1. Document in a constructive manner his or her performance weaknesses.
2. Document carefully that the employee understands the problem and has no legitimate excuse.
3. Document that you have given the employee a chance to improve.
4. Track the progress (or lack thereof) of the employee.

Throughout the process, you must continue to treat the employee with the same level of respect as you give all other employees—no blowups, no snide remarks. Then, if the employee still demonstrates incompetence, you can fire him or her without risking your own career's future.

Handling Incompetent Superiors

An incompetent person gets a senior position in a company for one of two reasons: he or she just got lucky or someone even higher up wants the incompetent person there. If you run into the former situation, remember that good luck runs out. Eventually the higher-ups will realize the incompetence of the person in question. Therefore, do not make it your job to get the incompetent person fired. I recently witnessed one of the most brilliant young engineers whom I have ever met leave a successful career because he had taken it upon himself to point out the incompetence of a senior engineer. The senior engineer, who was indeed incompetent, struck back by falsely alleging unethical conduct on the part of the young engineer. It degenerated into one of the ugliest professional situations I have ever witnessed, and, as usually occurs, the junior person lost.

If the incompetent person was not just lucky but was placed in his or her position for a specific reason as well—i.e., he is the son of the boss or she is the niece of the biggest shareholder—you run even greater risks if you try to hurt the person professionally. One phone call from the incompetent person to his or her protector, and your career is history.

Each of these scenarios leads to the same conclusion. You need to develop a constructive relationship with an incompetent superior such that the incompetent superior looks to you to keep him or her out of trouble. One great thing about incompetent executives is that they usually know they are incompetent. Consequently, they desperately seek someone to keep them from screwing up. If you become their confidant and savior, they will allow you to run the whole department. That fact will not be lost on those even higher up in the organization.

As the "rescuer," you must make sure the incompetent person does not commit professional malpractice, does not destroy client or customer relations, and does not engage in personal behavior that exposes the company to legal liability of the types that will be discussed later as well as those already discussed. The best way to do that is to carefully and deferentially explain to the incompetent superior the potential ramifications of ill-advised actions and to volunteer to "take some of the load" off of his or her shoulders by doing customer presentations and other key tasks around the office yourself. Many great careers have been built by those who covered for incompetent superiors.

Burning Bridges

You must be extremely careful not to permit a coworker to depart on nasty terms with you. Often, if the relationship is over, a departing employee wants to take one last shot at someone in the office, or, alternatively, someone in the office wants to take a parting shot at the person who is leaving.

The following true stories have led me to conclude that you should make every effort to stay on good terms with former employers and employees. The president of a large subsidiary of a huge company was experiencing some problems meeting corporate earnings projections. When it became clear that the parent company's management would force the president into early retirement, some of the president's advisers and senior assistants began to make their own calls to the corporate headquarters, backstabbing the president (complaining about his abilities and decisions) in order to save their own jobs. The president learned about these efforts going on behind his back and was so hurt that he refused to allow the company to give him a retirement party. He took off for Hawaii.

Four months later, a major competitor of the subsidiary hired the ex-president to run its company. Six months after that, the president's new company bought the very subsidiary where the president used to work. The president now had all of his former subordinate executives reporting to him again. Needless to say, some of them saw their careers rapidly fade into the sunset.

With the wave of corporate mergers going on, such scenarios are becoming more common. You may be working with or for a former coworker who you thought was out of your professional life forever. That person may resurface with a vengeance.

Here is another real-life story that reflects a situation that occurs more and more often. A young associate at a law firm got into a major conflict with some of the partners at the firm but had a good relationship with the others. The partners who did not like him yelled at him and belittled him in front of his peers. Eventually, the partners who did not like him fired him unceremoniously, telling him he was worthless and demanding that he be gone within two weeks. He left.

After a couple of intermediate jobs, the young lawyer found a job at one of the law firm's biggest clients—a major manufacturing company. The young lawyer performed well at the company and even got a promotion. At that point, with his position secure, he called one of the few partners at his old firm with whom he had maintained a good relationship. He told the partner that if he ever saw any of the partners who treated him rudely on any of the bills that the law firm sent to his company, he would pull the work from the firm and immediately give it to a competing law firm. He got his just revenge in a big way.

You never know when you will need to reuse a bridge that you thought was behind you in your career. Even if a professional relationship seems to be at an end, try to end it cordially so that you do not risk hurting yourself in the future.

Establishing Professional Equilibrium

Your first goal in your professional relationships is to bring the extremes to the middle—keeping appropriate distance in your relationships with people whom you like and exercising restraint in your relationships with people whom you do not like. Once you have done that, you have dramatically reduced your risk of a career crash due to your relationships with others on the job. There remain, however, a few additional actions you can take to better anchor your position with respect to coworkers, customers, and suppliers. I have developed the following phrases to help you keep these strategies clear in your mind:

1. power outsourcing
2. power insourcing
3. clique avoidance
4. loser avoidance
5. skip-generation relationships
6. accessibility control

Let's discuss them one at a time.

Power Outsourcing

A crusty senior accountant whom I admire very much often growls the following words to young accountants who want the firm to make them partners: "Partners don't make partners; clients make partners." The best way to anchor your position within a company is to have the customers and clients feel that you—your competence, work ethic, and professionalism—embody all of the positive characteristics of your company as a whole. The fact is that if your company's customers like your work, there is almost nothing a frustrated, disaffected, or arbitrary boss or coworker can do to hurt you on the job. Having your customers' respect is like an inoculation against the ugly aspects of the employment-at-will doctrine discussed earlier. As long as the customers and clients like you, you are virtually crashproof on the job. Learn, therefore, to derive professional strength from outside the company. I call it power outsourcing.

In order to achieve the benefits of power outsourcing, you need to be totally responsive and respectful to customers at all times—answer phone calls promptly, let the customers make the important decisions, be patient with the customers if you disagree with their ideas, and never bad-mouth customers to third parties.

Indeed, the best way to measure the likelihood that employees at any level within a company will be successful is by looking at how well they handle difficult customers. When you hear someone tell you that "you are going to find this client impossible," your eyes should light up. Consider it an opportunity to prove your value to your company.

Power outsourcing has its risks, however. Take this example. A computer hardware executive developed a great personal relationship with a senior vice president who procured computers for a large retailer. The two became very close, and the retailer bought all of its computer hardware from this executive. Yet four months after a $4 million sale, the computer hardware executive was out of a job. How could this happen?

Two reasons. First, the hardware executive had not counted on his counterpart at the retailer being promoted to senior vice president of international sales. The hardware executive's contact person left and went overseas. He had no relationship with the successor at the retailer. Second, the hardware executive had carefully protected his relationship with the retailer, not involving anyone else from his own company in the relationship, and he had even declined to inform his bosses about the status of various pending sales and marketing initiatives. His coworkers resented him greatly for this arrogance, and as soon as his contact person left, they let him go.

In order for power outsourcing to work, you must act as a representative of your company, not yourself, and you must develop relationships with multiple points of contact in your customers' organizations. If you are perceived as an empire-builder within your company, coworkers will be waiting to tear you apart like the barbarians did Rome as soon as any aspect of your empire weakens. Effective power outsourcing means embodying your company as a whole, not building a personal relationship that you guard from others in your company. As part of effective power outsourcing, you must promote the talents of others in your organization and expose them to the customer as well. Be a conduit for your company, not a roadblock.

In addition, as you develop your outside sources of power, you must look at other organizations as a whole, remembering that people move on to greener pastures. The average American worker will switch jobs as many as fifteen times in his or her career. You cannot define your entire relationship with a customer by your relationship with a single person who works for that customer. When you develop a relationship with someone who works for a customer, use that relationship to get to know more people who work for that customer—take your contact and his or her subordinates to lunch, attend customer social events. Only then will you achieve true power outsourcing.

Power Insourcing

You can also achieve stability and equilibrium at work by establishing a solid base beneath you. You must, therefore, have good relationships with subordinates throughout your company—including receptionists, copy machine operators, the night word-processing person, and anyone else who provides you support services. This is power *in*sourcing.

Learn the names of your support personnel, and if they help you a lot, make sure you send them Christmas cards, give them small birthday presents, let their superiors know of their good work, and give them something like tickets to a ball game after they have completed an especially difficult project.

Word gets around if you treat people well; most important, if the support personnel like you, they will go out of their way to help you in a crunch. You often need support personnel the most when your career is in a particularly precarious position. You do not want to encounter ambivalent or even hostile support personnel when you are trying to get an emergency project done under a tight deadline.

At the same time, do not adopt the pretense that everyone is equal on the job. As with any relationship on the job, you must keep some professional distance from your support personnel. Do not, for example, feel obligated to let all support personnel use your first name when addressing you, unless, of course, it is company policy or a well-established part of the corporate culture in which you work. Either way, if you get too chummy with support personnel, they may not respect your professional position; they may take advantage of your benevolence by coming in late or taking long lunches; and, in really bad cases, they may not feel the need to take your projects seriously. In sum, therefore, to get the advantages of power insourcing, show great professional respect and appreciation for others on the job, but do not feel that they have to be your best friends.

Cliques and Stones

I have represented companies in dozens of cases where a former employee accused some of his or her coworkers of on-the-job misconduct, from fraud to discrimination. When investigating the facts of these cases, I very frequently encounter sharply divided groups or cliques within small companies or within small departments at bigger companies. In a typical situation, a group of five or six in a department of fifteen people feel disenfranchised and start to gossip and complain to the point that the backstabbing destroys the group's ability to accomplish productive work. The disgruntled group begins to make a record of alleged instances of misconduct by the others. I once saw a disgruntled employee keep a log of how long the in-group took for lunch each day, neatly recorded on a grid. He then tried to make a case to upper management that the group had defrauded customers because they had been charging for eight-hour days, when he believed they were working only an average of seven and a half hours per day. Indeed, it is typical in such a situation that one of the unhappy employees soon quits, gets fired, or gets passed over for a promotion. Then, feeling a need to get revenge, at the exit interview the departing employee fingers the boss or other members of the in-crowd, or maybe the departing employee even files a whistle-blower lawsuit.

If you want to crashproof your career, you need to be able to deal with situations where your coworkers have lost their professional equilibrium. The people who ultimately survive such unfortunate situations are generally those who do not take sides. In order to avoid taking sides, without making everyone hate you, you first need to maintain communication with everyone in the group. Be a good listener, but when it comes to the backstabbing, make only neutral statements such as, "Well, I sure hope you two can work it out." Never cut off communication with any person or groups of persons with whom you work, and never join a clique.

You can avoid being perceived as having joined a clique by not having your office in their group of offices, as most cliques find ways to achieve physical proximity, and by not going to lunch with any clearly defined or exclusive group on a regular basis. While many people cannot choose their own office location, some people approach a boss and ask for an office vacated by a departing employee in order to get away from an office clique. You will be walking a tightrope, but many people navigate this difficult situation successfully. It should be heartening to know that these situations do not continue indefinitely: this kind of friction always leads to an explosion. Someone will bring the situation to a head; so your balancing act will not have to go on too long. You just need to position yourself so that you are not one of the casualties when the inevitable explosion occurs.

If it appears that you are being forced to take a side and you cannot deflect the issue, you should take a couple of days off—use your annual leave, don't lie about being sick—and see if the situation has changed any when you get back. If worst comes to worst—you are in the middle of the conflict and there is no end in sight—you may need to put in for a transfer to a new department.

If you work in a small office and you cannot transfer elsewhere, you should try to mediate the situation directly with those involved in the dispute—but only try one time. Assemble the entire group and let them know they are hurting the company, and demand that they learn to work together. This process has worked. If it does not work, go to a higher-level supervisor and see if he or she can resolve the problem. If you find you are still being pulled one way or another by office cliques, get out of there.

Beautiful Loser

This was a cruel section to write, but I had to put it in the book to keep the crashproofing strategies comprehensive, as I promised I would do at the outset. Invariably, you will find a person in your office who is worse than incompetent. This person has inadequate professional and social graces, or does nothing but complain all the time. It could be the hospital employee who repeatedly makes jokes at meetings about burn victims—yes, hold your nose, he calls them "crispy critters." It could be the person who buys little stuffed animals, writes the names of people he hates at the office on the animals, and sticks pins in the animals when he is particularly mad. At times, he also hangs the stuffed animals from his computer so they look as if he strangled them.

This is the office loser. Maybe this person is just in the wrong job, maybe this person is going through a rough period in his or her life, or maybe he or she is a sociopath. It does not matter. You have to keep your distance from this person—without letting him or her know it.

A downward professional spiral is like a whirlpool; it sucks other people in with it. If you associate with the office loser—even in an attempt to console that person—your career is at risk as well. For example, if the problem person complains about the CEO and you politely agree with him or her, word will get out to upper management that you are a complainer as well. The loser will go around the office saying that you agree with his or her assessment of the CEO. If the loser shows up late and you cover for him or her, you will not get much of your work done, and, in addition, others will perceive you as covering for someone who adds no value to the office. When you associate too closely with people who do not advance the company's interests, even if you are competent yourself, you will go from being a winner to being a loser yourself.

Always be cordial. Smile and greet the office loser with the same enthusiasm that you demonstrate for everyone else in the office. Never ignore the person because, if you do, he or she will then resent you and aim his or her loose cannon in your direction.

But keep a large gulf of professional distance between you and the destructive vortex known as the office loser. Never support one of his or her complaints, gripes, or grievances. Never participate in his or her "practical jokes," and just look down silently when he or she makes a totally inappropriate comment. Try to avoid being paired with him or her on work assignments. In short, smile and stay away.

Cultivating Skip-Generation Relationships

Almost every person I know who has enjoyed a secure professional career has attributed at least some of his or her success to the cultivation of skip-generation relationships. You can obtain tremendous structural support on the job if you make a conscious effort to get to know and learn from people who are older and younger than you are—regardless of your position and their positions in the corporate hierarchy.

There is a strong tendency within a workplace environment for people to associate primarily with people in their own age-groups. People in your age-group tend to share common interests, as they are at the same stage in life as you are, in such areas as having a family and developing social relationships. It is only natural that you would want to associate with these people because you always have something to talk about.

However, keep in mind that people of your own age-group are often your greatest rivals at work. They are competing for the same promotions and may not really want to help you too much professionally, even if you do have a lot of fun with them at lunch.

The success of a corporation depends upon implementing a combination of proven business practices and fresh innovative ideas. In order to get yourself well-anchored on the job, you need to expose yourself to these practices and ideas. The best way to get a more complete perspective on the operations of your company is to know people of varying levels of experience and different viewpoints. While I am a firm believer that older workers and younger workers are of equal value to companies, I think it is disingenuous to suggest that they generally have the same set of skills. What they tend to have are *different skills of equal value*. Sure, I know some seventy-year-old coworkers who are whizzes on their computers and could teach me a few things, but many more have never even turned on a computer. Similarly, I know some twenty-seven-year-old coworkers who demonstrate excellent strategic thinking in complicated situations, but many more have never even touched a complex matter and have simply not developed the ability to think strategically.

Senior workers have a wealth of experience that you need to know and understand if you want to be successful on the job. They have a sense of which strategies will work with established customers and suppliers because they have a tremendous knowledge base derived from their long years of professional experience. They also have the contacts within and outside the company that they will use to help your career if you work well with them. Younger workers, on the other hand, tend to know the latest technologies and trends. Therefore, they can make good suggestions on how to get out your corporate message in a way that customers of the future will understand. Young workers also often have a tremendous enthusiasm for new and daring projects. Of course, you cannot extend generalizations concerning younger and older workers too far, but to deny the aforementioned trends is to ignore that there are in fact differences between the bodies and minds of the young and the old—in terms of both energy and experience. Your job is to turn those differences into opportunities.

If you are early in your career, you should make it your goal at work to find a mentor, a more senior worker at your company (or even a client) who can lead you through the corporate or professional maze. There will be no competition with this person, so you will be able to trust him or her entirely. Your mentor will have a tremendous base of experience upon which you can build your career. In fact, it shall be seen throughout the crashproofing process that historical perspective is an important tool in understanding and avoiding risk. Senior workers can give you just that perspective on the job.

Have lunch with that person on a regular basis; run your strategies for work projects by that person; and take his or her advice very seriously, even when it runs contrary to your professional instincts. Also, make it a point to help your mentor stay attuned to what is going on with the younger generation at work. To work well, the relationship must be mutually beneficial. Seek advice, but also give it.

Then, as you progress up the work hierarchy, you should also make sure you develop solid professional acquaintances with younger workers, even those who are fresh out of school. While being careful not to force your advice on anybody, you should endeavor to become the mentor for others. If you are successful, your younger friends will support you tenaciously when you need their help, and they can provide you some fresh viewpoints on problems you face at the workplace. These junior people are not your rivals; they are your support system.

If you are somewhere in the middle of your career, between age thirty and fifty, you should have skip-generation relationships going both directions—older mentors and younger protégés. In my experience, these types of skip-generation relationships are a sort of secret weapon for crashproofing. Develop them, and you will have a combination of new ideas and sage, seasoned perspectives on the professional issues that confront you.

Controlling Accessibility

Another piece of the puzzle of establishing crashproof workplace equilibrium is properly controlling your accessibility. This is very tricky. Some people are too accessible and others are not accessible enough. For example, I am always running into people who are in a state of professional shambles because they are accessible to everything and everyone. I recently took a cab home from the airport. The cabby had three cell phones, a pager on his belt, the dispatcher's radio monitor in the car, and a Palm Pilot on the seat next to him. During the entire ride, he was being beeped, buzzed, or prodded by some electronic device so often that he was totally frazzled. At one point, I thought we were going to crash (literally) when he took his eyes off the road to try to figure out which one of his three phones was ringing. This man was too accessible.

At the other end of the spectrum is the accountant who lost a major metal-tubing manufacturing company as a client. When a client called his firm, the client got a recording asking the caller to enter the extension or name of the employee with whom the caller wanted to speak. Once through that exercise, the client was transferred to the accountant's assistant, not the accountant. If the assistant was not at her desk, the call went to voice mail and then to the operator, who was instructed to send the call to a different accountant's assistant. A client could go through four transfers without ever talking to a real person, even if the accountant was just sitting at his desk twiddling his thumbs. The CEO of the tubing company told me he eventually asked himself, "Who the hell does this guy think he is?" He took his large account elsewhere. This accountant was not accessible enough.

The objective is to become less accessible to people who hinder your progress and more accessible to those who can help you. This is obviously an exception to the general rule that you treat everyone the same on the job. However, if you do it right, *no one will know* you are treating different people differently. So, in some respects, the rule still holds. Here are a few basic principles that will help you avoid an accessibility crash.

No One Is Too Important for His or Her Customer or Boss

The accountant who made everyone go through a switchboard and a couple of assistants before becoming accessible made a common mistake that causes executives, business owners, and professionals to lose major clients and customers every day. The result can be a career crash. It is very common for people who have had some professional success to start thinking they are too important to answer their own phones. They think it adds to their professional aura to show everyone how many support people they have attending to their needs. In fact, however, it does nothing more than stroke their own egos while leaving customers and bosses incensed.

Your customers pay your bills, and your bosses pay your salary. Give them your direct-dial number and answer your phone yourself. Do not screen their calls. Have enough professional confidence that you do not need to impress yourself with your own inaccessibility. Having customers and superiors reach you immediately will cement the relationships that you need to protect your career.

When you are traveling, make sure that the customer can reach you quickly either through a secretary or assistant, or, in the case of very important customers or coworkers, directly through your cell phone. If you are going to be inaccessible (on a plane or at a meeting, for example), make sure that someone else can tell the customer exactly when you will become accessible and how to reach you at that time. Check your voice mail and E-mail regularly so you know who has been trying to reach you.

Limit Your Accessibility for Those Who Offer You Nothing

Balance your total accessibility to key people with reduced accessibility for the people with whom you do not need close professional relationships. Do so in a careful and tactful manner so that no one feels like you are cutting them out. To do so, develop circles of accessibility. The broadest circle, one that anyone can use, is to call the switchboard. The next level of accessibility is for customers and coworkers, all of whom get your direct-dial number at the office. Then you should place much greater limits on the number of people who get your cell phone or pager number. They should be only the most important people in your life—in my case, my wife, my secretary, and, on occasion, my biggest clients—five or six people in all. Let them know you do not give out this number to others. That makes them feel special and keeps others from finding out that you are giving a few people special treatment. If you have a secretary, remember that he or she can determine whether to call you on your cell phone or page you if someone of midlevel importance calls while you are away. As long as your assistant or secretary treats the others with respect and courtesy, those people will not feel deprived of access to you.

Finally, your home number should be off-limits to everyone except your secretary (if you have one), your boss, or in rare circumstances, your biggest customer. You may even consider an unlisted number to protect your time with your family. As long as your clients know that you check your voice mail regularly, you can tactfully deflect any requests for your home number.

As for everyone else, have them call the switchboard, or if you have a secretary, use him or her to screen their calls carefully. However, when you use staff to screen calls, the staff members must, again, be very well trained so that no one feels singled out for lesser treatment. Even the nuisance callers should be made to feel that they are getting the same treatment as everyone else. The screeners should treat everyone with courtesy and calmness. Don't let them answer "Hold please" or behave in an aloof manner. They should screen unknown callers carefully and respectfully to determine if they are potential new clients or other people with whom you should speak immediately. They should tell the cold-calling brokers and insurance salespersons that you will call them later, if you decide to call back at all, while putting potentially important calls through to you without delay. If someone complains that the screener is asking too many questions or rudely demands to be put through, the screener should put them through to you without resistance. As you can see, you must get the right person to screen your calls; it is an important job.

Do Not Become a Slave to Technology

Some people believe that technology solves all problems in the office today. These people are dripping with electronic devices that either make them too accessible (like the cabby with all the cell phones) or not accessible enough (like the accountant with the voice-mail system that kept callers from ever talking to a real person).

Remember a few basic points. Some people become so engrossed in workplace technology that they become slaves to it. They are always buying something new, upgrading something old, or testing new applications—and they do not get their jobs done. Do not let technology take on a life of its own so that it actually interferes with your job performance. This is a very real risk. I know a paralegal from a prominent law firm who lost his job because he allegedly spent all of his time experimenting with different computer applications instead of preparing cases for trial. He jovially volunteered to install software for lawyers and staff, but unknown to the recipients of his favors, he refused to do the work he was hired to do at the firm. Clearly, he had let technology take over his life, and it cost him his job.

Second, do not allow technology to impose your priorities on others. When you are at a meeting, the others attending are your *top priority*. Turn off your cell phone. Turn off the beeper feature of your pager and do not look at it even if it vibrates—until there is a break in the meeting. Customers and bosses never forget when their meetings are interrupted by someone's cell phone ringing right when they were in the middle of a thought, or even by something as seemingly benign as someone checking a pager in the middle of someone else's presentation. Even if you have other important calls you may need to take, make sure your assistant, receptionist, or—if you do not have those resources at your disposal—your voice mail lets a caller know that you will be unavailable until the meeting is over.

Third, never think that technology is better than humanity. Having a real person answer the phone instead of a robot or a techno-menu is always the preferable route. Having a human answer the phone may not be possible all the time, but it should be your objective. Similarly, a face-to-face meeting is better than a videoconference; a videoconference is better than a phone call. In many circumstances, a phone call is better than an E-mail. Indeed, some form of personal interaction often accomplishes a lot more than an exchange of E-mail, because you can reason and brainstorm much more efficiently during a conversation than you can during an exchange of writings. In most circumstances, you do not need to E-mail a person who is two offices down from you. Just go over and talk to that person. The exception, of course, would be a situation where you feel it is important to document an issue in writing. Use carefully considered judgment in deciding whether E-mail is really necessary.

These technology issues may seem minor in the entire scheme of things, but little things like cell phones going off at the wrong time or an important customer getting into an infinite voice-mail loop have cost companies and their employees important business many, many times. You can easily correct the problems posed by the overuse of technology by working diligently to prevent it from taking over your life, as well as the lives of customers, clients, and coworkers.

Do Not Fall Victim to Inconvenience Shifting

The final risk posed by other people to your professional equilibrium is what I call inconvenience shifting—i.e., attempts by coworkers to off-load their own tasks on you.

Effective workers prioritize their professional tasks by balancing three factors: the importance of the task, the due date for the task, and the amount of time it will take to perform the task. Entire books are devoted to the subject of task prioritization, and most of them provide formulas and case examples of how to balance these three factors effectively. This book, however, is not about how to make you a more effective worker; it is about how to prevent your career from crashing. It is assumed, therefore, that you have already developed basic task-prioritization skills. The crash risk comes when someone tries to derail your priorities system by getting you to do things you should not do.

Many careers have been done in when good workers had to rearrange their priorities in a manner that hindered effective job performance. Take this example, which a management consultant recently related to me. Susan's job was to advise corporate clients on the types of computer hardware macrosystems that would best suit their corporate needs. Susan's own company had a good computer hardware system in place, but the company was unhappy with its telephone system and was evaluating potential new telephone vendors. The head of the company office-systems group asked Susan if she would participate in a focus group to determine which phone system best met the needs of the company's consulting executives. Susan, of course, said that she would participate. However, after a couple of focus group meetings, the head of the systems group had Susan discussing pricing with telephone suppliers and attending marketing meetings. He ultimately pulled Susan into all of the administrative aspects of the telephone system procurement. As a result, Susan started falling behind in servicing her consulting clients. Most of the work she was doing for the office systems manager was work that the systems manager had been hired to do and was outside of Susan's area of expertise.

This is the common problem of "inconvenience shifting," and it can result in major disruption to your ability to get your job done effectively. You should do the job that you are hired to do, and you should always be willing to take on some additional tasks for the benefit of the company *in your area of expertise*. Had Susan been asked to help procure a new computer hardware system for her company, that would have been a whole different matter because she was a hardware procurement expert. However, it was the telephone systems guy's job to negotiate with telephone suppliers.

You should not take on tasks that fall far outside your job duties and simply shift the inconvenience from someone else to you. When people try to shift their inconveniences to you, learn to say no in a manner that is firm but not offensive to the "shifter." To do this, follow two simple steps: explain your higher priorities and suggest an alternative course of action. The best way to explain your higher priorities is to tell the other person specifically what you are working on and how important it is to you and your company. Never just say you are "too busy." You are never "too busy" to do something if it is your top priority, and people know that. Rather, you have to inform the other person that you have legitimate higher priorities. After you explain those priorities clearly, think of another way you could help the person without having the inconvenience shifted to you. For example, if a coworker wants you to take her to the airport because she wants to avoid parking her car at the airport lot, explain to her that you have a proposal to a major corporate client due that afternoon and offer to call a cab. She may or may not accept your offer, but she will not likely be mad at you, because you have both explained your higher priorities and suggested a legitimate alternative. In that way, you tactfully prevent her from shifting the inconvenience to you.

Learning to thwart attempts at inconvenience shifting is the final part of achieving workplace equilibrium. Developing this ability keeps you doing your job rather than someone else's job. If you combine this skill with the others discussed in this chapter—keeping your attractions and animosities toward others in check, properly controlling your accessibility—you will have professional balance in your dealings with others, and you will have successfully implemented the second major crashproofing structure that you need to protect your professional future.

3

Dealing with
Major Corporate Events

Convert Corporate Uncertainty into Professional Opportunity

While the data vary considerably, surveys indicate that up to 90 percent of Americans do not like their jobs. At the same time, 30 to 40 percent of Americans fear losing their jobs. Put these two statistics together and you arrive at a pathetic conclusion: *millions of Americans fear losing a job they hate.* The principal reason most disaffected executives are unhappy is that they feel their futures are not within their control. They are not worried about a professional screwup of the type discussed in Chapter 1, even if they should be. Nor are they particularly concerned about becoming the victim of an arbitrary boss or unhappy customer as was discussed in Chapter 2. Rather, over 50 percent of corporate executives feel that if they were to lose their jobs, it would be due to a corporate event beyond their control, like a merger or downsizing initiative.

People live in fear of being downsized, merged, outsourced, or consolidated out of existence. They feel their careers could be doomed at any moment by circumstances completely out of their control. This fear paralyzes them into inactivity. They do nothing to plan for such situations because they do not think there is anything they can do.

You need to adopt a totally different attitude toward major corporate events—a very active rather than passive approach. Every corporate event results in a shake-up. While many careers will crash during a shake-up, it is also the time when normally rigid corporate structure is in flux. When old structures collapse—be they political, economic, or social—new leaders invariably arise and take advantage of the uncertain situation. That means you have an *opportunity to advance* while everyone else is just worried about holding on to what they have. When it comes to your job, you must learn to convert the uncertainty created by major corporate events into opportunity to advance your career.

Here is an example of someone who did everything right when faced with corporate adversity. We'll go through the example and break down each step that you can take to prevent your career from crashing during trying corporate times.

In my law practice, I had the opportunity to work with a very savvy young executive who was a procurement manager for a company that made major components for fighter aircraft. He was also active in the local association of contracts managers. The executive had a three-year employment contract with a severance package that would give him the cash equivalent to either one year's salary and benefits or, if there was less than a year remaining in the term of the employment contract, half the salary and benefits he would have received had the term run its course.

The fighter program on which he was working was profitable, and he did a great job. At age twenty-nine, he was one of the youngest managers in the whole company. One day I asked him if he could attend a meeting at 5:30 P.M. to assist me in developing facts to defend his company in a lawsuit. He indicated he would have to meet with me some other time because he had to go to a different meeting—which seemed strange to me because employees of the company generally worked from 8:00 A.M. to 4:00 P.M. He explained he had volunteered to work on a "tiger team" that was providing a fresh look at procurement problems the company was having on a new and different fighter program. I asked whether he was doing that out of the goodness of his own heart. "Not at all," he replied.

He then explained he had done a lot of research on the state of the fighter program he regularly worked on, and he had had, as a part of his regular job responsibilities, many discussions with marketing people in his company. As a result, he had determined that when the current U.S. government contract for his plane ended in two years, there would be a strong likelihood that the U.S. government would stop buying the plane. The only possible hope for his production line was foreign sales, but a competitor had a much cheaper plane, which, although less capable, would meet the defense needs of foreign governments. He concluded that there would be massive downsizing in two years' time, when he would have only about eight months left on his employment contract. At that time, the company would be able to get rid of him by paying him only four months' salary and benefits.

With that in mind, he had volunteered to be on a troubleshooting team for another program that had a brighter future. He had picked that particular team because it gave him valuable exposure to a wide array of executives on the other program and because it allowed him to demonstrate his sharp analytic skills in resolving serious problems. As a result, he gained the respect of a whole new set of people at his company. In the meantime, he continued to do his regular job quite well.

A few months before the end of the U.S. government purchases of the old fighter and four weeks before one of the foreign governments announced which fighter it would buy, the young executive learned of a job opening on the new fighter program. It was only a lateral move, but all signs remained bad on the foreign sales front for the old fighter, so he took the position. Sure enough, four weeks later, the foreign government announced it would buy the competitor's plane, and his company announced massive layoffs on the old program.

The young executive had saved his job, but there was a more interesting development. When his company announced the downsizing initiative, many of his coworkers on the disbanded program were looking frantically for other career opportunities within the company. The new program needed some skilled workers, but its management did not know whom to hire. They looked to the young executive to help them decide whom to accept for a transfer, putting him in a position of great authority. The management of the new program deferred to his judgment, and he brought over a very grateful group of his former coworkers. Within a very short time, he had the respect of the new management and the gratitude of the old. This made him the most popular member of the new procurement group and the logical choice for a promotion, which he got within three months of getting the new job.

This young man had successfully converted corporate uncertainty into professional opportunity. To achieve security in times of turmoil, he took four actions:

1. He got an employment contract.
2. He kept himself very well informed of the potential for a major corporate event.

3. He developed multiple professional tracks.
4. He switched tracks at exactly the right time.

We will discuss each part of this crashproofing strategy.

Get an Employment Contract if Possible

The only sure way to defeat the employment-at-will doctrine is to alter it contractually. If you have an employment contract, you have the strongest professional crashproofing structure available. These contracts generally guarantee a term of employment and provide for substantial compensation in the event of early termination. In the case of our young executive, had he remained on the old program, the company could not have let him go unless it paid him four months' salary and benefits. While this was not an excessive sum of money, it gave the young executive two advantages. First, he knew he had a little financial breathing room if the worst happened, and therefore he could make rational, carefully considered decisions about his future. More important, the employment contract gave him a competitive advantage over the other workers, most of whom had not negotiated an employment contract. It would have been more expensive for the company to lay him off than to lay off his terminable-at-will coworkers; so the company would have been less inclined to lay him off than someone else, all other factors being equal.

The days where only the top executives get employment contracts are over. Companies thirst for high-quality candidates for complex jobs, and if you meet the company's criteria for employment, you have every right to ask for an employment contract. I have seen midlevel workers get employment contracts by very tactfully letting the new employer know the risks and sacrifices attendant to switching jobs—i.e., noting the hardship of changing geographic location, necessitating a spouse to quit his or her job. I have never seen anyone lose a job opportunity by asking for an employment contract. You may not get the contract, but it does not hurt to try.

Use Inside Information to Advance Your Career

Chapter 1 discussed that, in general it is illegal to trade the stock of a publicly held company when your trades are based on inside information. Yet people do it all the time. And many go to jail. However, there is no law against planning your career based on inside information. Yet people rarely do it.

It is essential that you stay extremely well attuned to what is going on at your company. Get to know a cross section of your company's employees: top executives, secretaries, marketers, lawyers, and engineers. Keep a solid professional network that will let you know about the prospects for such major corporate events as mergers, acquisitions, spin-offs, the ending of particular programs or product lines, and layoffs; and what the likely ramifications of those events are for your job.

Sometimes the people who are privy to major corporate deals are instructed not to discuss them with anyone, even other company executives, and you need to respect those policies, which are often based on legal necessity. However, even a statement that someone cannot talk to you about certain matters may tip you off enough for you to make your move inside the company. You do not have an insider-trading problem until you not only get information you are not supposed to have but also trade stock on that information or disclose it to people who are not supposed to know about it. You have no problem when you plan your career on the basis of inside information you obtain in the normal course of your job duties.

Once you learn that a major corporate event is likely, you must continue gathering information, particularly information on which parts of your company will most likely suffer the adverse effects of the corporate event. For example, some corporate departments are particularly vulnerable after a merger with a larger company. The administrative and corporate functions of an acquired company are almost always phased out after a merger. The acquiring company does not need two accounting departments, two facilities departments, or two marketing departments. Consequently, they vastly scale back these organizations. You need to get your head out of the sand and determine how vulnerable your job is.

Here is an example of good research into a corporate phase-out based upon a true story. An executive managed a branch of a medium-sized bank. She learned that a larger bank in town had made an attractive merger offer to the executives of her bank, all of whom would become fabulously wealthy if they accepted the deal. She concluded that the deal would likely be announced within a few weeks. Before the announcement of the merger, she went to the nearest branch of the acquiring bank, which was two blocks away from her branch. She saw that the nearby branch of the acquiring bank was bigger, had been newly renovated, and had a more updated computer system than her branch did. She knew which branch would survive the merger, and it was not hers! She transferred to a branch that was nowhere near a branch of the acquiring bank. Indeed, within two months of the merger becoming final, the acquiring bank announced it intended to close her old branch for good, putting about twenty people out of work from that branch alone. She had saved her job with awareness and planning.

Keep Your Career on Multiple Tracks

The aerospace executive who moved to a new fighter program got his new job because of "multitracking"—the process of keeping multiple career paths open at all times.

Most people do not multitrack. We live in a very linear world. People see themselves as progressing up the ladder or higher on the organization chart. They envision their professional progress as moving from one job to another—one single point to another—and they set their sights on the job or level of success just above the one they occupy now. Associates want to become partners. Managers want to become vice presidents. The owner of one restaurant wants to open a second one. This is linear thinking.

The problem with a linear approach to professional security is that if someone or something cuts that line, you will be out of luck. Your career will crash. The answer is multitracking. While you work hard to make your current career path a success, you need to concurrently develop *parallel paths* to which you could likely switch if someone or something cut off your current path of travel. There are two ways to accomplish successful multitracking.

Internal Multitracking

If you work for a large organization, you must multitrack within your company. Develop a second skill that you use on the job and that important people in the company know you have. Our young aerospace executive learned about a second fighter program and assisted people on that program after normal business hours. Similarly, I have seen cases where engineers worked closely with marketing personnel and shifted to the marketing function at the appropriate time. In some cases corporate attorneys worked closely with the management of a product line in manufacturing companies and eventually joined the business side of the company, becoming program managers and, in one case, a senior adviser to the president of the company.

You may need some additional education in order to multitrack successfully within your company. For example, a secretary took paralegal classes at night and jumped to a higher-paying law department job right as the company was downsizing its secretarial force. Similarly, a low-level manager spent five years getting an M.B.A. at night and was able to move to a much more senior management position when his company phased out his product line. Some companies even pay for higher education by putting employees in executive development programs. While it surely has happened, in sixteen years of dealing with dozens of corporations, I have never known a company to lay off someone who was in an executive development program. It makes no economic sense to cut loose a person in whom you have invested so heavily. Becoming part of a corporate development program is like buying job insurance.

External Multitracking

What do you do if you are the owner or employee of a small business? Generally, you have little opportunity for multitracking within your organization because the company is too small to create such opportunities. In fact, the real risk of working for a small company is that it can go out of business completely, in which case everyone is looking for new work. This is especially true of startup high-technology companies—90 percent of which will fail. If you work for such an organization, you *must* engage in external multitracking. Even if you work for a large organization, external multitracking is a good idea because it creates additional opportunities for your future. In developing external multitracking, you can take several routes.

First, join a trade organization. Our aerospace executive was active in the local contracts management association. Being active in this organization gave him a good network of job opportunities and even a chance to be part of the paid staff of the contracts management association. Many people who have found themselves unemployed have used these organizations to get themselves another job quickly.

But you have to do more. Trade organizations provide good leads for new work but no guarantees. You need to develop skills and activities you could transfer immediately into a new means of livelihood. Here is how I multitrack. I have always liked to write. While developing my law practice, I have also written books and worked hard to build a second career as a writer and lecturer. I am also a serious coin collector. While I do not sell my coins for profit, I have developed the expertise such that I could immediately become a professional numismatist if everything else in my life fell through. I would have another means of earning a living and maintaining my pride even if, for some unforeseen reason, I had to close my law practice tomorrow.

You may be an accountant who likes antique cars. Develop the skills that would allow you to service antique cars for profit if your accounting firm folded. I know an airline pilot who obtained an aerobatics license and became an airshow stunt pilot when it looked like the airline he worked for would go bankrupt. One senior vice president of a bank was in charge of corporate real-estate transactions and had handled a few such transactions for his relatives. Within days after being laid off after a merger, he became a Realtor. All of these people had successfully multitracked and transferred seamlessly into new professions when adversity struck their old professions.

Interestingly, when I talk to the subjects of these multitracking success stories, they are usually much happier in their new professions than they were in their old ones. Why? Because the new profession started off as a hobby, and people have hobbies because they like them. When the hobby became the job, they began working at something they really liked. In each case, the person used multitracking to turn corporate uncertainty into professional opportunity.

There are three common questions about multitracking. One question asked by employees who have heard me discuss multitracking is: Should I be multitracking with competitors, customers, and suppliers? These people want to know if they should be actively seeking offers from companies with which they interact while working for their current employer. Unless you have decided you are leaving your company no matter what, I advise that you keep cordial relationships with competitors, customers, and suppliers but that you refrain from initiating direct discussions of joining their companies. Word of these discussions almost always gets out and will make you look disloyal to your company, thereby undermining your own position. On the other hand, if a competitor, supplier, or customer takes the initiative and asks you to consider joining them, there is no harm in finding out what they would offer you. Once you determine what the offer is, unless it is so good that you decide to take it, politely decline the offer and tell the company you should keep in touch. Then tell your boss that they solicited you *but you told them you were not interested.* That makes you look more loyal to your company, but it also tells the people at your company that you are perceived by outsiders as a valuable asset. You have then increased your job security rather than given the appearance of disloyalty.

The second question people ask me—in fact, it is more of a statement than a question—is that they just do not have time either to volunteer to work on corporate activities outside their workplace or to take night classes. While some people—like new parents on family leave—truly may be unable to participate in outside activities during certain periods in their careers, my normal response to the "I don't have time" line is: baloney. Everyone I know—me included—wastes an inordinate amount of time watching "Survivor" and "Who Wants to Be a Millionaire," playing golf, drinking beer, or pondering which toothpaste to buy. The reason you do not think you have time for multitracking is that you see no immediate need to plan for financial disaster. I hope this book will convince you otherwise. Disaster creeps up on you, and you have to make planning for it a priority that is higher than the slothful tendencies that we all have. The fact is that you do have time to take a class on a Saturday morning or a Tuesday night. You do have time to stay at work an hour late a couple of nights a week. Stop moaning and get started.

The third question people ask me about multitracking is how they should handle an unfortunate interlude between jobs—i.e., a period of time that they actually spend switching tracks after a layoff. You must consider taking several actions when you are in between careers. Let's start with severance compensation. If, despite your crashproofing efforts, you are laid off from your current employer, negotiate the best severance package you can get. You have more leverage than you may think. For example, many employers will give a laid-off employee especially attractive severance benefits if the employee agrees to waive his or her right to sue the company for wrongful discharge. Unless you were the victim of overt harassment or discrimination, or you were pressured to engage in illegal activity, you should seriously consider agreeing to additional compensation in exchange for a waiver of your right to sue, because the employment-at-will doctrine makes it hard to recover against an employer anyway. Indeed, the simple fact is that most suits by employees against former employers are unsuccessful. In other cases, even a winning employee goes through years of emotionally taxing and highly disruptive litigation before obtaining any recovery. Consequently, agreeing not to sue in exchange for substantial additional severance benefits will work to the advantage of all employees except those who were the victims of the most outrageous workplace conduct.

My basic rule on this issue is that you should probably not sign such a waiver if you were treated *illegally*, but you should bite the bullet and sign such an agreement even if you were treated *unfairly*. If you are having trouble telling the difference between illegality and unfairness, it is worth the expense of an hour or two of an attorney's time to help you make the appropriate evaluation.

Following are other actions you should take when in between jobs:

1. If you qualify, take advantage of the federal law (called COBRA—the Consolidated Omnibus Budget Reconciliation Act) that allows you to

continue your health insurance coverage for a specified period—normally eighteen months—after you are laid off.

2. Negotiate special payment plans with all creditors before you miss a credit-card, student loan, or mortgage payment so that you do not ruin your credit rating.

3. Cut back dramatically on discretionary spending, including delaying vacations and car purchases.

4. Make judicious use of the cash reserves that we will discuss in Part Two.

Time the Switch to Coincide with Major Corporate Events

Multitracking presents the closely related issue of how to time a voluntary job change. Although surveys vary somewhat, a recent study reveals that the typical employee will hold twelve to fifteen jobs in his or her forty-five years in the workforce. A third of all employees say that they have no loyalty to their current employer and plan to leave soon. You cannot join this group. It is an essential part of crashproofing that you do not plan to change employers frequently, except where regular job changes are an established part of your industry (like advertising and publishing), a circumstance which is relatively rare. Normally, the more employers your resume has on it, the more likely it is that a prospective employer will view you as either disloyal or unable to work effectively with others. For example, when I was a young lawyer pondering a good offer from another firm, a partner at my firm told me the story of a bright young lawyer whom he had known many years earlier. The lawyer was quite competent and had many firms interested in him. He switched firms several times in his young career, always going to the highest bidder. As he switched firms over and over again, he began to get the reputation within the legal community as someone who could not be trusted, and he gained the reputation among clients as an attorney upon whom you could not rely—all because he continually announced a new professional affiliation. By the age of forty, he had no firm, no clients, no self-esteem, and a serious substance-abuse problem. His life had crashed in a big way.

The best time to switch jobs is when a major corporate event at your company is likely or imminent but has not yet adversely affected your job. You should try to make the switch before the downsizing or layoff or before the announcement that your bank branch will close, because you do not want to look desperate to the prospective employer. But you need to time the switch as close to the corporate event as possible so you can take advantage of any opportunities the event may bring your way—just as the aerospace and banking executives whom we discussed earlier did. Look at it as working a clutch. You go as far and as fast as you can in one gear, and when that track has just about run its course, you shift into a different and higher gear.

While you should never close your eyes to the possibility of switching jobs even in good times, I discourage people from continuously searching for a better job. The search process distracts you from your current job, and, as was said earlier, word will get out at your current place of employment that you are not there for the long haul. Of course, you may get what appears to be a great offer from another organization that is familiar with your work. In that case, you should consider the offer carefully but adopt a strong presumption that you will stay where you are. The reason you must adopt such a presumption is simple: you have a complete picture of your company, but you do not have a complete picture of the company that wants to hire you away. You want to make an apples-to-apples comparison, but the new company has control of all the information, so it takes the worms out of its apples. For example, the company that wants to hire you does not have an obligation to tell you—and will do everything it can to prevent you from learning—about its financial problems, management problems, customer relations problems, personality conflicts, and other negative aspects about its organization.

Therefore, if you have an opportunity that looks too good to ignore, you must take specific steps to learn the truth about the company making you this seemingly great offer. Here's how.

• *Research the New Company Outside of the Interview Process.* Review financial statements that might be available on-line; get an annual report if available (and read the footnotes, which tend to contain all of the bad news such as contingent liabilities and plans to close divisions); and do Internet and LEXIS-NEXIS searches to find newspaper articles and court cases that may discuss problems—financial and legal—that the company has had. If the company does business with the government, you can request information about the company's performance under the Freedom of Information Act (FOIA). Make such requests through an attorney, because often the government consults with the company to determine if exemptions from disclosure apply and you do not want the request traced to you. These sources will help you evaluate if the company is financially stable, committed to the product or service that you will be working on, and ethical and fair to its employees and customers.

- *Not only Study the Salary and Incentive Compensation Structure, but also Compare Benefits.* Often companies will lure you in with a high-sounding salary or bonus program but will also require you to pay higher costs or deductibles for health care, or have a pension or retirement plan that is not as lucrative as that of your current company. Do a careful comparison.

- *Ask Specific, but Tactful, Questions About Why the Job Is Open.* First, ask why the person whom you are replacing left. A vague answer such as he or she "didn't fit in" is always suspect and probably indicative of personnel problems in the department or organization. A specific answer such as "she was promoted to vice president" or "he moved to New York because his wife got a long-sought job as a curator at the Met" creates a neutral or even positive inference about your career prospects at that company.

- *Ask About Recent Major Corporate Events.* Determine whether there have been layoffs or downsizing activities recently and what areas of the company experienced them. If the company has engaged in a lot of restructuring, you need to ask point-blank what the company's future plans are. If you get a wishy-washy answer, you should be very reluctant to take the job. Someone I know told me he had asked a prospective employer if the recent wave of layoffs at the new company was over, and he got the response, "We hope that we're past the worst of it." That should set off spinning, red, neon lights in your head saying, "Don't take the job!"

- *Ask Why the New Place Is Better than the Old One.* Finally, you have to tell the prospective employer that you have a good job now and want to know why the new company would be better. If you get a "soft" answer like "we have really nice people," be careful. In any large group, there is a continuum of personality types. No company has a monopoly on "nice" people. You will find people whom you like and whom you do not like everywhere. When evaluating a potential new job, look to more objective criteria. Learn the background and experience of the people with whom you will be working. Are they well-educated? Do they have impressive work histories? Have they stayed at the company for a long time? Can you respect and learn from these people?

Then find out about the projects you will be handling. Are they challenging, high-profile matters? Who are the key customers and will you have access to them? Forget about how nice someone was at the lunch interview. Even the biggest jerk at the company is nice at a recruiting lunch. Make your decision based upon tangible, specific facts that will give you the information you need to determine whether the new employer has overcome the presumption you will stay with the old one. That approach will ensure that career moves enhance your security rather than increase your chances for a professional crash.

The Professional Crashproofing Checklist

We have now covered the essential rules of crashproofing your career. Here is a brief checklist of basic crashproofing practices you can use as guideposts as you set about the professional crashproofing process. It may take you a while before you can check each box off, but you should make it a goal to get there as soon as possible.

Act as if Your Worst Enemy Is Perched on Your Shoulder

Written Communications

____ I write E-mail with the same level of formality and care as any other document.

____ I never use profanity in my written communications.

____ I avoid images of violence or gratuitous sexuality in my written communications.

____ I never acknowledge legal liability in my written communications unless authorized to do so by my legal representative.

____ I respond decisively to offensive E-mail that I receive, telling the sender to stop copying me on such communications.

____ I am scrupulously accurate in stating my qualifications and accomplishments on my resume.

____ I do not overstate the capabilities of my company in marketing materials.

____ I respond to aggressive business letters with a well-structured, unemotional refutation of the allegations being made.

Oral Communications

____ I leave short, courteous voice mails after having carefully considered what I want to say.

___ I do not discuss company business in public places.

___ I run meetings at the appropriate locations, with set time limits and carefully defined agendas.

___ I rehearse oral presentations out loud at least twice before delivering them.

___ I begin oral presentations by telling the listeners how long I will speak and what I will cover.

___ I deliver oral presentations with varied intonation and visual assistance.

___ I conclude oral presentations by proving that I have covered what I said I have covered and by delivering a personalized story.

Professional Practices

___ I do not use the Internet or other on-line services for personal purposes at work unless given permission by an authorized person.

___ I do not misuse software licenses and other intellectual property owned by others.

___ I do not use information I gain about publicly traded companies to benefit me or others in the stock market.

___ I do not spend time conceiving or executing malicious strategies to drive other companies out of business.

___ I do not circumvent company procedures and/or government regulations concerning the procurement of professional goods and services.

___ I do not expose company trade secrets.

___ I do not pad the hours I work on a job, nor do I inaccurately shift hours between or among jobs.

___ I do not inflate expense accounts or entertainment charges.

___ I do not lie about illness or the reason for being late.

Professional Organization

___ I maintain a simple organizational structure for my files that prevents the piling up of important documents.

___ I have regular file-purging days.

___ I keep hard copies of important documents and drafts.

___ I use code words to protect sensitive documents.

___ I delete early versions of documents from my computer files.

___ I do not cover up or lie about mistakes I make on the job.

CRASHPROOFING LAW #2

Professional Emotion Is Like a Wet Rag: Wring It Out

Sexuality in the Workplace

___ I avoid overt displays of romance or sexuality on company premises.

___ I maintain physical and organizational distance from romantic interests at work.

___ I never sexually harass or create a hostile environment for another employee.

Professional Courtesy in the Workplace

___ I understand that it is part of my job to work well even with those whom I do not like.

___ I do not burn bridges with departing employees.

___ I obtain power within my company by maintaining good, but not protective, relationships with multiple points of contact among my customers and my suppliers.

___ I maintain healthy professional relationships with subordinates and support staff.

____ I avoid office cliques.

____ I avoid associating with office losers but maintain cordial, professional relationships with them.

____ I work to develop mutually beneficial professional relationships with older and younger coworkers.

Accessibility and Time Management at the Workplace

____ I make myself accessible to my customers and bosses by picking up my own phone.

____ I carefully limit my accessibility to others in accordance with their importance to me.

____ I never make anyone feel that he or she has less access to me than someone else.

____ I do not overuse technology (e.g., my cell phone is off during meetings).

____ I do not allow others to shift the inconvenience of tasks for which I offer no expertise from them to me.

CRASHPROOFING LAW #3

Convert Corporate Uncertainty into Professional Opportunity

____ I have an employment contract if at all possible.

____ I continuously gather information to learn of major corporate events and how they could affect me.

____ I have developed multiple potential career tracks, both inside and outside the company.

____ I switch jobs only after a careful assessment of the *objective* factors that would make the new job better than the old.

PART TWO

FINANCIAL CRASHPROOFING

Professional structures provide you income, but generating income is only the first of three steps you must take to crashproof your life. The next step is to convert that income into wealth. You can make money hand over fist, but if you cannot hold on to that money and build it into financial security, your life may still crash. This part of the book will discuss how to build the financial structures that create enduring wealth.

Let there be no doubt: *the forces of disorder hate wealth*. Why? Because wealth is the most powerful, disorder-resisting structure on earth. You can use wealth to build a home that protects you from the adverse forces of nature. You can use wealth to purchase insurance against disaster or to build back a home or business that disorder has destroyed. Wealth, therefore, actually reverses the disorderly direction of the universe.

Because wealth is so powerful, disorder has a million and one ways to take it away from you. Disorder will, for example, tempt you to gamble or drink your money away, encourage you to amass huge credit-card debt, and lure you into clever investment scams with false promises of riches. You do not have to fall victim to these tactics. Ensure you have the wealth you need by doing the following:

1. Bring wasteful spending under control.
2. Build solid savings and investment structures.
3. Protect those structures from those who want to destroy them.

I have a law of crashproofing that will help you accomplish each of these critical objectives. As you will see, I am not a financial adviser, so my laws have nothing
to do with picking hot stocks. Rather, my laws of financial crashproofing are based
on my experience as an attorney, prosecutor, and economic historian. You will learn
how to make law and history work for you to build a crashproof financial structure.

4

Bringing Wasteful Spending Habits Under Control

Your Worst Financial Enemy Is *You*

We will discuss the con artists and other sleazy people who want to take your money later in this book, but first you need to establish clearly in your mind that the main reason people crash financially is they are fiscally irresponsible. They have no one to blame but themselves. They do not save enough; they splurge their savings on pointless purchases; they run up destructive levels of credit-card debt; they waste hundreds of thousands of dollars on cigarettes, gambling, booze, and other habits that not only are unhealthy but also are bleeding financial wounds; they convince themselves nothing bad will ever happen to them that would require immediately available assets; and they delude themselves into believing they will never get old and need to retire.

When I was writing this chapter, I mentioned to a friend of mine that I had just put a few thousand additional dollars away for my retirement and the kids' college expenses. He replied, and I quote, "Retirement? College? You're only forty and your kids are not even ten years old. I'm forty-eight, I've got three kids—ages fifteen, twelve, and ten—and I'm gonna deal with those things when the time comes. You can't spend all of your time worrying. You have to just trust that things will work out over time."

This quote represents, of course, the faith fallacy discussed earlier—a blind belief that potential problems will work themselves out with the passage of enough time. As you should know by now, this approach—if it can be called an approach at all—does not work because it is contrary to the disorderly direction of everything around us. You need to be planning right now for all of the financial problems you can and will face down the road. Without your well-structured intervention, your situation will get worse, not better.

Having worked with and represented financial analysts, banks, accountants, and CFOs, I have no doubt that the only way to crashproof your finances is to implement structures that keep you away from your own money and that grow your money safely. Sure, you need money available to you so you can pay for daily expenses and essential purchases like cars and clothes, and you need to have funds available to have some fun, too. However, in order to crashproof your finances, you must structure your money and your mind so you do not even consider certain assets to be available for your day-to-day use. You need to separate yourself from your own money.

There are, of course, many ways you can force yourself to set aside money. Based upon my experience, as well as the interviews I did for this book, I have constructed a method that combines the best advice I have received from many financially successful people over the past sixteen years. You may find that a slightly different approach works for you, but whatever approach you use, you must put together a solid financial structure that combines four essential features: (1) denying yourself access to a large portion of your money, (2) spreading your money in a manner that reduces risks, (3) growing that money in a safe, methodical manner, and (4) being able to access that money in the event of a serious problem materializing in your life. Here is one way you can accomplish these goals: pyramid money management.

Introducing the Pyramid Financial Structure

Almost everyone in the world is familiar with the great pyramids. The Egyptians built the first one around 2800 B.C. for the Pharaoh Zozer. They built the last one around 1600 B.C., but several pyramids remain largely intact today. Many archaeologists and architects consider the pyramids to be the most enduring and awe-inspiring structures ever built. Nothing has resisted the forces of disorder more effectively than the pyramids.

Consider financial stability to be like a pyramid. You stand at a single point high atop the pyramid, and you get strong structural support from the four points at the base, which angle up to your position at the top. You will use the four bases of a financial pyramid to achieve a crashproof level of personal wealth.

In order to be crashproof at the earliest possible time, every American earning between $25,000 and $250,000 per year should save at least 20 percent of his or her after-tax income. This is a very high rate of savings. In 2000, the average American savings rate actually dipped into negative territory—after hovering between 3 and 9 percent during the 1990s. In Japan, however, the average citizen saves 13 percent or more of his or her income, even though the cost of living is higher and wages are generally lower than in the United States.

Although few people manage to do it, achieving the 20 percent savings level that can crashproof your life is not that difficult. The key to achieving a high savings rate is forced fiscal discipline. That is what the pyramid structure does for you.

Four Accounts Defined

The four bases of the financial pyramid are four accounts at a bank or other insured financial institution. This is probably a departure from your normal financial structure. Most Americans have only two accessible bank accounts—a checking account (that is out of money at the end of each month) and a savings account (with an average balance of just over $1,000). If you are in that situation or close to it, you are living at the top of a very thin pole, not on the solid pyramid base that you need. You are vulnerable to a big fall if there is just one gust of financial trouble in your life.

Pyramid money management envisions four well-funded accounts, not two underfunded accounts. Four accounts might mean a little more paperwork than two accounts and may result in some increased banking fees, but you will find that the cost of four accounts is only a few dollars a year more than the cost of two accounts, and the fiscal discipline the extra accounts create far exceeds the minor additional inconvenience they may cause.

Under the pyramid plan, the first two accounts control your spending and the second two accounts grow your savings. Your first account is the *limited-purpose checking account*. It will provide the funds for day-to-day expenses like home and car payments. You can convert the checking account you use now into your limited-purpose checking account simply by committing yourself to restricting the kinds of purchases you make with money in that account.

The second account is the *slush fund* in which you accumulate money first to wipe out your debts and, thereafter, to have fun and make discretionary purchases. Contrary to what some of these be-a-millionaire books say, you do not have to live life wearing cheap clothes, buying beat-up cars, and avoiding vacations. A part of crashproofing involves having the confidence and ability to be a little self-indulgent from time to time. The key to the process is keeping the slush funds separate from the funds you use for your basic expenses and savings, and to limit your spending on leisure activities to the sum you accumulate in that account. With the slush fund, you will learn how to separate your vices from the rest of your financial activity.

The third account is the *untouchable savings account*. That is your current savings account, but its purpose will be changed a bit, increasing substantially the amount of money you keep in that account and rendering that money unavailable to you for anything but true emergencies. The untouchable savings account will accumulate wealth that is immediately available to you in the event of (or to prevent) a crash, but you should never use that money for anything else as long as you live.

The final account is your *investment clearinghouse account*. As will be discussed in detail in Chapter 5, you use the money in this account to invest in various other forms of wealth—real estate, stocks, bonds, retirement funds, mutual funds, collectibles, and even some precious metals. The investment clearinghouse account can be a cash subaccount in a brokerage account, but for the purposes of structural integrity and discipline, it may be better to make this a completely independent bank account that is not accessible to your broker.

Direct Deposit

Before we discuss how to allocate the money you generate from your now-crashproofed career to each of these accounts, we must discuss a seemingly minor, but actually critical, mechanism in pyramid money management: direct deposit. You may already have one or two direct-deposit mechanisms in place—with money going directly from your employer to your checking account and maybe to a retirement account as well. For the strongest crashproofing structure, however, the money from your hard work should, if possible, go directly into four accounts, allocated in the manner that will be discussed shortly. Picture the direct-deposit process as the lines of the financial pyramid going diagonally down from the top of the pyramid, where you are, to the four bases that contain your assets. As simple as it sounds, research indicates you are much less likely to spend money that is directly deposited by your employer into bank accounts, bypassing you in the process. This is proof that the mere existence of structure resists the otherwise inevitable dissipation of wealth.

You need to have four direct-deposit structures in place, one for each of the previously defined accounts. Many employers will make such deposits if you give the payroll clerk or accounting department the requisite account information. Some companies will only deposit into a maximum of two or three accounts. However, if your spouse works, he or she can use the direct-deposit capability of his or her company to get your money directly deposited into the four accounts. And, if worst comes to worst, you can set up your own homegrown direct-deposit system. As soon as the paycheck comes in, you make the respective deposits into the four accounts—before you make any purchases or pay any bills.

Allocation of Deposits

Here is how to determine how to allocate the money you make at work among the four accounts. The first step is easy: determine your approximate total after-tax household annual income. To determine how much you actually take home, you should basically follow the same process you would when you fill out and file an itemized income-tax return. If you itemize, you may even want to use last year's return as a guideline. Take deductions for your children, mortgage, state taxes, and so on, and then apply your tax rate to the remainder. Deduct the sum owed in taxes from your total salary, and you have your approximate take-home income.

If you are just out of school and have no mortgage, children, or other income, you generally do not owe taxes at the end of the year nor get much of a refund. In such cases, you can probably just multiply the amount your employer pays you (after withholding) by the number of pay periods per year to get your total annual after-tax income.

So, for example, if a person makes $48,000 per year and the spouse makes $44,000, they have a pretax income of $92,000. With minor deductions, a federal tax rate of around 30 percent, and some state taxes, we will assume they take home $72,000.

The next step in allocating your money is to divide the take-home pay by ten, which, in the case of our couple making $92,000 and taking home $72,000, leaves $7,200. This sum of $7,200, or 10 percent of the take-home pay, is the basic unit by which the money will be allocated among the four accounts. This first step is quite easy. Then it is time to allocate the money to the four accounts. In each pay period, you put seven-tenths of the money into your limited-purpose checking account and one-tenth in each of the other three accounts. If both spouses are working, as in our example, you can divide the contributions of each spouse however you want, so long as the totals in each account are as have been described. For the couple with a combined annual after-tax income of $72,000, the checking account gets $50,400 annually (7 × $7,200) and the other accounts get $7,200 each annually. From the standpoint of their monthly or bimonthly direct-deposit instructions to their employer or employers, here is how they should proceed:

Account	Total Annual	Monthly Direct Deposit	Bimonthly
Limited Checking	$50,400	$4,200	$2,100
Slush	7,200	600	300
Untouchable Savings	7,200	600	300
Investment	7,200	600	300
Total	$72,000		

This family instructs its employers or banks to make the monthly or bimonthly deposits to the requisite accounts in the sums listed on the chart. If there is a shortfall in the total you are able to put away each pay period—for example, you expect part of your take-home income to be in the form of a tax refund—you should allocate the shortfall to the checking account and reduce the amount direct-deposited into that account accordingly. Then, when the refund comes, put that sum in the checking account to even things out. So, for example, if our family expects a tax refund of $4,800, they should reduce the bimonthly deposit into the checking account by $200 (i.e., $400 per month or $4,800 per year) so that the other sums can remain as they are on the preceding chart. When the refund comes, they put that sum into the checking account. You will also need to recalculate the sums you put in each account every time there is a substantial change in your income—a raise, you hope.

Legal Structures Create a Disciplined Mind

As has been discussed, bank accounts, direct deposit, and specific percentage allocations to accounts by your employer are facets of a legal structure that holds your assets. The process is simple. Your hard work generates income. The income is stored energy or wealth. You then direct that wealth to accumulate in four distinct accounts.

The purpose of this legal structure, however, is to make it easy for you to restructure the way you *think* about money. The pyramid system places absolute structural limits on how and when you can spend your money. As you will see, each of the four categories has some flexibility, which is necessary for any structure to last; but if you are to crashproof your finances, you have to structure your mind as rigidly as you structure your accounts: the limited checking account pays for day-to-day expenses, the slush fund covers extraordinary expenses, the savings account accumulates cash available for emergencies, and the investment account grows your wealth and builds your long-term security. You cannot use money in one account to cover a perceived shortfall in another. Use the clear legal structures to create clear mental structures that will prevent you from dissipating your wealth in the way the forces of disorder want you to do.

The Four Corners of the Pyramid

Once you have instructed your employer to deposit the appropriate sum into each of your four accounts, you have to determine how and when you can use the money in each account. What follows here is the condensed, combined wisdom on this subject that comes from many very bright, knowledgeable people who have successfully crashproofed their finances. You may decide to vary this approach a bit. That is fine, as long as you strive toward a disciplined structure that gives you savings of around 20 percent of your after-tax income. The key to successful financial crashproofing is that once you have come up with a plan you know will work for you, you need to stick to the plan no matter what. The following is an approach I know will work.

Limited-Purpose Checking Account

The money you have your employer deposit into this account pays your taxes, as well as the following specific categories of expenses: (1) rent, mortgage, and other regularly payable home-related expenses such as homeowner's insurance; (2) car payments and insurance; (3) food, clothes, and children's supplies; (4) utilities; and (5) other miscellaneous recurring expenses, from child-related costs such as day care to routine entertainment costs such as movie rentals and family dinners at a restaurant. To qualify as "routine," the total amount you can spend on entertainment should not exceed about 5 percent of the sum that you put in the account. In the case of our example family, that would be about $210 per month (5 percent of $4,200). You do not use the money in this account for any other purchases, such as jewelry, new appliances or electronic devices, or any of the other truly discretionary expenses. Those purchases come from the slush fund that we will discuss later.

Before we discuss how to keep these five categories of expenditures within the 70 percent after-tax income limit, here are a couple of ways that disorder will tempt you into cracking and maybe even destroying the limited-purpose checking-account structure. The first threat is something we all have: the evil *automatic teller card*. It should be no surprise to you that the forces of disorder want you to be able to withdraw your funds anytime, anywhere. The more access you have to your checking funds, the more likely you are to dissipate them. That is why you find automatic teller machines in casinos, expensive malls, and other places where you are likely to get weak-kneed and make a big withdrawal to make some useless expenditure or take a big gamble. Some banks will even cover over-withdrawals and charge them to your bank credit card so that you can begin making exorbitant interest payments almost immediately.

It is a small step but an important one: you must learn to exercise great discipline in your use of the automatic teller card. Take out money only in small increments for preplanned activities, such as a movie or weekly lunch money. Never use the card to make an impulse purchase, and never withdraw more money than you have, even if the bank will let you get away with it. Properly used, this card is a convenience, but it can rapidly become an enemy if you use it too often and withdraw too much. Easy access to cash is a siphon for the forces of disorder; you have to keep that fact in the forefront of your mind at all times.

But it gets worse. It seems as if every year, technology makes it more difficult for people to maintain structural distance from their money. For example, a radio commercial for a large financial institution bragged about "banking without boundaries" and promised customers that they would "never need [their] checkbooks again." The phrase "banking without boundaries" really means "banking without structure," and while it appears high-tech and convenient, it actually plays right into the forces of disorder that try to separate you from your money. Crashproofing requires *banking with boundaries*.

That ad was a bank promotion for debit cards. When automatic teller cards appeared in the 1980s, for example, they converted the process of diminishing your funds from three steps to two. Before automatic teller machines, you would write a check, cash it, and then spend the cash; it took up to three steps to separate you from your money. With an automatic teller card, you only needed to get the cash and then spend it—a two-step process.

Apparently that was not easy enough for the forces of disorder. In the 1990s, we were introduced to the *debit card*, which takes money directly from your checking account to finance a purchase—a one-step process. Crashproofers do not use debit cards at all. Debit cards effectively eliminate all of the structure and distance that crashproofers place between themselves and their money. There is no place for a debit card in the financial crashproofing process because they are totally astructural.

That is not the worst of it. I have not yet mentioned credit cards, which allow you to spend money that you do not even have. Our discussion of credit cards will come later, however, when we cover antistructural and destructive financial devices. For now, just remember that plastic and crashproofing are in many circumstances incompatible.

Keeping in mind, therefore, that you should use your automatic teller card sparingly and your debit card *never*, let's see what the experts say about keeping your home and other living expenses within the 70-percent-of-take-home-pay limit that your account structure establishes. Most people do not keep their household expenses down to 70 percent of their income—in fact, most people spend in excess of 90 percent of their income on household expenses. Yet discussions with everyone from mortgage brokers to realtors, car dealers to apparel store owners, reveal that achieving this spending limit is actually quite easy if a few basic tips are followed. Most encouraging, you do not even have to sacrifice your quality of life to achieve these spending limits.

Some of the following advice you may have heard before, while other advice will probably be new to you; either way, only a small percentage of Americans actually implement these money-saving practices. Make these practices part of your personal structural discipline and you will easily live within your limit under pyramid money management, with virtually no sacrifice in your lifestyle.

Properly Purchase and Finance Your Home

Let's start with the largest expense and investment that most people have: the home. Properly purchased and financed, your home can be your greatest weapon against a crash. As shall be seen later, if you can build real estate equity rapidly, you will have the most enduring and stable asset a person can buy. If, however, you make unwise decisions in the purchase and financing of your home, your home can be the fastest route to a crash. It can be a crushing weight on your shoulders instead of the solid financial foundation it should be.

LIVE IN A RIGHT-SIZED HOME. In fact, millions of Americans have lost their shirts on their homes. One of the most serious crashes in recent times occurred in Texas in the late 1980s and early 1990s, when oil prices tanked and the Texas aerospace industry hit rock bottom. People who had overextended themselves financially due to the thriving late 1980s economy found themselves without jobs in the early 1990s because of massive downsizing initiatives by financially strapped oil and aerospace companies. Thousands of homes went on the market simultaneously, prices crashed, and people were left with huge mortgage deficits. The situation became so desperate that it was common for once-successful people to simply abandon their homes and move to other states, allowing banks to foreclose on their dreams and causing bill collectors to hound them from location to location. You cannot let this happen to you.

The fact is that millions of Americans live in homes that drain too much of their wealth. The first step in crashproofing, therefore, is to live in a home you can *easily* afford and to have enough equity in your home that you could sell it without owing money in the event of a real estate crash.

PURCHASE RATHER THAN RENT. It is generally better to purchase than to rent because you build up equity when you purchase. There are exceptions, however. If, for example, you believe you might have to move on very little notice or you plan to take major career and financial risks (i.e., quit your job as an accountant to pursue a career as a painter), you are safer not to be locked into a long-term real estate commitment. For many people, therefore, particularly the young and unsettled, it may be a good idea to rent for a couple of years. However, it should remain your goal to build up some real estate equity at the earliest possible time.

Substantial crash risks, however, are associated with purchasing a home. One of the most unfortunate aspects of the recent economic boom is the ready availability of mortgage credit. Mortgage companies and other financial institutions— spurred on by Realtors and developers— inundate us with ads, mailings, E-mail, and even house calls trying to convince us to buy the largest and most expensive home for which we can "qualify." Indeed, there has been a focused effort among these organizations to replace the word *afford* with *qualify*.

Do not fall into this trap. Many people can qualify for a home loan that they really cannot afford. Countless dozens of professionally successful people I know—many of them making upward of $150,000 per year—are in the largest homes for which they could get a mortgage approved. In fact, many developers and their financiers are letting people into their new neighborhoods with as little as 5 percent down, and mortgage companies are qualifying people for loans equal to six or seven times their annual incomes—a practice almost unheard of only fifteen years ago. The people who fall into this financial situation have positioned themselves for a major crash if there is just one shake-up with their jobs or families or if there is a national or world recession.

It is easy to become giddy with your own self-importance when you see how much home the banks and developers are willing to let you buy. You must remember that wealth and success are not measured by how much debt others are willing to allow you to amass. The forces of disorder around you want you to get into as much debt as possible; that is why people make it easy for you to do so. There is absolutely no honor, prestige, or glory in it.

Unsurprisingly, those who do overextend or "overleverage" themselves are often a sorry group of people—with high rates of divorce and emotional illness. They may throw lavish Christmas parties to show off their spacious homes, but when the guests are gone, the pressure of their precarious financial positions takes an exorbitant emotional toll on their families and on their personal emotional health. They have nothing that you don't have, other than a cloud of debt hanging over their lives every day.

DETERMINE HOW MUCH HOME YOU REALLY NEED. You must, therefore, live in a house you can truly afford. Some basic financial formulas will help you determine what to spend, but first look at the situation from a slightly different perspective. Ask yourself, "How much home do I really need?" Most people find they can afford what they need. Do not buy space you do not need. In fact, the universal forces of disorder love *wasted space*. Rooms that you do not need or use drain away money like a sewer sucks in water—from heating and air-conditioning bills to the cost of painting, plumbing, higher insurance premiums, and roof problems. Disorder also revels in oversized yards that siphon away money at an alarming rate—including the costs of trimming trees, planting flowers, and killing all of those poor moles. These homes deplete wealth, time, and energy. The more house and yard you have, the more routine maintenance costs you will incur and the greater the likelihood of costly occurrences such as leaks, falling trees, flooding rooms, and the like.

One of my friends has a huge house with five bedrooms the family never uses. Something is always going wrong with the house—usually in one of the rooms they do not use. They have a crisis every week. What will it be this week?

Once they came home from a party to find thousands of termites flying around the kitchen, mating over the dishwasher. It took $4,000 to turn the termite love nest back into a kitchen. The next time we were over to their house for a party, the entire family room flooded, and we spent the last hour of the party trying to vacuum up enough water to prevent the flood from spreading to the rest of the house. Almost inevitably, your decision to live in too much home will result in such crazy things happening to you. It is part of the way universal disorder works.

You should consider a variety of sociological issues when deciding how much house you need. Consider, for example, how much a closely knit neighborhood is worth to you. You may have noticed that on Halloween the kids who live on large estates almost always go to real neighborhoods—with more modest houses. These estate kids do not even know their own neighbors, who often live a couple of acres away. In fact, living in a closely knit neighborhood has tremendous advantages—you and your kids will make friends quicker and find it easier to have a social support system in such surroundings. Your kids will also get more candy on Halloween.

I am not saying, of course, that you should never buy a big house. But the first step you should take in determining how much house you can afford is to check your ego at the door and figure out how much house will give you and your family the comfort you desire and the values you want to foster in your household. What you should never do is put yourself at financial risk just to get the precarious and highly questionable rewards of showing off a large home to your coworkers or your best friend from college.

PUT A SUBSTANTIAL SUM DOWN, 25 TO 30 PERCENT IF POSSIBLE. Once you have decided what you really need, you will find it much easier to apply more tangible financial guidelines for crashproofing your home-buying process. By cutting out the unnecessary amenities, you will likely find yourself more able to afford a house that gives you what you need. Prior to the mortgage boom of the 1990s, the conventional wisdom was to put 20 percent of the home's cost down in cash and finance no more than three times your annual pretax income. This is a not-less-than formula, meaning you should never put down less than 20 percent. In my experience speaking with successful crashproofers, however, most say they put between 25 and 30 percent down and limit their mortgages to two and a half times their annual income. Many do better than that. I know a millionaire who lives in a modest two-bedroom house. He told me he lives there because he has no kids and he could afford to pay for the whole house in cash.

While most of us cannot afford to do that, his attitude represents crashproof thinking at its best. Scale down the home; scale up the equity.

While the money for your monthly mortgage payment comes from your limited-purpose checking account, your down payment can come from your investment clearinghouse account (which will be discussed later) because, as we shall see, real estate still represents the most time-honored and reliable of all investments.

USE FIXED-RATE MORTGAGES. Fixed-rate mortgages are a must for crash-proofers. Mortgage brokers will entice you with variable-rate mortgages, which start low but can creep up if interest rates increase, or "balloon" mortgages, which hit you hard on the back end. From a purely financial perspective, variable-rate mortgages may provide some advantages if, for example, you plan to move before the payments increase. Real estate or mortgage brokers will also tell you that you may be able to refinance your variable-rate mortgage at a reasonable fixed rate before the big payments kick in. These statements are true, but they interject a dangerous element of chance and a high degree of risk that crashproofers simply do not allow in their lives. What if you decide not to move before the high payments start? What if interest rates go up a lot and the variable rate doubles the payments you make? Part of financial crashproofing is attaining peace of mind, and fixed-rate mortgages are the only way to get there.

The crashproofer's approach is to lock into a fixed-interest rate—i.e., one that can never change, no matter what happens to national interest rates and no matter what bank or company might buy your mortgage. The standard term for a fixed-rate mortgage is thirty years. A fifteen-year mortgage is better if you can afford it, but it is not essential to attaining security. As you shall see shortly, if the crashproofing process goes well, you will soon have sufficient funds to pre-pay your mortgage, meaning you will have your house paid off long before the thirty-year term of the mortgage. Consequently, it is important that your mortgage documents have no penalties or hidden fees associated with prepayment. Most do not, but some still do, so you have to read the fine print in the loan agreement carefully—something that few people do.

Consider refinancing your loan early in the loan term when the interest rate drops 1 percent or more below what you are paying now without any "points" (points being an up-front premium payment, with one point equal to 1 percent of the loan sum). Paying points on the initial loan allows you a lower interest rate, so you should consider it; however, paying points on the refinancing could effectively eliminate the advantage you get from the lower rate.

To summarize, the following are the basics of keeping your home payments in check so you can keep your limited-purpose checking expenditures within the 70 percent target:

1. Cast aside your pretensions.
2. Take no pride in the amount of debt that banks, realtors, and brokers want you to incur.
3. Decide what you really need in terms of space.
4. Purchase rather than rent.
5. Put at least 20 percent down.
6. Get a fixed-rate mortgage with no prepayment penalties.
7. Refinance if the rates drop more than 1 percent below what you are paying with no points.

If you follow these simple guidelines you will have taken the first step toward crashproofing your finances, and you will be able to live within the means provided by your limited-purpose checking account.

Control the Car Purchasing Process

The second expenditure that comes out of your limited-purpose checking account funds is your car payment and insurance. The key to keeping your car payments in line is to control the purchasing process. Car dealers use a well-known and well-established structure to get you to buy the most car for the most money. You can commandeer that process and come out ahead.

BUY RATHER THAN LEASE. Assuming you cannot pay for the car in cash (which you in fact will be able to do once your crashproofing program has been up and running for a few years), you can either finance a car purchase or lease the car. For the vast majority of people, loans are better than leases for a couple of reasons. First, a crashproofer wants to have extended periods of time in which he or she makes no car payments at all; i.e., the car is paid off. If you finance the car, you will eventually pay it off and have no payments at all for some time. In fact, most conservative purchasers do a lot of research on-line or in magazines on the service history of various models, and they buy car models with the best long-term service histories. They get three-year loans but keep the car for six to eight years. This means they have not only no payments most of the time but also little in the way of repair costs. This process allows them to save huge amounts of money over extended periods of time.

If you lease, you will always be paying for the car. People who lease usually keep the car for a short period of time—two or three years—after which the dealer tempts them with a newer and more expensive car. Some people who are self-employed will realize the tax benefits from leasing a car they use primarily for work, but the actual number of people who can benefit financially from this arrangement is small. Your accountant can tell you whether you would benefit from leasing. Otherwise, buy.

RESEARCH THE SERVICE HISTORY OF THE MODEL YOU WANT. If you are going to buy the car rather than lease it, you need two obvious results: a good car and a good deal. Yet surprisingly few people do even the most basic research to determine whether they are getting either. Finding yourself with exorbitant monthly payments and/or excessive repair costs can seriously set you back in your efforts to build the requisite assets for crashproofing your life. With the way money grows over time, even just a few thousand dollars in unnecessary car expenses when you are young can take away $100,000 or more from your ultimate net worth later on in life.

To get the right car, you need to do careful research. Use on-line services or trade publications that are not affiliated with any particular car manufacturer. Look for models with the best warranties and the best post-warranty service histories. The crashproofyourlife.com website has links to some of these services.

CONSIDER A MODESTLY USED CAR, BUT BEWARE OF SALES TRICKS. Once you have decided which models are the most reliable, you need to decide whether you want to buy a used car or a new one. There are tremendous advantages to buying a low-mileage used car. First, cars are not an investment, even though hundreds of dealers advertise them as investments. The moment you drive off the lot with a new car, the car loses between 15 and 30 percent of its value— hardly what could be characterized as an investment. Consequently, if you buy a slightly used car, you can reap the benefit of this rapid depreciation without sacrificing much quality. Three of my last four cars had just a few thousand miles on them when I bought them, and I saved thousands of dollars by going this route. The cars still had extensive warranties left on them, and even after the warranties expired, the cars remained virtually trouble free.

However, you must eliminate a couple of risks if you decide to buy a car with a few thousand miles on it. Remember, there is a *reason* why someone turned in a car after only driving it for a few thousand miles. The problem could be the owner or the problem could be the car. If the problem is the owner—he went bankrupt or his spouse just hated the color—you probably have nothing to worry

about. If, however, the car is a lemon or was rebuilt after being in an accident—
as many used cars are—you need to know that. All cars have a documented service history. If you get the vehicle identification number (VIN) of the car you
are considering, you can access its service history on-line for a fee. There is recommended reading on this subject at the end of the book, as well as links to such
research sites on the crashproofyourlife.com website, but the dealer can certainly
get this information for you. Dealer representatives often tell customers that they
have no service history on a used car. If you hear that line, question the dealer
carefully on why he or she has no such history, because you are probably dealing
with a liar. If you do not get a credible answer, leave immediately. Once you have
the service history, study it carefully to determine if the car had major mechan-
ical problems or was in an accident and hastily repaired, shined up, and put back
on the lot. You will be surprised at how many "slightly used" cars were in a slightly
huge accident. Do not buy these—no matter how good the price looks.

Once you know the service history, you should try to learn the *use* history of
the vehicle. From my law practice, I have learned of several cases where dealers
systematically lied to vast numbers of customers about what the cars were used
for prior to being purchased by the dealer. This practice is particularly common
among dealers who sell low-mileage "program cars." Disreputable dealers will
give you a story like "most of our program cars were driven by VIPs in a golf
tournament," when in fact many such cars were used by car rental companies
and driven roughly by dozens if not hundreds of people. You need to get a statement from the dealer telling you exactly who used the car and for what purpose
before it arrived on the lot. In some cases, dealers buy at auction and do not
know the use history of the car. These auctions can be a cover for battered-up
rental cars. In other cases, however, the dealers know exactly what they have,
and they may try to keep that information from you.

For example, I recently learned about a successful stockbroker who bought a
low-mileage program car from a supposedly reputable dealer. He did not ask for
the service history on the car, and he did not ask for what purpose the car had
been used before the dealer got it. A couple of days after he bought it, he found
a business card under the front passenger's seat. The card said "John Jetter,
Instructor, Indianapolis Amateur Auto-Racing School." The stockbroker called
Mr. Jetter in Indianapolis and asked him what make and model the school used
to train aspiring race car drivers. Sure enough, the school used the same make
and model that the stockbroker had just purchased from the dealer as a low-
mileage program car. Mr. Jetter told the broker, "We race them for three thousand miles and then sell them as junkers—by that time, the transmission is shot

and the whole car is falling apart." As it turns out, the dealer had purchased many of these cars from the driving school, slapped on a new coat of paint, and then passed them off on unwary consumers as slightly used program cars. This dealer got into trouble, but who knows how many have gotten away with such fraud. You can avoid such a situation by being thorough in your research.

OWN THE TRANSACTION. You are entitled to know the service history, the chain of title, and the accident history of any car you buy. Getting this information is the most important part of taking control of the transaction when you are buying a used car.

If you decide to buy a new car, however, you must take control of the negotiating process as well. Dealers have a whole series of tactics they use to get you to spend too much money. These tactics are decades old, but they work time and time again. First, price and interest rates are fungible. Dealers will cut the price of the car, hemming and hawing about how good a deal you are getting, but then they will get the money back from you by charging you a higher interest rate than they charge to other customers. Alternatively, they will tell you they are giving you a huge break on the interest rate, while jacking up the price of the car. They will always find a way to get what they need to make a decent profit. You need to determine what the monthly payment will be because that reflects the combination of price and interest. Comparison shopping among dealers must focus on the monthly payment for a specified term.

Second, dealers misuse terms like *invoice*. They tell you they are selling you the car at $500 over their invoice, but there are documented cases of dealers having more than one invoice for the same car. Also, these invoice prices often do not account for various incentive programs that the automakers offer the dealers if they sell a certain volume of cars. If they tell you they are so desperate that they are selling you the car at invoice, they are probably lying. There are websites that purport to have the real cost to the dealer of every model of car; some people have questioned the numbers on these sites, but these numbers are more reliable than what the dealers will tell you, so I recommend you use them as guidance. The crashproofyourlife.com website has links to some of them.

Finally, almost every salesperson will use another salesperson as the "manager" to whom he or she goes when you have reached a price impasse. By having the salesperson bring out the "manager," the consumer gets the false impression that he or she has really been driving a tough bargain that needs special approval. It is all just a sales tactic. Salespeople routinely agree to serve as the "manager" for each other.

In order to avoid falling victim to financial gimmicks and sales ploys, you must take immediate control of the purchasing process by doing something like the following. First, come up with a written specification of exactly what you want—including make, model, color, accessories, and financial assumptions (how much down, how many years of payments). Second, go on-line and find the lowest price and monthly payment offered there (the crashproofyourlife.com website has links to carbargains.com and carsdirect.com, two of the most well-known car-selling websites). Third, fax local dealers your specification and tell them the lowest Internet price that you could get. Fourth, tell the dealers that the lowest bidder gets the sale. Many dealers hate Internet purchasing, so they will do their best to beat that price (studies, while mixed, show that many deal-ers will undercut the Internet price by $500 or so), plus they are competing with other dealers, so you will really force the best price out of them quickly. Once you have the lowest price, call the dealer and ask if he or she could sweeten the deal just a little more. If you do that, I guarantee you have purchased the car at the lowest possible price, you have avoided the potential fraud and games, and you have saved a lot of valuable time.

When it comes to crashproofing the car-buying process, therefore, you must

1. Research the service history of the model you wish to purchase.
2. Lean toward buying rather than leasing.
3. Consider a modestly used car, after researching the service and use histo-ries of the particular car you want.
4. Control the purchasing process with a fax of the exact specifications you want and the best Internet price you can get.

When you take these simple steps, you have moved that much closer toward crashproofing your finances.

Basic Necessities: Stay Away from the Glitz, and Shop Around

The next category of expenses for which you use funds from your limited-pur-pose checking account is clothing and food. This concerns basic necessities—not evenings at formal French restaurants or expensive evening gowns. The latter expenses come from the "slush fund," which we shall discuss later.

Some of those be-a-millionaire books contend you have to wear cheap clothes and avoid expensive tastes in order to become financially secure. All they are really saying is frugality, frugality, frugality—although they find about fifty dif-ferent ways to say it. Having had the advantage of working with both garment-industry and grocery-industry executives, I have no doubt you can dress and eat well while remaining within the financial constraints imposed by the pyramid financial structure.

Reducing clothing budgets without looking like a slob is remarkably easy. To do so, simply avoid the seemingly overwhelming lure of the high-overhead, glitzy gallerias that have sprung up in most major cities. These places use marble floors, fountains, and elaborate displays for one purpose: to get you to pay more than you should for clothes. Effectively, they use their structures to destroy your structures. Instead of buying your clothes there, find the less pretentious warehouse stores that sell the same clothes without the glitz. These stores get the closeouts and the leftover items from the glitzy stores. They tend to have rows and rows of garments—a huge selection offering the same suits and dresses as the glitzy places for up to 50 percent less money. These places carry Nieman-Marcus, Armani, and other top-of-the-line brands. You will have to learn to live with a little less of the (often arrogant) service personnel at the expensive shopping centers, and you have to be willing to shop at a place that looks more like a barn than a palace. I get most of my suits at one such place, and coworkers have showered me with compliments on these distinguished-looking garments. The only awkward moment comes when I run into five people I know at these places and they look embarrassed to see me there. They should be *proud* of their smart approach to clothes. So should you.

We have seen it time and time again: one of the greatest obstacles to crash-proofing our lives is our own pretentiousness. Keep in mind that it is much more satisfying to feel financially secure than it is to act like you are just too cool to be seen at a discount store. If you want to restructure your mind to be crash-proof, you have to work hard to eliminate the cobwebs of arrogance that cloud intelligent financial judgment. Buy the same clothes at a different place and you will save thousands of dollars over the course of your life; and you will be able to stay within that 70 percent limit imposed by your limited-purpose checking account.

Now let's discuss food and meal purchasing. First, as with clothes, stay away from the premium outlets. Many people feel as if they have to buy a four-dollar cup of coffee every morning—that represents tens of thousands of dollars in retirement money sipped away. Sure, you can indulge yourself from time to time; just do not make trips to the pretentious food and coffee outlets a regular habit until you have reached a comfortable level of financial security.

In addition, even the more modest food-shopping locations have vast differences in prices. Most people shop either at the stores closest to their homes or the stores where their parents shopped. However, the research I did for this section was truly eye-opening for me, indicating that proximity and habit should not be the basis for your decision on where to buy your food. Food-industry experts and consumer groups have done extensive research into the variations in food pricing, and these statistics are stunning. They recommend you conduct an experiment like the following. A shopper wrote down sixty items that she most often buys, including the brand names she preferred. She then went to several local supermarkets and wrote down the prices of each item. She returned home and totaled the items for each chain. The totals, rounded to the nearest dollar, ranged from $113 to $178. Assuming the shopper bought those items every two weeks, careful shopping could translate to a yearly difference of over $1,600 on just those items. Invested safely over twenty years, the savings she would realize on those items alone would total over $60,000. One day of comparison shopping allowed her to take a nice step toward crashproofing her life. Not bad for one morning's work. No matter how successful you are, it is worth that little bit of time to learn who is trying to gouge you and who is not. You may want to repeat the process every year or so to make sure you take advantage of any price changes.

In the aforementioned experiment, the shopper bought the brand names and product sizes she liked. Many people attempt to save additional money by buying generic products and large-quantity containers. While this strategy can help, be careful. Studies reveal that generic foods and medicines are cheaper than their brand-name counterparts and are of equal quality. Generic drugs, for example, run 30 to 55 percent cheaper than brand names. However, while generic products are cheaper, the prices of generic products tend to vary much more than the prices of brand names, so comparison shopping is very important if you are to realize the true savings potential of such products. The reason generic product prices vary so wildly is simple. A reputable store will mark up the generic product by its normal rate of profit. So if it pays $5 for a generic food product and $10 for the name brand and generally charges a 20 percent markup, it will price the generic product at $6 and the name brand at $12. However, research indicates that less-reputable stores will buy generic products at very low prices but mark them up to levels where they are just a tad under the prices of the name brands. These stores will, for example, charge $12 for the brand-name item mentioned earlier but charge $11 for the generic item—a whopping 120 percent profit. Some pharmacists mark up generic drugs between 1,000 and 2,000 percent. Comparison shopping for generics may, therefore, be even more important than comparison shopping for brand-name products.

Next, a word about volume purchasing. Most people believe volume purchasing is financially sound. That is why people buy the huge boxes of cereal or the fifty-pack of tissue paper. Interestingly, however, buying products in large volumes often *does not* save money. For some products, the purchase price for large-volume containers or packages is ounce per ounce more expensive than purchasing the same product in small containers or packages—sometimes significantly so. Packaging costs, as well as the difficulty in getting retail shelf space for larger items, mean that the retailer often has to charge a higher price per ounce for the larger product in order to make a profit. You need to study the per-ounce price of each product and determine what the optimum size is by dividing price by weight. This process can also be a real money saver that allows you to keep within your 70 percent limit for the checking account fund without ever sacrificing quality.

When it comes to clothes and food, therefore, you can stay within the appropriate financial limits if you make your clothing purchases at the closeout stores and not at the glitzy malls; do regular comparison shopping, especially for generics; and learn the optimum sizes for saving money on the products you purchase. These easy steps make crashproofing a painless process.

Reduce the Number of Utility Players in Your Life

The fourth expense covered by your limited-purpose checking account is utilities. Companies that conduct utility "audits" for private homeowners report that the average homeowner could save over 20 percent on utility bills by taking some very painless steps to reduce these costs—once again, without sacrificing lifestyle. They include properly insulating inside walls and ceilings, replacing old furnaces with more fuel-efficient ones, installing split-level heating and air-conditioning for two-story homes, and shutting off computers and other high-energy-using devices when they are not in use.

But there is a more important and perhaps less obvious way to reduce your utility bills. You have to ask yourself whether you really need all of the utilities that various companies tell you you need to have. As was discussed before, it seems as if everyone has a couple of private phone lines, call notes, call waiting, two or three E-mail addresses, a cell phone or three, a Palm Pilot, a Nextel direct communication phone (a walkie-talkie to those of you over fifty), a pager, cable TV with five premium channels, a VCR, satellite dishes, a dedicated service line for their computers, and personal websites. Last month I saw a man paying for his groceries with food stamps while talking on a very expensive, snazzy cell phone the whole time. He was talking to a friend about a show he saw on Home Box Office. Even people of modest means routinely spend $100 to $200 per month on premium utilities.

You do not really need all of these utilities and premium amenities. I get by on an unlisted regular phone line, a cell phone that is usually off, a home computer without E-mail, basic cable, and a VCR—and I think I am technologically overextended. A friend of mine who is a senior executive at a high-tech company does not even have a VCR. Her family reads books at night. That is a rather quaint concept. Ask yourself whether these devices add efficiency and structure to your life or just complicate matters. Having four hundred TV channels, three phones, two E-mail addresses, and a pager would make my life miserable. As in the case of buying a home, success is not measured by how much money you can spend; nor is it measured by how often you can be interrupted at dinner. Sit down, analyze all of the services you have, add up the fees you pay, and determine which services you can cancel without any real degradation to your quality of life. It will save you a lot of money and further advance your efforts to stay within the pyramid financial structure.

Recurring Child-Related Costs and Routine Recreation

The final category of expenses for which you use your limited-purpose checking-account funds is child care and basic recreation. If you use day care or otherwise pay for someone to look after your children, the money for such care comes out of the limited-purpose checking account, just as your other day-to-day costs of living do. I realize that day-care costs have skyrocketed, and the financial burden that day-care costs impose will make it harder to keep your total recurring monthly costs within the 70-percent-of-income limit set by the limited-purpose checking account. However, the alternative is for one spouse not to work at all, which would presumably make staying within the limit even more difficult because the family would lose an income. If, therefore, I expect single-income families to stay within the 70 percent limit, I certainly expect dual-income families with day-care costs to do the same. If you are to crashproof your life, you simply have to scale back house, car, and utility payments to the point where you can fit your day-care costs into the 70 percent limit set by the checking account structure.

You also use the money in the limited-purpose checking account for minimal, routine entertainment costs. While I may sound very rigid in my insistence that you stay within the structural limits you set for yourself, there is no doubt that you need to have some fun while you build the crashproof life. The category of routine entertainment expenses includes baby-sitters, video rentals, a family dinner and movie, a ballgame, and so on. Put a 5 percent limit on your spending for routine entertainment—that is 5 percent of total checking-account funds available. Using our example family that makes $92,000 per year and puts $50,400 in the checking account each year, this family can spend over $2,500 per year on these expenses without risking so much as a crack in their pyramid financial structure. That is a fair amount of fun.

Vacations, special restaurants, summer camps away from home, and new VCRs can come out of this fund if there is some money left over, but you will accumulate additional funds for these more extravagant activities from the slush fund, which will be discussed next. The limited-purpose checking account needs only to cover recurring, routine entertainment expenses.

The Slush Fund

The limited-purpose checking account covers your day-to-day living expenses. You do not need to use the money in the checking account to make extraordinary purchases. Money for those purchases comes from the next account, which is the second corner in the pyramid financial structure: the slush fund. I am not sure when the phrase "slush fund" first came into the English language, but it became a household term during the 1970s when President Nixon allegedly used secret bank accounts for political payoffs during the Watergate scandal. The phrase "slush fund" has come to mean money that is available for illicit purposes.

We all have frailties, temptations, and the like, and we must admit that fact up front. We cannot spend our lives focused entirely upon lofty personal, professional, and financial goals. We need our own slush funds. Not to do illegal things, of course, but to do things that may not, from a purely objective standpoint, advance our crashproofing goals. As you know, many of these get-rich books and seminars tell you that you have to live a frugal, austere life in order to accumulate wealth. They say this for two reasons: first, from the standpoint of the person giving the advice, it is a lot easier to say "never spend any money" than it is to come up with a more reasoned and measured approach to financial security. Second, from the perspective of the person getting the advice, it is a lot easier to do nothing but save money than it is to put into place a more complex and comprehensive crashproofing plan.

I don't know about you, but I do not want to die rich and miserable. If you take the time to reduce your expenditures in the manner discussed earlier, there will be enough money left over for you to have some fun, too. Indeed, the slush fund provides the flexibility that is critical to any viable, long-term structure. Flexibility resists the adverse effects of the disorderly trend of everything around us, which makes the slush fund a critical component of your financial crash-proofing plan.

The flexibility of the slush fund manifests itself in two ways. First, the slush fund is flexible because its purpose changes over time. It starts out as a means to eliminate some of the bad structural defects that may exist in your financial foundation. There are certain vices that you must try hard to eliminate in your financial life because they hinder your financial progress by destroying the structures you are building. They are like termites in your house, like grave robbers in the pyramids. You first use the slush-fund money to eliminate these highly destructive habits.

The second form of flexibility in the slush fund is spending discretion. Once you have eliminated the financially counterproductive aspects of your life, you will have plenty of money available for enjoyable activities that may not advance your wealth accumulation process but do not destroy it either. You get to choose them. In sum, the slush fund transfers money from counterproductive activity to nonproductive activity of your choosing. You cannot afford the former, but everyone needs a bit of the latter.

You will direct-deposit 10 percent of your after-tax income into your slush fund. For our couple making $92,000 per year and taking home $72,000, that amounts to $7,200 per year. During the first year or two of their crashproofing plan, they will use much of this money to help them stop their financially destructive habits; afterward, they will be able to use that sum to enjoy themselves.

Eliminating the Spending Threats

For most people, the greatest threats to the integrity of their financial structure are credit-card and other high-interest debt and binge and impulse spending. The big three traditional vices—cigarettes, gambling, and alcohol—also contribute extensively to the financial ruin of many people. Stunningly, if the typical young American couple that smokes eliminated their credit-card debt, stopped binge and impulse spending, stopped smoking, and cut gambling and alcohol expenditures in half, that couple could have close to *$2 million* in additional retirement money. With that kind of extra security in the works, spending some money on a Caribbean cruise or a trip to Disneyland would pose no financial problem whatsoever. That is the philosophy of the slush fund: eliminate the most costly vices, and free up money for some of the finer things in life.

TRADITIONAL VICES. At the outset, let me reiterate the point I made at the beginning of the book: issues of morality and health are for the most part beyond the scope of this book. I do not care if you enjoy wallowing in the neon of Vegas or smoke until your lungs look like tar paper. I spend a few bucks at the roulette table whenever I give seminars to groups in Vegas, so this book claims no moral high ground. What is undeniable, however, is that cigarettes, gambling, and alcohol are bleeding financial wounds. A two-pack-a-day smoker who starts when he or she is a teenager throws away well over $1 million of retirement money. A typical beer drinker throws away another $500,000. Add up the direct costs of these vices and multiply by the interest you could have received on the money had you invested it conservatively. (I have done this in the notes at the end of this book.) You will see why these habits often mean the difference between a secure future and a complete crash for hundreds of thousands of people.

Then there is gambling: the only "investment" you can make with your money where the odds are *always* stacked against you. It is not a complex analysis. The casino makes money by making it easier for you to lose than to win. If you put your money into gambling, you will slowly burn it away.

Finally, all three of these habits are addictive. You may get in, but you may not be able to get out. That separates them from other leisure expenditures, like vacations, which tend to be one-shot deals. Consequently, traditional vices represent an antistructural, downward spiral, and they are completely antithetical to crashproofing. If you have a problem with any of them, use as much slush-fund money as you need to get professional help to overcome your addiction. It should be your highest *financial* priority, if nothing else. Enough said.

HIGH-INTEREST DEBT. Reliable studies indicate that the average American family carries almost $6,000 of credit-card or similarly financed debt. The average interest rate on this debt is 14 percent per year at a time when the prime interest rate is under 7 percent. If you pay the typical minimum monthly payment on $6,000 of credit-card debt (usually 1.5 to 5 percent of your debt), it will take you many years to pay off the debt even if you never charge another item. When it is finally paid off, you will have written checks to the credit-card companies totaling up to $25,000.

People like credit cards because of the way the credit-card companies market them. The companies lead us to believe that having the card is in and of itself indicative of wealth—we are so solid financially that these big companies are offering us impressive credit lines of $5,000 to $10,000. They encourage our spending by taking advantage of how we would like to perceive ourselves rather than how we really are.

Any mechanism that encourages the depletion of wealth is an ally of universal disorder. Credit-card debt is like a large, leaking hole in the vase of roses that I discussed at the beginning of the book. Therefore, a principal purpose of the slush fund is to eliminate any credit-card or other high-interest debt you may have. The minimum payment that you have been making comes out of the limited-purpose checking fund, but then you write a second check from the slush fund to pay off the financed debt until it is gone.

Avoid for-profit enterprises that claim they can get you out of debt. Using the slush-fund money to rid yourself of credit-card debt means you do not need the services of the various for-profit organizations that bombard you with commercials telling you they will save you for a fee. They come in three basic types: companies that provide daylong seminars that run $100 or more, in which you are told the "secrets" of debt elimination; debt-restructuring companies that charge as much as $2,500 to take over the servicing of your debts; and bankruptcy lawyers who run those tasteful television ads with the blinking graphics saying, "Stop the debt collectors in their tracks!"

The daylong seminars revealing the "secrets" of debt elimination almost always make the same five points:

1. Stop charging and start paying cash.
2. Consolidate your debts to the credit card with the lowest interest rate.
3. Pay more than the monthly minimum on your cards.
4. Try to negotiate a lower interest rate with the credit-card company.
5. Consider a low-interest home equity loan to pay off the high-interest credit card.

This is sound advice, and you just got it for a lot less than $100. The first two points are self-evident: you are going to avoid further debt if you start paying cash, and you should move your debt over to the card with the lowest rate. In fact, a crashproofer will cut up all of his or her credit cards except the one with the lowest interest rate, and maybe a backup card that he or she will use only in emergencies. Remember, however, credit-card companies often charge a fee for debt consolidation that can be up to 6 percent of the balance you transfer to them. You must factor in both the interest rate and the consolidation fee when you determine which card you will use. Then you should consider the one principal card that you keep as nothing more than a convenience that prevents you from carrying a lot of cash around, and you should never charge a sum greater than what you have available in your checking account.

The third point made by the seminars—paying more than the minimum—is also a very basic proposition. The problem, of course, is getting enough money to do so. Having the structurally separate slush fund helps solve that problem. The slush fund gives you the ability to pay off the debt in a systematic, well-structured manner. Every month your employer direct-deposits money into a fund that you use to eliminate your debt.

The next point, trying to negotiate a lower rate, is worth a try. It sometimes works, although many credit-card companies will not budge on their interest rates. Finally, a home equity loan is a viable option—you will without question be paying less interest (and probably getting a tax deduction) if you borrow against your home and pay off your credit cards with that money. The problem is, as shall be seen later, owning your home must be one of your primary investment objectives, so, while borrowing against your home may mitigate your spending problems, it undermines your investing strategies. Consequently, you may be better off just using as much of your slush-fund money as possible to get rid of the debt rather than shifting the debt to a home equity loan. You should certainly get a home equity loan before taking more drastic actions such as filing for bankruptcy.

Private debt-restructuring companies are companies you pay to take over the whole process of paying off your creditors. They usually take a percentage of the interest that they save you; for the typical debtor, the fee will exceed $1,000 and may be as high as $2,500. As you can see, by having someone else do what you could do yourself, you can lose thousands of dollars. These companies claim to be worth their high fees just for providing you with the discipline they presume you lack. Crashproofers have the necessary structure and discipline in their lives, so they do not need to pay others to give it to them. Save the $2,500 and do it yourself.

Then there are the bankruptcy lawyers. In one of their TV ads, a smiling bankruptcy lawyer urged people to hurry up and declare bankruptcy before the law changes and it becomes too late! Lawyers like him claim to have the secret formula, the magic potion that will cure you of your financial woes: declare bankruptcy, pay the lawyer a fee, and either be released of your debts forever (a Chapter 7 bankruptcy) or have your debts reduced and consolidated (a Chapter 13 bankruptcy). Huge numbers of Americans are availing themselves of this "opportunity"—over a million per year in 1998, 1999, and 2000—despite unprecedented economic prosperity. Many of these people had a lot of paper wealth and a lot of income at one time or another, but they have found themselves unable to meet their financial obligations, often due to the failure of risky investments. The high number of bankruptcies is proof of just how devastated our friends and neighbors will be if the economy goes into a prolonged tailspin. Right now millions of Americans are teetering on the edge of a financial abyss.

Bankruptcy is a mistake unless you are in an absolutely hopeless situation. If you declare bankruptcy, your credit rating is shot to hell for ten years, making it virtually impossible to finance a house or car. The various state bankruptcy laws also place severe restrictions on what you can keep (for example, a small home and only one car per family). Plus, as an added bonus, there will remain the social stigma associated with bankruptcy. People talk, and you might think that you do not care, until your kid comes home from school crying because another kid made fun of his bankrupt dad. It has happened to good people. Finally, if you declare bankruptcy, you may be precluded from certain jobs or job assignments. Financial institutions, companies that do certain types of government work (such as defense contractors), and other companies that require financial background checks will steer clear of applicants who have a bankruptcy in their pasts. Bankruptcy is a ball and chain, inscribed with the words: I Lost, Disorder Won.

If you are so bad off that those bankruptcy commercials are beginning to look appealing, go to a nonprofit, consumer credit counseling bureau first. Most cities have them. Although they are funded by the credit-card and finance industry, the nonprofit, consumer counseling organizations are far different from the private debt-restructuring companies discussed earlier. Consumer credit bureaus charge no fees, so they are not trying to make any money off your misfortune. They will contact your creditors and work out a payment plan that better suits your available cash. Often creditors will agree to accept substantially less than 100 cents on the dollar, which is something no seminar can do, and it avoids the tremendous liabilities associated with bankruptcy. Credit-card companies support these organizations because they know they will get at least some of the money owed to them, whereas if you declare bankruptcy, they may get little or nothing. Do not hesitate to use them. (See the crashproofyourlife.com website for more information on this topic.)

BINGE AND IMPULSE SPENDING. The slush fund will provide you the funds you need for purchasing gifts, appliances, and personal luxury items. But in order to stay within the limits of the slush fund, you will have to eliminate binge and impulse spending. Most families could save thousands of dollars annually with more controlled spending on leisure and luxury items. Indeed, binge and impulse spending are a major cause of dangerously high credit-card debt. Interestingly, however, small cash transactions often account for a lot of inappropriate buying as well.

A "binge" spender spends more than what is necessary to get the desired result. If you can spend less than you do and get the same result, you are a binge spender. For example, if Grandma would have been just as happy with a $35 wool sweater for her birthday, why did you buy her a Versace blouse for $350?

An "impulse" spender buys something totally unnecessary on the spur of the moment—like my daughter's twenty-eighth Barbie doll, which I bought last week when we were supposed to be shopping for a birthday present for her mother. Binge and impulse spending tend to occur when people buy gifts, most often around the holiday season, although there are many year-round bingers. The average American adult spends over $800 for Christmas and other holiday gifts, meaning that the average family spends in excess of $1,500. You can reduce these costs substantially.

The first step is to look back on all of the holiday presents you *received* last year and determine how many of them you actually used for any purpose whatsoever. Here is how it went in my house. The coffee-table book of breathtaking photographs from the Alaskan tundra that we got from Aunt Jessie went right into a box in our less-than-breathtaking basement. My eight-year-old daughter never once wanted to play the board game she got from her cousin, so we gave it away. My three-year-old son preferred the packaging to any of the actual toys he received. We also got all manner of sweaters and schlocky jewelry with reindeer and candy canes on them, which can only be worn a few days out of the year.

Looking at what you did with what you got should send you a message about your own spending habits: quit wasting your money on expensive things people do not want! Perhaps the best way to avoid the binge expenditures is to realize you should never impose your taste on someone else. Most people are very pleased to receive a less expensive gift that defers decisions of taste to them—a gift certificate to a music or bookstore or a small gift of china in the pattern they picked when they got married. People appreciate these low-key, simple gifts much more than expensive, subjective gifts like a life-sized plastic Santa or a framed print by the modern Crayola artist Ximbini from the "large breast" period of his career.

Then there is the question of shopping for your more immediate family— yourself, your spouse, and your kids. This generally presents the problem of impulse buying. I can speak from experience. At last count, my eight-year-old daughter had those twenty-eight Barbies mentioned earlier, as well as six American Girl dolls, twenty-seven Beanie Babies, thirty-three miscellaneous stuffed animals, and five musical instruments. She plays with one or two of each. My son just turned three and he has eighteen toy airplanes. My wife and I purchased most of these toys on impulse when we were going to a movie or buying some undershirts. I do not even know where to put all of these things, as they have taken over the house.

I am trying to improve. These kinds of impulse purchases not only waste tremendous sums of money but also devalue the entire process of gift giving. I remember when most kids had only one Barbie and one G.I. Joe. Kids treasured these toys; they played with them until they were worn out or fell apart. That is why these old dolls can be worth $500 in good condition today.

We do this impulse buying for ourselves too. My wife and I have seven Christmas CDs and at least twenty-five other CDs—classical, rock, and pop—that we have never even listened to one complete time. We have ten ornate picture frames sitting in boxes, books we bought but never bothered to read, a couple of unopened computer games, and a host of other impulse buys that represent completely wasted money. And we go even more loony on vacations—buying iridescent sunglasses, sunflower ceramic plates, and piles of T-shirts that now reside in that distant spot at the back of the closet that no one can reach.

The best way to reduce binge and impulse spending is to think about why you are going to the store and *stick to that thought*. If you are going to the store to buy some new and necessary casual china, you must hold to the plan. If, when you get to the store, you are tempted to veer away from the plan because you are overwhelmed with the beauty of a four-foot papier-mache parrot, stop for a second and think about what that purchase will likely mean to you a month from now. That thought should halt you dead in your tracks and cause you to resume your quest for the china that you really need.

In addition to eliminating the truly useless expenditures, consider gifts that can actually increase in value. I very much appreciate gifts of savings bonds to our children. Anyone can buy spectacularly beautiful gold coins with panda bears or maple leafs on them that they can put into jewelry very inexpensively. These gifts—which come in all sizes and prices—are investments.

One of the best ways to avoid impulse purchasing on your behalf is to develop a hobby or avocation involving the collection of items that tend to retain or increase in value. If you collect coins, stamps, baseball cards, or antique cameras, your relatives can buy you something you like that actually may be worth more in ten years than it is now. I know one couple who have amassed a small fortune by collecting memorabilia from the American Civil War and another who collect antique valentines. When it is birthday or anniversary time in their households, they ask their families to provide them something for their collections. If friends and relatives do not have the expertise to pick out something like that, they give gift certificates from the dealers who sell these collectibles. Everybody wins.

"Mutual agreement" gift buying is a must for crashproofers to stay within the limits of their slush fund. If you are tiring of that nineteen-inch television and you really want to go to thirty-six inches, make an agreement with your spouse that the new TV will be your joint anniversary gift to each other. If discretionary money is really tight under your crashproofing plan (because, for example, you are using most of your slush fund to pay off the credit cards), you may have to bring the whole family into the mutual-agreement gift buying process for a couple of years. Get the whole family to agree that the main family Christmas gift is going to be the camcorder or the VCR.

If you have a large extended family, you may want to bring them into the mutual-agreement gift buying process as well. An acquaintance of mine has her extended family (siblings and in-laws) draw names from a hat. Each family member then buys a single gift for the person whose name he or she drew from the hat. Each gift is then deemed to be "from" all of the other family members. Many very well-off families purchase gifts with some variation on mutual-agreement gift buying. How do you think they got to be so well off?

Playing in the Slush

If you use the slush-fund money to eliminate your consumer debt and otherwise control your bad habits, you may have a year or so without having much fun. But eventually you will start to build up some serious money in the slush fund. This extra money is yours to enjoy; however, your expenditures can never exceed the amount in the fund.

Some people take the extra slush-fund money and invest it. That is fine but really not necessary. Shortly, we will discuss the untouchable savings account and the investment clearinghouse account. These accounts will provide you more than enough in savings and investments.

It is important to use the slush-fund money for vacations and other fun events. Here is why. Many years ago, I became acquainted with a couple who saved every penny for retirement. He was a successful doctor and she was a well-paid illustrator, but the couple almost never took vacations. They drove an old car and wore very unpretentious clothes. Soon they had amassed more than four million dollars. Finally, when the doctor turned sixty-one, they retired to the life in Florida that they had planned for many years. Nine days after they arrived in Florida, the husband died of a massive heart attack. His widow lived a sad, lonely life for another twenty years. She told me time and time again how she wished that she and her husband had enjoyed their wealth a little when they were younger.

As the preceding example illustrates, lives can crash even when there is financial security. Within your slush-fund limits, you really should live a little for today. Moreover, you can make your slush-fund money go a long way these days if you take advantage of such new opportunities as special Internet fares offered by airlines and websites that do rapid comparison shopping for you on air fares, hotel rates, and other leisure costs or that allow you to bid your own price on vacations. You may not know exactly where you are going until close to the time you have to leave, but the discounts are so great that it is hard to pass them up. I know a couple who decide each year that they will take a vacation at a certain time, but they do not decide where to go until two or three days before the date of departure. At that time, they pick the best Internet fare to any fun location they can find. They know airlines and hotels post very low Internet prices at the last second to fill vacancies that cannot be filled at regular prices. Last year they went from Tucson to Brussels with a round-trip fare of $198. Similarly, I told my wife on a Wednesday last year that we were going to Paris on Friday, thanks to a $298 Internet airfare the airline advertised the week of the trip. I encourage you to become proficient at using the Internet to get these amazing values out of your travel dollars. Such opportunities demonstrate that you can adopt a careful, structured approach to managing your money while still enjoying the finer things the world has to offer. There is a list of some of the relevant websites on the crashproofyourlife.com website.

Charitable Gifts

Your slush fund also provides you money that you can give to charities. How much and to what charity you give is a very personal decision. However, there can be no doubt that helping other people whose lives have already crashed is not only a kind act, but it will also help you strengthen your own crashproofing program. When you see how easily other lives have crashed, you will redouble your own efforts to plan for adversity that could strike your own life.

A good approach to charitable contributions is to research two or three charities and make most of your donations to those groups. This approach has a couple of advantages over giving small amounts to many charities. First, if you adopt a special charity during your life, you will not feel obligated to give money to everyone who calls you, sends you a leaflet, or stops by the door. Remember, many of these cold callers are frauds. They take your money and pocket it for themselves. For example, a fireman in my area recently told me that his organization was not affiliated with *any* charity and that all of those people calling me to make a contribution to the local "Relief Fund" and the like were simply con artists. Similarly, a couple of years ago I learned of a man who dressed in a phony policeman's uniform and went door to door soliciting money for a nonexistent policeman's charity. It happens all the time.

If you research carefully the charities that you will benefit and give generously to them, then you will not feel obligated to give money to questionable organizations that come knocking at your door. In addition, when you decide among legitimate charities, always ask them how much of the money they receive really goes to the individuals whom the charity benefits, as opposed to administrative costs. Many charities spend so much on paying their staffs and advertising that very little actually goes to the cultural activity or disadvantaged group the charity is supposed to benefit. You must spend your charitable dollar as wisely and carefully as you spend your other discretionary funds.

Finally, when you carefully research and then support a small number of charities, you have the opportunity to become integrally involved in their operations. You can attend their galas, maybe even volunteer to help them in their fund-raising or planning, or you can serve on their boards of directors. Becoming actively involved in the charity will strengthen your crashproofing mind-set even more than giving money does, and it will allow you to impart your crashproofing knowledge and discipline to very special organizations.

5

Building Wealth to Achieve Security

Once you control your spending by setting up the first two corners of the pyramid financial structure—the limited-purpose checking account and the slush fund—you are no longer your worst financial enemy. You keep your home, car, and other household expenses under control, and you eliminate your credit-card debt and impulse spending. You limit your expenditures on vacations and extravagances to the amount that accumulates in a specific account set up for those purposes. You are a financially responsible person. Or are you?

The Financial Pyramid, Continued

The limited-purpose checking account and the slush fund cover your expenditures, which amount to 80 percent of your after-tax income, but you still have to figure out what to do with the rest of the money you make. The final two corners of the financial pyramid take the remaining 20 percent of your after-tax income and invest it in a manner that will allow you to achieve a high level of financial security.

Even with your spending under control, your life will still crash if you do not develop the proper savings and investing structures. However, a very different law of crashproofing applies here. When discussing your spending habits earlier, we operated on the principle that you are your worst financial enemy—and that is quite true. People like to spend money. In sharp contrast, however, you will find that when it comes to your saving and investing habits, you are in fact your best financial friend.

Other people give you a lot of advice on what to do with your savings and investment money. They counsel you to take big risks on such investments as "hot" new stocks, speculative limited partnerships, or volatile commodities futures. As soon as you hear about these "opportunities," you probably experience an almost instinctive reaction that *you should not do it*—it just doesn't sound right. Yet many people go ahead and take these unnecessary risks because of the promise of big financial returns and the pressure others put on them. You have to learn to follow your initial instincts and resist the pressure and temptation to invest in speculative ventures just because some yahoo is promising that you will get rich quick.

In this discussion of the last two corners of the pyramid financial structure, you will find that your basic instinct for self-preservation and security should be your guiding light. If you are saving 20 percent of your after-tax income, you are putting away a far greater percentage of your money than the typical American does. So you do not have to take a lot of risks to achieve financial security. Follow your inclination to play it safe, and you will have succeeded in crashproofing your finances.

The Untouchable Savings Account

With your expenses under control, you need to build a solid foundation of immediately accessible cash savings. The third of your four accounts in the pyramid structure is, therefore, the untouchable savings account. The purpose of the untouchable savings account is to provide you risk-free cash that you can access immediately in the event of an unexpected crash. That is its only purpose.

Try to Save Enough to Live a Year Without Income

Many investment advisers recommend you have cash savings equal to three months of your salary. For a crashproofer, however, salary is not the best standard by which to measure what you should save. You should base your savings on how much you need to live, not how much you make. First, establish your own personal comfort level. Decide how many months worth of living expenses you would need to have in the bank in order to ease your concerns about the kinds of crashes that would be most likely to materialize in your life. So much of crashproofing is *feeling* secure, and only you know—based on your unique personal and professional circumstances—how much spare cash you need to have.

While ultimately it is a personal decision, here is some guidance on how much to put into the savings account. This advice is based on conversations I have had with a wide cross section of American people whom I have met on my lecture tours. On average, people from ages twenty-one to sixty-four, making anywhere from $25,000 to in excess of $150,000 per year, tell me they would feel secure about their futures if they knew they could live an entire year at their current standard of living without having any additional income and without touching the money they have invested for their retirement and children's education. In the minds of many hardworking Americans, that sum would give them enough time to get back on their feet if some life crash occurred. In our example of the family that makes $92,000, one year's worth of living expenses (i.e., the total deposited in the limited-purpose checking account per year) equals just over $50,000.

If you directly deposit 10 percent of your after-tax income into the savings account, as depicted in the chart at the beginning of Part Two, you will accumulate one year's worth of living expenses in less than seven years. That is a very solid crashproofing goal and a very reasonable amount of time in which to achieve that goal. I recommend, therefore, that you try to save one year's worth of living expenses over a seven-year period, and we will operate on that assumption as we proceed. If, however, your financial situation is tight, you may want to set a goal of saving six or nine months' worth of living expenses and adjust your financial plans accordingly.

Make sure that the money is directly deposited into an insured savings account that pays money-market rates. At current rates, the interest will not be substantial, but getting even a little interest will accelerate the achievement of your savings goal by a few months. In fact, once you have six months' worth of living expenses put away—which should take just under three and a half years— you should consider putting the rest of your savings into certificates of deposit (CDs) at the same stable bank where you keep the general savings account. The CD will pay a higher interest rate than the money-market savings account pays. If a crash does occur, you do not have to worry about running out of money before the CD becomes due. If you find you need to use the money, you can first access the six months' worth of cash savings in the savings account. By the time that money is gone, the six-month CD will have come due, and then you will be able to use those funds without penalty.

Ignore the Leverage Mongers

Some people will tell you that it is crazy to leave as much as $50,000 languishing in a money-market savings account, or even a six-month CD, when the average return on stocks has been much higher than the return on CDs in many recent years. The prevailing wisdom is that you should incur the risk to seek high returns on your money unless you are very close to retirement. For crashproofers, however, this is flawed reasoning. First, if you set up strong financial structures such as the pyramid plan, there will be plenty of money to invest in other forms of wealth, including stocks and bonds. In fact, the next part of the pyramid structure that we will discuss is the investment clearinghouse account, which will give you the opportunity to be more daring with a carefully allocated portion of your assets.

The main reason why people overleverage themselves with high-risk investments is that they spend too much and consequently, they have very little money to invest. As a result, they have to incur a lot of risk to get the returns they need. Indeed, if you are only saving 3 or 4 percent of your income, you will need a big return or you will have nothing when you retire. If, on the other hand, you adopt a pyramid structure that forces you to save a large percentage of what you make and instills greater care in the way you spend money, you will have so much extra money available that you will be able to afford to be more conservative with your investments. Keeping a year's worth of living expenses in cash becomes affordable, therefore, when you manage your money with the structure and discipline that crashproofers do.

The second reason you should ignore those who preach against having large sums in a low-interest savings account is the need for accessibility of funds. Crashproofers recognize the tremendous value of *immediately available cash*. Under the pyramid plan, the money in your savings account will always be there, available on a moment's notice, to help you through the really hard times. With that kind of peace of mind, it is worth sacrificing the few potential interest points you might otherwise gain if you placed that money in riskier investments. However intangible it may seem, there is real value in the security you get from knowing you have a big chunk of cash just sitting there in the bank gathering dust. Once you try it, you will see that it simply feels right.

Finally, in these days of low inflation and low interest rates, people often forget that one of the possible "crash" scenarios that could occur is a spike in inflation and a correspondingly rapid increase in interest rates. In such a situation, the interest rate on your savings would skyrocket while the prices of stocks would probably plummet. If this happens, when all the people caught up in market mania are licking their wounds, you will be safe and secure with a solid base of cash earning a high rate of interest on which you can live. The goal of saving one year's worth of living expenses, therefore, makes a lot of sense to anyone who adopts the kind of comprehensive crashproofing structures that form the basis of our plan.

Stop Depositing When You Reach Your Savings Comfort Level

Assuming you want a year's worth of living expenses in the bank, you will have achieved your goal after about seven years of direct depositing 10 percent of your after-tax income into your savings account. You will have enough money in the bank to give you the comfort and security that you desire. At that point, you can cease depositing money into that account or sharply reduce the sums that you deposit there. You can virtually forget about the money you have in the savings account. You need only to ensure that the interest rate you are getting on the funds in that account stays in line with inflation so that the purchasing power of your savings remains steady. And, if necessary, make occasional deposits into the account to keep its purchasing power constant.

Once you get your savings to where it should be, redirect the amount for the savings account into your investment clearinghouse account. So, for our family that makes $92,000 per year, after one year's living expenses ($50,000) are safely in the savings account, the family should distribute the money as follows: $4,200 per month in the checking account, $1,200 per month in the investment account, $600 per month in the slush fund, and nothing in the savings account. Have a little party when you hit the appropriate savings sum; you deserve it. Of course, you must use slush-fund money to pay for the party.

Investment Clearinghouse Account

The process of building a crashproof financial structure is very methodical. First, you learn to live on about 70 percent of your income by being more careful in the way you spend money on your home, car, food, clothes, and entertainment. Then you learn to eliminate serious financial vices and keep leisure and extraordinary expenses to about 10 percent of your income. Next, you build a cash reserve of up to one year's worth of living expenses. The fourth and final corner of the pyramid is learning how to invest the remaining funds in a way that will maximize financial growth and minimize financial risk.

Establish Your Investment Structure

Your investment clearinghouse account is, like your other accounts, a basic interest-bearing account at a federally insured bank. As with the other accounts, you have your employer deposit the money directly into this account. Or, if your employer limits the number of accounts to which it will make direct deposits, simply write a check yourself each month from your checking account to your investment account. If you must adopt the latter approach, make sure you write that check to your investment account on a designated day each month soon after you get paid—and do not make exceptions. If you cannot use direct deposit, you must ingrain in your mind the process of doing it yourself, making it the equivalent of direct deposit. It takes a lot of discipline to use these mental structures rather than legal ones.

Then you let the money accumulate for a little while. For our family making $92,000 per year, the employer deposits $600 per month in the investment clearinghouse account. After the family has accumulated $50,000 in its savings account, the employer will increase the amount deposited in the investment account to $1,200 per month, because the family will divert the money that previously had been deposited into the savings account to the investment account. That is a good chunk of money to have available for investments.

Because of the low rate of return you may get on any bank account, you should never let the investment clearinghouse account accumulate very much money before you use the funds in the account to purchase an investment. You already have a savings account you use to accumulate cash. My advice is, if your family income is between $50,000 and $100,000 per year after taxes, then when your investment clearinghouse account has $2,000 in it, you should start thinking about making investments in stocks, bonds, real estate, or commodities. If you have a higher income, wait until you have more money in the account and make bigger investments; if you have a lower income, do not wait until you have $2,000. It may be better to invest the money $1,000 at a time because you do not want the money sitting in the investment clearinghouse account too long.

Investing in stocks and bonds will also require that you have a brokerage account and a retirement account. About 50 percent of Americans have at least one such account. You need both. We will discuss a little later how to allocate your investments between your brokerage account—which gives you the advantage of accessibility of funds—and your retirement account—which gives you tax advantages at the expense of accessibility. For the purposes of establishing the correct structural basis for your investing, you must have both types of accounts. If you do not have them already, plan on having these accounts available as avenues for investing some of the money that accumulates in your investment clearinghouse account.

Do Not Assume You Can Outperform Efficient Markets

The framework for your investing has now been established: you will directly deposit 10 percent of your after-tax income into your investment clearinghouse account each pay period. You will make an investment from the funds in that account whenever the account has accumulated $2,000, with appropriate adjustments depending on your income. You will open a brokerage account and a retirement account so that you have a mechanism to make your investments.

Now you must consider your investment options. First, consistent with the crashproofing strategy, you need to know what *not* to do. Then this section will provide a general framework for safe investing, which ultimately allows you to make the final decisions. Remember, this is not a book about picking hot stocks or making a killing in the bond market. Crashproofing involves first eliminating the negative, and then learning what positive opportunities you may have; and you make the final decision on which path to take. This process works equally well with investing.

People have many investment options, but most of these options are not good for crashproofers. In simple terms, most investments are too risky. If you keep your finances structured according to the pyramid plan, it will not be necessary for you to take big risks in order to get enough money to achieve financial security.

Learning to avoid risky investments is not easy. The typical investor has heard the interviews with the homemaker who invested $2,000 in Amazon.com when it was a new company and sold out less than five years later at $240,000. Consequently, investors expend a tremendous amount of energy trying to figure out the "next big thing"—like tech stocks a few years ago. Investors focus their investment energy into trying to determine which investments (usually stocks) will outperform the rest of the market in the coming weeks and months. In fact, many people have completely lost interest in "boring" investments like real estate, bonds, or even established blue-chip stocks. Rather, they scour the business media hoping to find the "big one" that will make them rich and allow them to retire next summer. Some of them make trades on an almost daily basis, constantly shifting their money to their latest finds.

Jackpot hunting and day trading are completely antithetical to crashproofing. There is a reason why the lady who invested $2,000 in Amazon.com cashed out at $240,000: *almost no one else figured out that the stock was going to do so well during that limited period of time.* Once people realized there was great potential in the company, millions of people started buying the stock and the price of the stock soared. But what does that fact pattern mean? It means that most people got into the stock when it was too late to make any more money than they could have made on safer investments. In fact, a large percentage of people who bought Amazon.com lost money because, once the average investor heard the stories about the profits a few people had made, the market went into a frenzy and overvalued the stock. As I said earlier, no one interviews the losers. And there were plenty of them.

Crashproofers never think they are more clever than all of the other investors out there. Rather, they adopt a much more conservative approach based loosely upon a well-known but controversial economic premise called the "efficient market." At several points in this book, history has given us some perspective on the crashproofing process. In that tradition, this section will discuss some economic history that should discourage you from incurring unnecessary investment risk and wasting valuable time trying to find the super stock of the future.

Around 1900, economists began espousing what they called the "theory of speculation." They claimed, rather simply, that the market price of an investment always reflects the proper value of the investment; therefore, there is not much you can do to outperform the market. Under this theory, people should invest in a broad, diversified spectrum of stocks that reflects the market as a whole and give up on the idea that they can somehow pick stocks that will perform better than the market.

The reasoning supporting the efficient market theory goes something like this. People make a decision to buy a stock based upon the information they have available to them about the company issuing the stock. They have three types of information available to them: the past performance of the company, the company's predictions about its likely future, and the evaluation of that data by scores of investment advisers. An individual investor assimilates the information available to him or her and then decides whether to buy shares in the company. Every other investor does the same thing. The price of the stock, therefore, necessarily reflects the collective judgment of all investors based on all information in the marketplace. By definition then, the market price of the stock always reflects the best possible estimate of its value because it is the culmination of all the wisdom of every investor.

This theory gained momentum throughout the first several decades of the twentieth century. In 1922, legendary economic theorist William Peter Hamilton espoused a similar proposition, saying that "market movement reflects all real knowledge available." Similarly, in 1932, the eminent Robert Rhea opined that "industrial averages afford a composite index of all the hopes, disappointments, and knowledge of everyone who knows anything of financial matters, and for that reason, the effects of coming events are always properly anticipated in their movements."

By the 1960s, this efficient-market theory had solidified into a major economic discipline. Burton Malkiel made the classic statement, "A blindfolded monkey throwing darts could select a portfolio that would do just as well as one carefully selected by the experts." He reasoned that, because the market price of a stock reflects all publicly available information, there is no way any one individual can consistently beat the market except by blind luck; so you might as well have a monkey pick your stocks.

People then tested this theory. For example, the *Wall Street Journal* has on more than a hundred occasions compared the performance of stocks picked by the experts with the performance of both randomly picked stocks and the Dow Jones Industrial Average. The randomly picked stocks have outperformed the experts almost 40 percent of the time; the Dow Jones Industrial Average has outperformed the experts about 47 percent of the time. In fact, many local and regional news organizations have done the same test and had results where the "monkey" actually outperformed the experts. This monkey test, among others, supports the fairly sensible conclusion that you as an individual are not likely to have more or better information than the market as a whole. The monkey studies confirm that the price of a stock usually reflects its current value based upon all available information, and there is little you can do to pick investments that will do better than the market as a whole.

Many people disagree with efficient-market principles. They point to investment managers like Peter Lynch or tycoons like Warren Buffet who have consistently outperformed the market. In addition, economists who dispute efficient-market principles have done studies to demonstrate tiny inefficiencies in the market that they claim could have allowed an insightful investor to outperform the market. Efficient-market theorists respond that simple laws of probability dictate that there will always be a few people who do better than the market and a few who do worse, but the overwhelming majority of people will be somewhere in the middle and that skill in investing has little or nothing to do with these variations in performance. They note further that respected studies confirm that very few investment advisers outperform the market as a whole over a period of ten or more years. When the market does well, so do they; when it performs poorly, they do too.

You may not want to believe the efficient-market theory, nor do you have to believe it. But this is a book about crashproofing, and if the efficient-market theory turns out to be true, then you are setting yourself up for a crash every time you increase your investment risk by following hunches, acting on "tips," and putting too much money into one particular investment or investment sector. True or not, it is indisputable that an efficient-market approach represents a very conservative, safe, and unpretentious way to look at investing. By adopting an efficient-market approach, you accept that the price of an investment represents the best guess at its value and that you will not have any better insights on the issue. Therefore, if you believe in the efficient market, your investment goal is to pick a balanced, diverse group of investments that will reflect the market as a whole.

Whether the efficient-market theory is in fact right or wrong, crashproofers should assume that it is true. If it is wrong and you follow it nonetheless, you might miss the jackpot no one else saw, but you will still have a safe, well-balanced portfolio. On the other hand, if the efficient-market theory is right and you ignore it by following your hunches and taking risks, you could easily find your financial situation crashing and burning. Therefore, play it safe and assume that markets are efficient.

With this assumption in mind, you should avoid three kinds of behavior that can contribute to a financial crash. First, you should not waste your limited time and energy looking for undervalued investments. People devote tremendous amounts of time to studying the market in an effort to make the great find of the future. Some people sneak onto the Internet at work eight or ten times a day to follow the market and look for stocks. You are better off excelling at your job, rather than wasting your time (and risking your livelihood) trying to pick stocks while you are at work. Sure, you should monitor your investments to keep abreast of your financial progress, but do not become a slave to the market such that you sacrifice other, more important aspects of your life in order to make the big find. There are many market junkies out there; do not become one of them.

Second, never act on a supposedly "great tip" someone offers you. It is amazing how many people will run out and buy a stock or mutual fund on the recommendation they received from a stranger in an airport, a college buddy, or a coworker who does not seem to be doing a whole lot better financially than they are. If you are going to crashproof your finances, you must assume that the person with the tip, whoever he or she may be, is no better at predicting the market than the collective wisdom of everyone else who is looking at the market. For example, in 1929, two weeks before the stock market crash, the respected economist Irving Fisher stated, "stock prices have reached what looks like a permanently high plateau." If he could not get it right, neither can your brother-in-law.

The only exception to this rule is if the person has "inside" information—i.e., material nonpublic information. If you get inside information, the efficient-market theory says you will be able to outperform the market because the trading price of the stock does not reflect inside information. So if you make the trade, cash in quick because you will need the money to pay your lawyers and support your family while you are in jail. As I hope you remember from Part One, trading on inside information is usually illegal.

Finally, do not incur a lot of transaction costs. Every time you make an investment, you have to pay a transaction fee. Stockbrokers charge trading fees. Real estate brokers charge a fee of usually about 6 percent of the transaction value. For mutual funds, you may have to pay a sales commission that averages 5 percent and can be as high as 8 percent of the investment. That means you could invest $10,000 in a mutual fund and only get $9,200 in equity. The stock has to go up over 8 percent in value just for you to break even. Moreover, when you sell at a profit, you have to pay capital gains taxes on that profit. The longer you hold a profitable security, the longer you defer the tax payment.

In fact, the efficient-market theory holds that excessive transaction costs and management fees put people into positions where they *underperform* the market. The facts confirm the theory. In 2000, two professors at the University of California, Davis, released a study indicating that, during the five and a half years ending in 1996, frequent traders obtained an average return on stock market investments of about 11.4 percent annually, while buy-and-hold investors got a return that averaged 18.5 percent. Both the theory and the empirical data indicate, therefore, that following hunches and tips leads to excessive trading, and excessive trading leads to lost income.

Crashproofers must adopt a buy-and-hold strategy because it reduces transaction costs. By the same token, once you become comfortable with the process of buying securities, you should use low-cost brokerage services and purchase investments with low up-front fees so that you do not put yourself deep into a financial hole every time you make an investment. Then you have taken full advantage of the efficient market.

Learn the Histories of the Spectrum of Investments

By now you should be willing to discard the idea that you are going to make a quick killing in the market that would let you retire early. Rather, you have some real work to do. You have to put together a low-risk portfolio of investments.

Many people get the misimpression that efficient-market principles prove that you might as well just buy a monkey at the pet store and have that monkey throw darts at the *Wall Street Journal* to make your investment decisions. After all, the monkey often does just as well as the investment advisers, right? People hear this theory, think it makes some sense, and just throw up their hands and give up.

Do not lose heart. True, efficient-market principles suggest that you cannot use skill to outperform the market. However, even operating under these principles, you must still pay close attention to what you buy. According to many theorists, even in an efficient market, you can still reduce the risk that you will suffer a financial crash or seriously underperform the market. Because of the stellar growth of the economy over the past century, the odds on making money just performing at market levels are pretty good. So, while you cannot consistently outperform the market, you can—even in an efficient market—reduce the risk that you will underperform the market and lose your security.

Consequently, while crashproofers do not waste time trying to outperform the market, they do study risk carefully and invest in a manner that minimizes underperformance. Here is a hypothetical example that explains the difference between a doomed philosophy that tries to outperform a market, which is contrary to the efficient market and crashproofing, and an intelligent approach that tries to minimize market risk, which is consistent with both the efficient market and crashproofing.

Let's say you are looking at two stocks: E-moon and General Appliances. E-moon is in the business of building the first commuter spaceship to the moon. E-moon plans to have a test launch of its first prototype commuter spaceship next year. At the other end of the spectrum, General Appliances builds refrigerators and has done so for several decades. Both stocks are trading at $100 per share.

The efficient-market theory says that the price of the stock reflects all information available about each company, and both are valued at exactly the same sum. However, even though the market values the two stocks at the same price, equal valuation does not mean that the two stocks carry the same risk. Obviously, on its face, the space venture is a lot riskier than the appliance venture. In this case, the reason General Appliances is trading at $100 is that according to the collective wisdom of the market, if all goes well in the refrigerator business, a year from now the stock might be trading at $110. However, if General Appliances experiences a business downturn, it might slip to $90. It is a low-risk stock because the company is in the rather mundane business of making refrigerators, a business with fairly predictable market trends. Consequently, the current price averages out at $100 with little upside or downside risk.

E-moon is trading at $100 for a very different reason. No one outside the company knows if the test of the prototype moon rocket will go well. To the market, it has a fifty-fifty chance of success. If, in fact, the test of the prototype does go well, the market wisdom says the stock will jump to an astonishing $10,000 per share. The company will be a pioneer in a whole new business and it will take off in a big way. However, the market also believes that if the prototype rocket crashes and burns, the price of the stock will also crash—to about $1 per share—because it will prove that public travel to the moon is a long way in the future. Those two potential scenarios—one where the stock will trade at $10,000 in a year versus one where the stock will trade at $1 in a year—average out to a current stock price of $100 per share, just as the two potential scenarios for the appliance company average out to $100 per share. As you can see, however, just because two companies are accurately valued by the efficient market at $100 per share does not mean they are equally risky. The market knows that the space venture is much riskier than the refrigerator venture. Therefore, even though the market accurately values an investment, and even though you cannot consistently outperform the market, you can, by buying the appliance stock rather than the space stock, adopt an investment strategy that reduces your risk.

The following section will discuss how to allocate your investments in a manner that keeps risk to a minimum while still gaining a healthy return. The key to risk-averse investing is understanding which types of investments are most likely to hold their value over time, i.e., which investments have shown the greatest stability over time. In order to achieve this understanding, crashproofers need to know the history of each of the major categories of investment—and not just the recent history but also the long-term history. Once you understand why certain types of investments hold their value better than others, you will be in a position to spend your investment clearinghouse funds in an intelligent, risk-averse manner.

Therefore, we'll discuss the history and risk levels of the four major categories of potential investments for your investment clearinghouse funds: real estate, commodities, government securities, and corporate securities. We will put each type of investment into its historical context and use that context to come up with some general guidance for where each type of investment should fit into your crashproofing plan. Then you decide what to buy and when.

REAL PROPERTY. The oldest and original form of wealth is real property, or real estate—land and home. Long before there were stock markets and junk bonds, there was only one true measure of wealth: how much land you owned. One of the most treasured phrases of the English language as it developed in the Middle Ages was *fee simple absolute*. It meant that you had the ability to do anything you wanted with a piece of land, including passing that land on to your heirs. Other phrases that meant you had a temporary right of occupancy to a piece of land, a partial interest in that land, a lease interest, or a future interest also appeared in early English texts; but it was the goal and dream of nearly all people in the Middle Ages to be able to utter the phrase "fee simple absolute" when describing the land that they occupied. The English Middle Ages' version of today's American Dream, the phrase appeared throughout the early English documents because it was what everyone coveted.

Land is the original investment. You live on it. You can grow vegetables or livestock on it. You can rent it out. Or you can just relax under a tree and take a nap on it. Land is also the most structural of all investments. You can survey your land and measure exactly what you own or build a house on it and measure the square footage. You can put a fence around your property and a roof over your head and keep many of the forces of disorder out of your life. Because land ownership is so solidly rooted in history and so structural, it is a powerful foe of the universal tendency toward disorder that wants to make a mess of your life.

Crashproofers take full advantage of the power of property. Indeed, to a crashproofer, land is the most powerful of all investments. For most Americans, their homes will be their biggest and best investment. In many neighborhoods across the United States, homes have increased in value 1,500 percent over the past thirty years. In the minds of many, land remains today the most stable and desirable of investments.

Moreover, if you own your home and yard free and clear, you are far less vulnerable to economic catastrophe than someone who does not own real estate, even someone with plenty of other investments. If, for example, there were a major inflationary recession or depression, the prices of stocks would plummet, and, under many scenarios, the bond market would suffer serious setbacks as well. You could lose your paper investments quickly.

Of course, with higher interest rates, real estate prices might go down, too. The difference is that you cannot live in a municipal bond or twenty shares of IBM. If real estate prices go down, you still have a tangible asset; whereas when stock and bond prices go down, you have nothing left. Indeed, by owning real estate, you still have your most important asset when a crisis hits—a home. If you have no property or you have a big mortgage, you may find yourself without a place to live.

This is not a far-fetched scenario. At many times during the history of the United States, economic crises threw many once-prosperous Americans into homelessness. Read the newspapers from the four or five days preceding the panic of 1837 or the stock market crash of 1929. These papers covered the banal social engagements and breezy stories that often blossom during times of economic prosperity. Virtually nobody was listening to the few naysayers who believed that economic crisis was imminent. Yet within days of these pleasant stories, the lives of the same people mentioned were thrown into turmoil. It has happened before and it will happen again.

It is essential, therefore, that you obtain free and clear ownership of some piece of property—preferably the one containing your home—at the first possible opportunity. This viewpoint is, in some respects, contrary to conventional wisdom espoused by the "leveragers." Many of these investment experts say you should keep a high mortgage and put your money in other investments. Their reasoning is simple. When you borrow for your home, the interest is tax deductible, meaning you are paying a very low rate of interest on money you borrow for your home. So you may have a 7 percent mortgage, but your tax deduction may make the effective rate more like 5 percent. Leveragers see no reason for using hard-earned income to pay off a loan that may have an after-tax rate of 5 percent per year when you could be investing that same money in a stock that could pay 20 percent per year, with much of the gain tax deferred until you sell it and a low capital-gains tax rate once you do cash it in. This reasoning is the most simple application of the principal of leveraging—borrowing at a low rate and investing at a higher one.

This philosophy is fine as long as the economy is good and other investments are yielding higher returns than your after-tax mortgage rate. But the reasoning is flawed to a crashproofer for three reasons, based in the previously discussed history. First, you are less likely to need to spend your accrued investment wealth when the economy is strong and stocks are doing well. You will need to cash in your investments when there is a crisis, which is when stocks and bonds often lose their value. So, at the exact time when you really need the money, you may not be able to reap any of the benefit of the paper gains these investments have afforded you. On the other hand, real estate, as a more stable historical investment, may well hold more of its value when paper investments fail.

Second, investment advisers often ignore that real estate has a use and purpose independent of its market value. You live on land, your kids play on it, and you can even raise food on it. Stocks and bonds are pieces of paper. They have no use beyond their market value. Land has such a use, indeed many such uses, that the market price never fully reflects. So even if real estate prices crash as badly as other investments do (or worse for that matter), you still have something of substantial value to you.

Finally, it is human nature to seek tangible security, and real estate provides it. You will get a far greater sense of personal security being in a home that you own outright, sitting in the living room on your favorite chair, than you will get from reading your monthly brokerage statement. People feel better about life when they are surrounded by the security of their own land and homes. And they should.

Crashproofers make real estate ownership a primary goal of their investment strategy. In order to accomplish this goal, you should accelerate the home ownership process. The first step to home ownership is, as was discussed earlier, to buy a home and piece of land that you can afford. Figure out what you really need, and keep in mind that the forces of disorder thrive in wasted space. Once you have determined the piece of land you want and can afford, you make the monthly mortgage payments out of the limited-purpose checking account, as outlined earlier.

However, you should then go a step further. Use some of the funds in your investment clearinghouse account to "prepay" your mortgage so you can own the land sooner. Your goal should be to make at least one, if not two, extra payments per year, thereby increasing the equity you have in your home and reducing the term of your mortgage. Here is how it works. Once or twice a year, write a check from your investment clearinghouse account in an amount equal to one mortgage payment and send it to the bank. Include a note stating that this is an extra payment and the full sum should be applied to reduce the *principal* on the loan, not the interest. Ask for a printout of your loan schedule to confirm that the bank or mortgage company properly applied the extra payment to the principal. The printout will show that you have more equity and have shortened the term of your loan.

This process can greatly reduce the amount of time you have to wait to own your home and substantially lessen your interest payments. Say, for example, you have a $100,000 mortgage to be paid over thirty years at a 7.5 percent fixed rate. If you increase your principal ownership by making one extra payment per year, you will slash almost $40,000 in interest off of your debt and reduce the loan period from thirty years to just over twenty-three years. This is crashproofing at its best.

You should use the structural discipline that you have developed to prepay the mortgage without outside assistance from a lending institution or other financial organization. Some banks and other financial institutions offer what are called "accelerated mortgage" or "equity builder" plans. They tell you they will help you reduce the interest that you ultimately pay and shorten the term of your loan if you allow them to administer a plan where you pay a little more each month than the mortgage requires. You may also be approached with this type of a plan by a "cash management" company that is not even associated with your lending institution and about which you know absolutely nothing (other than what they tell you).

You do not need equity builder or cash management plans. They are just a cover for the same prepayment concept we have been discussing, although the institutions administering them usually have you make the prepayments in small monthly increments rather than through one or two larger payments each year. The problem with these plans is the financial institutions or cash management companies that set them up and administer them charge hefty fees to help you do exactly what you can do yourself for free. Often they charge hundreds of dollars up front just to set up the plan and then a monthly fee on top of the start-up fee.

Moreover, the cash management companies that are not affiliated with your lender can be real fly-by-night operations. They can take your money and then fold up like cheap lawn furniture. One organization recently advertised on the Internet that by taking a seminar just about anyone can make tens of thousands of dollars from forming a cash management company that does nothing but "help" people set up prepayment plans. Would you trust your money to some guy whose only qualification to administer your mortgage payment plan was that he had attended a three-hour seminar he learned about on the Internet? With pyramid financial planning, you already have a more reliable and far less costly structure in place to administer your own prepayment plan. Do not waste your money allowing others—often of questionable credentials—to do it for you.

Once you own your home, you should also consider spending some of your investment clearinghouse money on other real estate investments, particularly undeveloped property near growing metropolitan areas. While such purchases can be risky, land near cities has historically increased in value, as developers tend to buy it up for new housing ventures. Investing in rental properties is also an option, but it is also risky because of the substantial amount of time and money involved in finding good tenants and keeping up the property. Consequently, crashproofers generally shy away from undeveloped and rental property until they have a very solid base of other investments and a lot of time to devote to their property business. Whatever you decide to do, as you work through the various stages of the crashproofing process, keep in the forefront of your mind the historical fact that land has always been a measure of wealth, and it therefore represents a basic and essential part of any crashproofing plan.

COMMODITIES. Here is a subject even more controversial: what, if anything, should you invest in commodities? Commodities include livestock, timber, and the various metals—from tin to platinum. For the purposes of this discussion, however, I will assume you do not intend to buy a herd of cattle or a truckload of aluminum. The following discussion of commodities will be confined to precious metals, gold and silver in particular.

Commodities are the second-oldest form of investment. Until a few decades ago, leading world economies operated on the gold standard: the value of their currency was tied directly to the price of gold. In fact, while civilizations have valued everything from glass to seashells at one time or another, almost every civilization has considered gold to have great value. The recognized value of gold and other precious metals developed independently in civilizations as far apart in time and space as the ancient Egyptians and the Aztecs.

Gold and silver seem to have a unique quality, one that is not found in any other form of investment: *intrinsic value*. They have value that is independent of their industrial or trade use. In today's society gold has industrial value in, for example, the wiring of high-tech devices, and silver has for decades been of value in developing photographic film. But early societies did not need precious metals for any industrial purposes, yet they continued to place high value on them. Even their beauty for jewelry and ornamentation cannot explain the enduring value of gold and silver, because other metals and alloys like lead, copper, and brass are visually attractive but carry nowhere near the value of gold. Rarity alone also cannot explain the value of gold. Four-leaf clovers are rare, but they do not form the basis of the economic structures of entire civilizations. While industrial use, rarity, and beauty have contributed to the value of gold and silver, civilizations have in some sense valued gold and silver just because they are gold and silver. That is intrinsic value.

The historic popularity of gold and silver, combined with their strange, intrinsic appeal, earn them a place in the financial structure of a crashproof life. The appeal of gold seems to transcend time, space, and the cultural idiosyncrasies of any civilization. The wealth inherent in gold and silver has resisted the forces of disorder around us better than almost any other tangible item on earth.

Many financial advisers detest gold and silver as investments because precious metals produce no interest. That is a legitimate concern and the principal reason why gold cannot form a major part of any sound investment structure. However, because of their historic stability, precious metals remain an essential, albeit small, part of the crashproofing picture. Indeed, gold and silver remain the best weapons against inflation, and inflation remains the greatest threat to economic stability in our country and the world. From 1970 to 1980 when interest rates crept up to 14 percent and inflation was rampant, gold went from $35 per ounce to $800 per ounce. Silver also went up dramatically, although part of that increase was the result of an attempt by a few individuals to corner the market. The prices of these metals fell equally dramatically as the rate of inflation decreased in the mid- and late 1980s. Crashproofers always keep in mind that it is during trying economic times that people will most need wealth, so gold and silver represent unique protection that is available for periods of great inflation. They will never be an investment with a steadily rising value, nor will they be a good investment during good times.

I recommend you use your investment clearinghouse account to purchase gold or silver in a sum equal to approximately 5 percent of your annual living expenses. You can learn how to go about making such purchases by checking the recommended reading section at the end of the book. So, our family making $92,000 per year with annual take-home pay of about $72,000 and living expenses of $50,400 should have put away in a safe-deposit box about $2,500 in gold and silver. If, for example, we experience another inflationary recession like we did a couple of decades ago, that gold would likely be worth between $10,000 and $15,000—a nice cushion for you and your family in the event that you are struck with a crisis during such economic hard times. If we experience a major world catastrophe and the kind of inflation that other countries have experienced in recent years—sometimes 100 percent or more annually—that gold could be worth a fortune, $100,000 or more. In effect, the value of gold and silver is inverse to that of paper investments. Gold and silver tend to hold their value when paper loses its value. For that reason, you cannot afford to be without some gold and silver in your balanced, risk-averse allocation of investments.

GOVERNMENT SECURITIES. You have probably seen government securities, and you may own some. As we consider where they fit into the crashproof investment structure, let's think about what they really are and how they came to be. Government securities—principally bonds—are notes issued by government entities such as the U.S. Treasury, individual municipalities, and foreign governments. A government entity borrows your money in return for its promise to pay you interest over a specified period of time and to return the principal sum at the end of that period. The government puts its "full faith and credit" behind these notes but unless it gets the obligation insured, it gives you no other guarantee that it will pay you back.

In general, investors feel that bonds—particularly U.S. bonds—are very safe investments because they have produced stable returns for the past several decades. However, while many government securities are fairly safe and should be a part of your crashproofing plan, there remain serious risks associated with government securities—with some being far more risky than others. You need to know and understand these risks before you decide how much of your investment clearinghouse funds to invest in them.

While government securities are the third-oldest form of investment, they have a much more checkered past than real estate or precious metals. Let's discuss, therefore, how we got from gold to paper as a unit and measure of wealth and thereby learn the pitfalls of investing in government paper. By understanding the historical risks associated with government securities, you will be better able to decide which securities to make part of your crashproof investment structure.

We will start the analysis all the way back in the ancient world. While the earliest civilizations used land as the principal measure of wealth, they also traded to a limited extent in ingots of precious metals. The problem with these ingots was that they were heavy, unwieldy, and of varying purities. Consequently, anytime someone used an ingot of precious metal to pay for goods or services, assayers had to weigh the ingot and measure its purity—a time-consuming process. For that reason, gold and silver were not of much use in small, day-to-day transactions, which were generally consummated with barter.

However, starting around 675 B.C., the Greeks established the use of precious metals as an effective means of day-to-day currency. Asian and Greek city-states stamped small pieces of gold or silver (or an alloy of the two) with the name or emblem of the city or ruler that issued them—be it the owl of Athens (500 B.C.) or the idealized face of Alexander the Great (325 B.C.). These imprints on pieces of precious metal represented the guarantee of the government issuing them that the metal was pure and of a specified weight. We call them coins.

Coins represented the first time that governments guaranteed the value of currency. If you trusted the government that issued the coin, you did not need to weigh the coin and you did not need to test the purity of the metal. Soldiers and traders accepted the coins of trustworthy governments without question. This made the process of conducting commerce and paying for wars much more simple.

However, the value of the coin was only as good as the reputation of the ruler who issued it—a very important lesson that remains instructional today as we analyze the safety of the bonds and currency issued by various modern governments. At several points in ancient history, when countries or rulers had depleted their wealth or amassed tremendous debt (as occurred in Athens after the Athenians lost their war against Sparta), their governments attempted to leverage their past prestige by putting their imprint on silver coins they had debased with copper—a metal with very little intrinsic value. The issuers hoped the debased coins would trade at the same value as the pure coins had. Some ancient cities and rulers, desperate to rid themselves of their debt or obtain supplies they could not otherwise afford, stamped out large quantities of these low-quality coins. The plan did not work. Soldiers and traders demanded increasingly greater quantities of these coins to cover the debts owed to them or to provide new supplies and services. As a result, governments had to mint more debased coins to buy the same supplies and services they had previously purchased with fewer pure coins. This process—whereby it took more money to buy the same thing—was one of the most notorious discoveries of the ancient world. We call it *inflation*.

For many centuries, no one would accept a coin at a value any less than the value of the gold or silver in the coin, so inflation reared its head every time a ruler or country tried to pass off a debased silver coin at a value greater than the real worth of its metal. Debased silver or copper coins circulated with unstable and often unclear values. However, during the late years of the Roman Republic and the early years of the Roman Empire, the government of Rome finally succeeded in getting the army and the public to accept a copper coin at a value of one-quarter of a silver coin, even though the copper in the coin was worth less than the value the government decreed the coin to have. The Roman emperors were so powerful and the people had so much faith in the future of Rome that the people, including the army, accepted the imprint of the emperor's face on the coin as a guarantee of its stated value, regardless of the actual value of the metal in the coin. People accepted, on a much larger scale than ever before, currency that had *symbolic* value but no *intrinsic* value. Rather than containing actual wealth, these copper coins were merely representative of wealth that resided in the state.

The circulation of bronze coinage at a value far above its nominal metallic value achieved limited success during the rest of the Roman Empire and during the centuries following the Roman Empire. Then, some seventeen centuries after the great Roman experiment, a brilliant but doomed financial adventurer named John Law came up with the idea that he could help the French government retire its extensive national debt by selling *paper* certificates that represented the ownership of gold that the French intended to mine on its land in the New World. His "money" had no metal in it at all. While others had experimented with paper money before Law, the Law notes caught on like wildfire. For about five hundred days in 1719 and 1720, Law's paper notes actually circulated as wealth, increasing in value twentyfold during that period. Soon, however, the investing public realized that the real money they had invested in this paper money was lining the pockets of Law and the French nobility, and there appeared to be no plan to actually mine the gold in the French territories. The people lost faith in the government issuing the Law notes, and their value plummeted. Law had to flee France to avoid the angry throngs of fleeced investors. He died in poverty, and many of his investors experienced total financial crashes.

Only a couple of years after the Law debacle in France, England experienced a similar disaster known as the South Sea Bubble. The South Sea Company promised to pay off the British national debt in return for the exclusive right to trade in the Pacific, and people investing in the company received notes, hoping that the profits from trading in the South Seas would bring them great riches. The notes were in high demand until the investors realized that Spain, not England, controlled the South Seas, after which the notes quickly became worthless. Similarly, during the American Revolution, the fledgling government of the United States tried to finance the war against England with the famous Continental Currency, paper notes allegedly secured only by the patriotic fervor of the citizens of the revolting colonies. As the costs of war increased, the money presses went wild, and once again, rampant inflation rendered the money almost worthless. In the same tradition yet again, the revolutionary government of France during the French Revolution tried to finance its wars by issuing *assignats*—paper notes allegedly secured by land that the new French government had confiscated from the Church. They printed notes that had a face value far exceeding the value of the confiscated land, and they, too, became worthless in a cycle of voracious inflation. The same story played out once again when the Confederacy issued paper money during the American Civil War and again when Germany's Weimar Republic issued huge sums of paper money to cover its debts after World War I. These notes also became as worthless as Monopoly money.

That is, in a nutshell, the early history of the move from money with intrinsic value to money with symbolic value. The concept of wealth guaranteed by government but separated from the intrinsic value of land or gold had a very rough start across the board—from the early coins of the Greeks and Romans, to the first notes issued in eighteenth-century France and Britain, to the currency issued during the early decades of the United States. The risk inherent in paper or symbolic wealth is that the issuing government does not have the stability or economic power to deliver on the stated value of the paper. When the public loses confidence in the ability of the government to make good on its promise of value, the value of the paper decreases, usually in a cycle of tremendous inflation.

The more recent history of paper wealth explains why we consider it so secure today. The concept of paper wealth did not achieve sustained acceptance in the United States until the late nineteenth century. Even then, the government tied the value of the paper money to the price of gold, and the government circulated gold coins that anyone could get in exchange for the paper. It was not until the 1930s that the U.S. government felt as though American citizens would accept currency that was not tied to the price of gold. The country went off of the gold standard. It issued paper money that did not guarantee the bearer that the notes could be traded in for gold or silver, and it took gold coins out of circulation. The plan worked, and other stable countries did the same thing.

With the people weaned off of the gold standard, the government no longer had to secure its paper notes with any precious metal. That made it easier for the government of the United States to extend its "deficit spending"—issuing debt securities to fund the operations of government with no backing beyond the "full faith and credit" of the government of the most powerful country on earth. What the Greeks had started, the Americans had finished. People now accepted paper as having value, with nothing but the promise that a stable and powerful government would honor the money and no means to obtain gold for the paper that represented wealth.

So when you accept paper money for services, you are stating that you trust the economic power of the government that issues it. Similarly, when you buy a government bond today, you are saying you have enough faith in the issuing government to purchase nothing more than a paper promise of that government to pay you back with interest.

Consequently, as has been the case throughout history, crashproofers must determine how much faith and trust they can reasonably put in the government that issues securities that they consider buying. If history is any indicator, a government that is straddled with debt and instability will try to pay its debt by printing a lot of money and selling a lot of bonds. That in turn will cause inflation and a rise in interest rates. The inflation and interest rate increase will reduce the principal value of your bonds, and you could find yourself the victim of a financial crash.

For example, say you buy a long-term bond from an unstable government for $100 at a 7 percent annual interest rate. Obviously you will get $7 each year for your investment. Now say that the very next day the desperate government that sold you the bond experiences tremendous financial hardship and prints a lot of money to get itself out of debt. Inflation and interest rates jump to around 14 percent. With interest rates at 14 percent, you can now get the same $7 per year interest from a $50 bond (because $7 is 14 percent of $50). Obviously, the value of your $100 bond that pays $7 per year will plummet because anyone can now get the same return for half the investment. That is the risk of investing in the securities of an unstable government. If worst comes to worst, the government might just default on its bonds and not pay you anything.

With these risks in mind, the following are your options as you consider what kinds of government securities you should make part of your crashproofing plan: bonds issued by the government of the United States, bonds issued by municipalities within the United States, and foreign government bonds.

U.S. Debt Securities. The government of the United States issues a variety of types of securities, each of which operates under slightly different timing, payment, and taxation scenarios. The principal forms are treasury bills, treasury notes, treasury bonds, and savings bonds. Take note that when the United States has budget surpluses, it may refrain from issuing some of these securities for certain periods of time, and the interest rates that government securities pay are ever-changing. You will need to check the crashproofyourlife.com website for up-to-date information on which options and rates are currently available to you. Moreover, the dollar thresholds listed in the following paragraph are current as of the time I wrote the section; I recommend using the links on the crashproof yourlife.com website to get the most up-to-date information on dollar thresholds as well.

Treasury *bills* are very short-term securities (with terms of one year or less). Instead of getting traditional interest, you buy them at a "discount": you pay less than the face value for the bill and then cash it in at the full value when it matures. Treasury *notes* are intermediate-term bonds (with maturities of more than one year but less than ten years) that are the federal equivalent to a privately issued certificate of deposit. Treasury *bonds* are the same as treasury notes but with longer terms until maturity—up to thirty years. Last, U.S. savings bonds are a form of government savings account with no fee. They pay lower interest rates as determined by a complex government formula. You can buy savings bonds in very small increments—as little as $25, $50, or $100—whereas there is at least a $1,000 minimum purchase for other types of U.S. government securities. Most financial advisers agree that once you consider all factors, the various forms of U.S. securities are not much different, but the overall best value for the money is the intermediate-term treasury note, and the worst value is the savings bond. You can purchase these securities directly from the U.S. government for no fee. See the links on the crashproofyourlife.com website.

What is important from the crashproofers' perspective, however, is that most investors and their advisers consider any form of U.S. debt security to be the safest of all possible investments because the U.S. government is the most stable in the world and the U.S. economy is the most powerful. It is true that the odds on a default by the United States on its securities are nearly zero, so U.S. government securities represent the most reliable form of paper investment out there. Consequently, you should definitely invest some of your investment clearinghouse funds in U.S. treasury bonds, bills, or notes.

However, despite recent budget surpluses, the United States still has a $6 trillion debt that depends upon a broad tax base to pay the interest. Many respected economists predict that the burden of that debt may well increase within a couple of decades as the baby boomers retire. If in the future the U.S. economy fails to perform as well as it has over the past few years, there is a chance, albeit a small one, that the government may have trouble raising enough tax money or borrowing enough new money to pay off its bond interest. In such a case, as history has shown, the likely result is inflation and the reduction of the value of the bonds you may be holding. This scenario may seem impossible in light of the low inflation we have had in recent years, but it was less than two decades ago that the United States experienced double-digit inflation.

There is now a way you can hedge your bets. As of a few years ago, you have another option from the U.S. government: inflation-indexed securities, or "I" bonds. When you purchase such a bond, depending on the type, either the principal sum or the earnings rate of the bond is periodically adjusted to account for the rate of inflation. This eliminates the risk of the bond value plummeting when an inflationary cycle hits. However, there can be some tax disadvantages to inflation-indexed securities. You should check the links at the crashproofyourlife.com website for details.

In order to balance the inflation risks with accessibility, interest rate, and tax concerns, a crashproofer should consider splitting his or her purchases of U.S. securities evenly between standard securities and inflation-indexed securities. With the inflation-indexed securities, you have some money that is inflation-proof, thereby eliminating the greatest historical risk associated with government debt. By having regular U.S. government securities as well, you have some money that would protect you in times of deflation and which can, depending on the type of bond, give you some additional protection (or at least deferral) from taxes—the other great government threat to our well-being.

Municipal Bonds. The second most popular government security today is the tax-exempt municipal bond. Instead of being issued by the federal government, these bonds are issued by various subsidiary government entities—cities, counties, school districts, etc. Municipal bonds pay interest that is free from federal taxes and exempt from state taxes in the state of issue. Consequently, to realize the maximum tax benefit, you should buy municipal bonds issued by entities located within your state of residence.

Some municipal bonds are "callable" at a certain designated time before their term is over, meaning that the issuing municipality can cash out your bond if interest rates drop to a level such that your bond is paying significantly above going rates. Being "called" right when you seem to be doing well can be a real source of frustration to the holder of a municipal bond.

As with any situation where a government is guaranteeing the value of paper, you have to carefully assess the stability of the issuing municipality before you buy a municipal bond. Fortunately, bond-rating services can help you with this process. These services rate the bonds from AAA to C based upon their assessment of the financial stability of the entity issuing the bonds. You will get a much higher rate of return on a C bond than on an AAA bond because the municipalities have to entice you with greater interest, but you will also incur a lot more risk. An AAA bond will pay a lower rate of interest, but AAA bonds are insured, so you have very little risk of losing your investment.

In order to diversify bond risks, crashproofers—particularly those in high tax brackets—should purchase some municipal bonds because they protect the holder against the propensity of the government to overtax its citizens when times are rough. No federal bond provides tax benefits as extensive as municipal bonds do. You should increase the mix of municipal bonds in your portfolio as you move into higher tax brackets because the higher your bracket, the greater the advantage of the tax-free status of the bonds.

Crashproofers also stick with AAA municipal bonds. You now know how over the centuries many unreliable governments have defaulted on their promises to guarantee the value of the notes, currency, and coins they have issued. Not only could this situation still occur today, it has happened very recently. In 1998, eleven municipalities in California alone defaulted on their municipal bonds. In 1983, the $2.25 billion bond default of the Washington Public Power Supply System (abbreviated WPPSS, but eventually called "whoops") left thousands of investors in a financial bind. That is not a risk a crashproofer takes. Therefore, you must purchase highly rated, insured municipal bonds.

Foreign Bonds. Just as the federal government of the United States and individual municipalities within the United States issue bonds to raise money, foreign governments and municipalities do the same thing. The foreign bond market is generally not for crashproofers. Many foreign governments are not stable, and you do not get the same tax benefits from foreign bonds that you can get from domestic bonds. Getting reliable information about the risks associated with these bonds is also more difficult than it is with domestic bonds. In fact, it is often easier to get information about foreign private companies than it is about foreign governments. For that reason, as shall be seen later, while there is a small place for foreign stocks in a crashproofing investment strategy, there is no place for foreign government bonds.

Government Bond Allocation. Before moving on to the fourth major type of investment—corporate securities—we should discuss briefly how to allocate between U.S. government securities and municipal bonds. We have already established that you should split your purchase of U.S. securities about evenly between regular securities (bills, notes, and/or bonds) and inflation-indexed bonds. But in order to diversify your government securities holdings, you should also divide your purchases evenly between U.S. government securities (both standard and inflation-indexed) and municipal bonds. Simply make alternating purchases—buy a U.S. bill, note, or bond one time and an AAA municipal bond the next time. If you are in a low tax bracket, tilt that balance toward U.S. government securities and away from municipal bonds.

You should also purchase bonds with varying maturity dates to give yourself both the liquidity of short-term investments and the extra return offered by long-term investments. This process is called building a "bond ladder."

To sum it up, therefore, if you want to be as crashproof as possible, start with the assumption that your government securities holdings should consist of 25 percent regular U.S. securities, 25 percent inflation-indexed U.S. securities, and 50 percent AAA municipal bonds. If you are in a low tax bracket, shift that balance towad taxable bonds; if you are in a high tax bracket, shift toward municipal bonds. The 25/25/50 allocation—appropriately adjusted for tax rates—renders an already safe investment even safer. The more general issue of how to allocate among government bonds, corporate bonds, and corporate stocks will be addressed after we cover the latter two forms of investment.

CORPORATE SECURITIES. The next category of investments, and a very popular one, is corporate securities—stocks and bonds issued by private companies. To get the perspective crashproofers need on corporate stocks and bonds, it is important to take a step back and consider what a corporation really is.

Our states have passed laws that allow for the creation of the legal structure known as a corporation. A corporation is a fictitious person. It has all of the legal powers of a real person. Like a person, a corporation lives and dies; it makes contracts; it earns and spends money; it sues and can be sued. It can act ethically or it can commit crimes. A corporation's brain is its board of directors and operating officers. Its nerves are its executives. Its heart and other vital organs are its employees. Its bones are its facilities. It builds muscle through the successful sale of goods or services.

But the lifeblood of a company is capital. Money, pure and simple. If you buy *corporate stock*, you provide capital and in return you obtain ownership of a piece of the company itself. You have a "share" of the company. You then get to vote and otherwise participate in certain corporate affairs. When you own corporate stock, your success as an investor in stock is entirely dependent upon how the rest of the corporate body functions with the lifeblood you have provided it. You are turning yourself over to the talents and abilities of those who run the company.

The risk, therefore, is that the company officers and employees may not perform to your expectations or to the expectations of the market as a whole. Many high-flying stocks have lost up to 85 percent of their value during the past couple of years because of uncompetitive products and second-rate service. But often the reason a company loses value has nothing to do with the quality of the product or service it is selling. Stocks have taken huge hits due to inaccurate earnings predictions, management corruption, or questionable accounting. Indeed, during 2000 and 2001, several seemingly sound companies plunged into a financial abyss due to accounting problems that had nothing to do with the quality of their products or services. Often the stock of these companies completely crashed in just a day or two, leaving investors devastated. Another well-known company—the former Columbia Healthcare—saw its stock drop during the late 1990s from $44 per share to $20 due to allegations of widespread management corruption, even though the fundamentals of the health-care business remained sound. Indeed, most of the value of a stock is not in the value of the company's assets but in its earnings potential—which is really just the level of trust that you and other investors have in the company management's ability to make an honest profit.

Many investors make their investment decisions based upon a stock's price-to-earnings ratio (P/E)—the ratio of the stock price per share to the earnings per share. Companies with high P/E ratios (once considered to be anything over 15:1, now considered to be more like 30:1 or higher) have little in the way of profitable products now. They trade at high prices almost entirely because of the earnings *potential* of the company—a potential that the company cannot realize unless the company management comes through for the investors. Indeed, some high-tech companies have P/E ratios of 100:1 or higher, and others have no earnings at all—meaning that the stock is just a little piece of paper and a lot of hope. As will be discussed later in this chapter, crashproofers put most of their stock investments into companies with lower P/E ratios; but there is a proper place for some purchases of high-potential, lower-earning stocks as well.

In contrast, when you buy a *corporate bond*, you are not purchasing a part of the company. Rather, you are simply lending the company money in return for a fixed rate of interest. You will not lose your principal unless the company goes under entirely; although the sale value of the bond on the market will be subject to the same forces (such as inflation and interest rates) as the government bonds discussed earlier. As with government bonds, various organizations rate the corporate bonds based upon the financial stability of the issuing institution. Some get high "A" ratings, whereas others are classified as "junk" bonds—they are unsecured and very risky. Crashproofers stick to highly rated bonds. Because highly rated U.S. corporate bonds are almost as safe as municipal bonds and U.S. treasury securities, you should allocate your bond portfolio evenly among the three types.

Because the performance of corporate securities depends upon the success of a small group of managers, corporate securities are the most risky of all the investments that have been discussed. However, with proper allocation among the different types of stocks and bonds available, you can reduce your risk levels to their absolute minimum while reaping the benefits of the normally higher returns that corporate securities have provided when compared to government securities. Later we will discuss methods for allocating the money that you place in these investments so as to keep the risk to a minimum. First, however, we must briefly look at the other investment options you have and why you should stay away from them.

OTHER INVESTMENTS. Real estate, commodities, government securities, and corporate securities represent the core investments available to crashproofers. Other possibilities, however, include limited partnerships (where a general partner guides a group of limited partners to invest in any one of a variety of investment types), as well as variations on investments already discussed, such as options on stock and commodities futures. These will not be covered in any detail for one simple reason: none of them are good for crashproofers. They are too risky because they are either inherently volatile or they lack transparency.

An inherently volatile investment is one that, by nature, fluctuates wildly in value. Purchasing an option to buy a stock at a stated value at a certain time is, by definition, a high-risk exercise. Options tend to be short term, meaning that you are abandoning the safe, long-term, buy-and-hold strategy that crashproofers employ. The price of the option will fluctuate, often significantly, as the market establishes how likely it is that the option will have value when the time to exercise it comes. It is high-stakes gambling. Options have no place in our solid investment structure unless your employer simply gives them to you as part of a compensation package.

An investment that "lacks transparency" gives you little insight into its level of risk. Stocks and bonds are heavily regulated by federal and state authorities, so the companies issuing them have a duty to make public filings and disclosures that tell you how well they are doing, how much capital they have, etc. Because the market has a lot of information about them, they are relatively "transparent," so their market price is reflective of their value.

In contrast, limited partnerships, investment trusts, and small, closely held corporations have fewer reporting requirements and are far less transparent than corporate entities that issue publicly traded stocks and bonds. When you invest in these less-transparent entities, you do not know much about what the people managing these entities are doing with your money. Also, it is very difficult for you to check up on the truth of what they are telling you. Investing in them is like playing roulette, and until you have a big cushion of financial security, you should stay away from these investment "opportunities" entirely.

Allocation of Investments

We have already discussed some general guidelines on how much of your investment clearinghouse money should go into the various types of investments. I suggested you try to make one or two mortgage prepayments per year. I also suggested you put away 5 percent of one year's living expenses in gold or silver.

Within the context of U.S. government bonds, I recommended that you divide those investments evenly between regular U.S. securities and inflation-indexed bonds. Finally, I indicated that dividing your bonds evenly among federal bonds of all types, AAA municipal bonds, and highly rated corporate bonds is a safe, simple approach to asset allocation.

These "micro" allocation suggestions should be helpful, but they need to be put into the larger allocation issue: how to diversify your various stock investments and how to allocate between stocks and bonds generally. In making these broad allocation decisions, you have two options: have someone else do it for you or do it yourself.

MUTUAL FUNDS. When you invest in a mutual fund, you are paying a professional manager to invest your money in a group of stocks, bonds, money-market accounts, or some combination of them that the manager picks to achieve a stated investment objective. In effect, you trust the manager to diversify your investments for you. If one stock or bond in the portfolio of a mutual fund loses substantial value, the overall loss of value of a share of the mutual fund will usually be insignificant because there are many other stocks or bonds in the fund that spread the risk.

Among the least risky funds are those that approximate the market as a whole. Index funds tend to reflect the efficient market and therefore carry a relatively low level of risk, as far as stock investments go. Other funds, while diversified, purchase securities from certain specific sectors such as technology or health care and therefore depend upon a narrower cross section of the market. These funds will generally carry greater risk because they are tied to the fortunes of a much smaller cross section of the economy. Still other funds deliberately concentrate on risky investments such as junk bonds or low-rated municipal bonds. While they still spread risk among many investments, these funds have greater inherent risk because every one of their individual holdings carries a high degree of risk.

Crashproofers should consider mutual funds, especially lower-risk index funds, because of their convenience. However, as was discussed earlier, there are some problems with mutual funds that cut into the rate of return that investors could get if they allocated the money themselves. First, unless you buy directly from the fund, you will have to pay your broker an annual fee called a 12b-1 charge that typically runs 0.25 to 1 percent of the value of the investment. That means you are starting the race from a few yards behind the blocks. Second, if you buy "load" funds, the investment manager also charges you an entrance fee that can be as high as 8 percent. All funds also charge a management fee—typically 1 percent of the value of the investment per year and sometimes as high as 2 percent. Moreover, the mutual fund distributes profits every year—profits on which you pay taxes. When you buy stocks yourself, you pay capital gains tax only at the time that you sell the stocks. Finally, sometimes fund managers do not invest the way they told you they would, and you can find yourself with big losses you never expected. For example, in 2000, a money-market fund—supposedly the safest of all—reportedly lost 40 percent of its value because the manager had invested in some risky institutions to increase the yield.

Even if you invest in index funds, there is a good chance that you will underperform the market by a few percentage points due to the fees you pay. Those points can add up to a lot of money over two or three decades of investing. You have to decide whether your time is better spent on endeavors other than managing your own investments. Can you make more money by freeing yourself up to pursue professional multitracking and having a money manager take care of your investments, or is it worth it to you to manage your own money and get a few extra interest points per year on your capital? Only you can make that decision.

ANNUITIES AND VARIABLE ANNUITIES. Traditional annuities are contracts between you and an insurance company. Charitable gift annuities are agreements whereby you give your money to a charity and the charity agrees to pay you a yearly sum, either fixed or variable. When you purchase a fixed, tax-deferred annuity, you give the company or organization selling the annuity your cash, and the organization promises to pay you a set sum—effectively a guaranteed rate of interest—each year until you die. Depending on the policy, upon your death, your heirs can choose to continue to receive income or to take a lump-sum payment as specified in the policy. With some policies, however, you can choose a higher payout in return for cutting your heirs entirely out of any distribution. Choose and read your distribution selections carefully.

The advantages of fixed annuities are twofold: first, they take the guesswork out of investing because you get a guaranteed return, and second, the money accumulates tax-free until you actually take the guaranteed payments out of the account for your personal use. However, you pay both taxes and a penalty if you withdraw the money before the age of fifty-nine and a half. If you can live on the income that an annuity company is willing to pay you, you should study annuities as an investment option. You have to research the financial stability of both the company selling the annuity and the company that insures the payments. However, the law requires that companies selling annuities keep a substantial cash reserve, so most annuities are quite safe. The guaranteed return can provide the sense of security that crashproofers work so hard to get.

There is a problem with fixed annuities, however. The companies that sell fixed annuities make money by investing your money at a higher rate of return than they will pay you. That simple fact means that you can do better investing the money yourself. As a general rule, when you consider the sum the annuity company pays you and factor in that you or your heirs will get a limited lump sum after the term of the annuity has run out, the return you get from your annuity may significantly underperform the return you can get with good, safe self-investing. By purchasing an annuity, you effectively trade income stability for lower overall returns.

A variable annuity gives you the option of putting some of your money in subaccounts that the company invests in mutual funds. The fixed account earns a guaranteed rate of interest, and your principal is fully protected. Premiums that you choose to invest in the subaccounts are subject to market fluctuations, and your principal remains at risk. However, these products give you the opportunity to get a higher rate of return if the stock market does well.

In the past, the fees charged by companies selling annuities and variable annuities—which include up-front broker commissions and management fees, as well as fees for withdrawal of funds that exceed set limits in set time periods—have been so high that a vast majority of financial planners have considered these policies to be very poor investments. However, competition among companies offering various annuity products, combined with government investigations and class action lawsuits against these companies concerning their aggressive sales practices, has led the companies to be more open about their fee structures and has also led to a reduction in their fees. Consequently, the annuity products are clearly better than they once were, which explains why investors have put hundreds of billions of dollars into annuities in recent years.

Nevertheless, when you buy these products, you are still paying a lot of people a lot of money to do what you could do yourself. Moreover, if you buy a variable annuity, you are putting a lot of trust in the investing savvy of the people managing your money, which can lead to unfortunate results. For example, late in 2000, the press reported how an organization tied to the Lutheran Church had allegedly mishandled money that faithful Lutherans had put into variable charitable gift programs, hoping to live off of the interest. Many of the donors had to scale back their lifestyles extensively when they received interest payments far below projected rates, allegedly due to investing mistakes made by those to whom they had entrusted their money. For these reasons, the balance still tilts in favor of learning how to allocate your investment money yourself. You can do it and be just as secure, if not more so, than you would be by entrusting your investment money to someone else.

SELF-ALLOCATION. While it takes more work, crashproofers can achieve personal financial security quicker if they choose to allocate their investment money themselves because reducing the fees you pay others to invest your money is the best way to get greater returns. In fact, according to the conservative efficient-market principles we have adopted, reducing fees is the only way you can consistently improve the returns you receive when compared to those of other investors.

In determining how you should allocate your investment clearinghouse money among the various investments available to you, we start with the premise you have previously read in this book: personal comfort. The reason people lose their money in risky investments is that they hear isolated anecdotes about risky investments that paid off and outright lies about the money-making potential of other investments, and these stories cause them to sink their money into companies and projects that go under.

Go back to your basic desire for personal security. As stated at the outset of this chapter, you have a natural—almost primal—instinct to keep yourself and your family safe. If you trust your basic instinct for self-preservation, you will naturally adopt a safe investment allocation strategy. As you consider how to spread your investments among the many options you have, always start by asking yourself a simple question: what will let you sleep at night?

Sometime in late 1998, I ran into an old acquaintance, a forty-year-old business professional. We started talking about investing. He claimed he loved to play the stock market. Although he admitted he had a big house with a big mortgage and huge large-car lease payments, he said he felt financially secure because the paper value of his investments in "hot" Internet stocks exceeded his debts by several hundred thousand dollars. I asked him whether he ever considered using his stock profits to pay off his mortgage or buy some treasury bonds. He laughed and looked at me as if I was stupid. He pointed out that he had a 7 percent interest rate on his mortgage and that most of his monthly payment was tax-deductible, so he was really borrowing at less than 5 percent. He also noted he was averaging between 18 percent and 30 percent per year on his stock investments when treasury bonds were paying less than 7 percent. "Why would I pay off a 5 percent loan or invest in a 6 percent bond when that same money is earning 18 percent to 30 percent in the stock market every year?" he asked. I smiled and moved on to another topic of discussion.

A few weeks later, I saw the same man taking a nap in a chair at a local athletic club. After he woke up, I told him he looked wiped out. "I never get much sleep," he said. When I asked him why, he said—in marked contrast to what he had told me before—that he worried a lot about "the kids and the house and all that stuff." I looked at him and said, "Get rid of the mortgage and buy some T-bills." He smiled and dozed off again.

About four months later, I got a call from him. I did not know him well, but he felt he needed to call me. He told me he had paid off his mortgage and shifted some of his money to less risky investments. He could sleep well at night and had more time to spend with his kids since he was not monitoring and worrying about his stock investments all the time. He came home to a house that was really his. His new positive outlook on life had spread to his family as well.

The very next day, I had breakfast with a successful investment adviser whom I was interviewing for this book. I asked him how he would allocate investments if he wanted to crashproof his clients. He explained to me that he could put together a group of corporate stocks that would resist almost every form of economic downturn imaginable. He did not mention any investment other than corporate securities. "What about bonds or real estate?" I asked him, fully expecting to be chastised again for an overly conservative view of investment allocation.

I got a different reaction. "Well," he replied slowly, "I own some farmland. And we planted some walnut trees on the land." I looked him in the eye and asked, "Why?" He replied, "So I can sleep at night." He went on to describe how secure the land made him feel. "If everything goes to hell," he said, "I can always drop what I am doing and come out to this farm. We can grow our walnuts and sit under the trees drinking lemonade all day long."

In two days, I had heard two people, who do not know each other, talk about the value of allocating investments so that they could "sleep at night." This is a good context in which to make your investment allocation decisions. How much you allocate among real estate, commodities, stock investments, and bond investments must occur in the broader context of making sure that you, too, can sleep at night. That might mean that you make more than the one or two mortgage prepayments per year that were discussed earlier. Or, maybe you will choose to buy a lot of government securities and invest only a little money in the market. The fact remains that if you are saving or investing 20 percent of your income, you have the luxury of making these safer investments if you sleep better doing so.

There are some more specific investment allocation structures. In response to the growing concern over stock and bond market volatility, many successful investment advisers have developed investment models designed to resist the various economic forces that could cause the value of your investments to crash. These models balance investment purchases so that if one type of investment suffers, others are likely to gain in value or at least hold their own so you do not suffer catastrophic consequences. You should follow two basic concepts:

1. Buy more bonds if you have less time.
2. Buy stocks or stock funds with low cross-correlation.

Bonds and Time. The first principle relates to the proper balance between stocks and bonds in a risk-averse investment structure. By saying you should have more bonds when you have less time, you are acknowledging, as you did in Part One, that any disorder-resistant structure must have some flexibility in it. Consequently, the relative mix of stocks and bonds in your investment structure should change as time passes.

After you have put your money aside for real estate and commodities, you have to allocate the remainder between corporate stocks and bonds—both corporate and government. Historically, U.S. government bonds, insured municipal bonds, and highly rated corporate bonds have been safer investments than stocks because they are less volatile. They provide predictable returns and the principal is rarely at risk.

However, the average return on stocks has been higher over the long term than the return for bonds. So stock investments may actually prove safer than bond investments if you can wait for a long period of time—twenty or thirty years—before you cash them out.

Several conservative investment advisers have developed a nifty rule of thumb for safe allocation between stocks and bonds: own 1 percent in bonds for each year of your age. So, if you are twenty-five years old, you should have 25 percent bonds and 75 percent stocks. At a young age, you can afford the higher volatility of stocks because you have a long time to wait to cash them out to support yourself in your retirement. On the other hand, if you are sixty-five years old, you will want 65 percent of your money in bonds and only 35 percent in stocks because bond returns are more predictable and there is little risk of a total flameout in their value. By the time you reach a hundred years old, you should be totally into bonds.

This approach is entirely consistent with crashproofing with one possible exception. You may wish to skew the mix more toward bonds when you are about to make a big expenditure prior to your retirement—such as sending your kid to an expensive college. You will want financial predictability and stability when you are preparing to shell out that kind of money, so you should consider keeping a larger percentage of your funds in bonds during that time period.

Attaining Low Stock Cross-Correlation. Next, you should reduce risk within your stock holdings by making sure that you have stocks with low cross-correlation. Obtaining investments with low cross-correlation means that you pick stocks (and mutual funds, if you go that route) that tend to operate independently of each other. For example, highly capitalized companies (large caps—companies that are very big and have a lot of money) and companies with lower capitalization (small caps) have historically operated with a substantial degree of independence. In some years the large caps do well; in others, the small caps drive market growth. Large-cap and small-cap stocks have low cross-correlation.

You should have a mix of large caps and small caps in your holdings so their risks balance out. However, because small caps can be riskier than large caps, you should tilt the mix toward the large-cap stocks. A conservative investor will have 70 to 80 percent of his or her stock holdings in large caps with the remainder in small caps to provide cross-correlational balance without depending too much on the performance of smaller, less stable companies.

Foreign and domestic stocks also have low cross-correlation. Even though stocks of companies headquartered in foreign countries tend to be riskier than stocks of U.S. companies, you actually incur greater risk by holding only U.S. stocks because you have failed to achieve maximum cross-correlation. For example, a recent study reveals that if you invest only in the S&P 500—a group of leading U.S. companies—your holdings would have a "standard deviation" (the measurement of likely fluctuation) of 16.4 percent. That is low to moderate risk for a crashproofer. If, on the other hand, you bought an evenly balanced group of only foreign stocks, you would have a much higher standard deviation of almost 23 percent. Logic would suggest that if you moved down a continuum from holding all U.S. stocks to holding all foreign stocks, you would find the standard deviation moving steadily from 16.4 percent to 23 percent.

Not true. While there is an increasing correlation between U.S. and foreign stocks, there remain enough differences between our economy and foreign economies that there are some cross-correlational advantages to owning a small percentage of foreign stocks. For example, if 80 percent of your stock portfolio is in an American S&P 500 index fund and 20 percent in an evenly balanced international fund, the study indicates that your standard deviation drops to 15.4 percent—a risk level that is lower than the risk level of a portfolio holding only S&P 500 U.S. stocks. So even though foreign stocks are riskier, there is enough of a disconnect between U.S. and foreign stocks that you can often reap some benefits in foreign markets when U.S. markets decline. Once your allocation of foreign stocks goes above 30 percent, however, your risk levels are higher than you would have if you invested only in U.S. stocks. You should, therefore consider investing up to 20 percent of your stock holdings in foreign stocks.

One more note about foreign stocks. Because of the difficulty you may have in adequately assessing the level of risk individual foreign stocks pose, your efforts to achieve minimum cross-correlation may best be served by biting the bullet and investing in a mutual fund that invests in a balanced group of foreign stocks. Picking your own foreign stock is quite difficult, so you should consider mitigating the risks with a balanced foreign-stock mutual fund.

The final cross-correlational consideration is "value" versus "growth." A value company is one that has substantial earnings, pays a decent dividend, and usually provides a product or service that is well-established and time-honored. Traditional telephone services, staples, and other "boring" products and services normally form the backbone of a value company. These companies also tend to have relatively low P/E ratios (under 25:1)—meaning that the price of the stock is not a vast multiple of the earnings or, stated a little differently, that the price of the stock neither anticipates nor requires vast growth in the future.

Growth companies generally have lower earnings, spend a lot of money on research, and claim to hold the key to the future. They would include biotechnology, computer software, and leading-edge technology stocks.

From a crashproofer's standpoint, value stocks represent a solid past while growth stocks represent the limitless future. Value and growth stocks also have relatively low cross-correlation, so buying a mix of the two will keep your risk of a financial crash to a minimum. However, just as it is important to weight your investments toward U.S. stocks with a lighter counterbalance of foreign stocks and large caps with a lighter counterbalance of small caps, it is equally important for a crashproofer to tip the balance toward value stocks over growth stocks. While you need some growth stocks to keep your cross-correlational risks low, you should base your investment structure on a foundation of companies that make proven, profitable products; you should avoid "supergrowth" stocks (with P/E ratios of 100:1 or higher) because they are entirely speculative.

While I have not conducted a scientific study, my conversations with attorneys, brokers, and clients in the financial industry have led me to conclude that a mix of around 80 percent value stocks and 20 percent growth stocks represents the most crashproof structure possible.

GOLDEN YEARS. The last allocation issue is how to decide the amount to put in your retirement account. You can contribute to your employer's tax-deferred 401(k) account (or 403(b) account if you work for a nonprofit company), which normally gives you the choice of several funds or money-market accounts in which to place your retirement money. About half of all employers offer this important benefit, and many provide "matching" funds to a specified limit. Legislation passed by Congress in 2001 gradually increases—over the next several years—the maximum annual contribution you can make from $10,500 to $15,000, with additional opportunities for senior workers. As these rules are ever-changing, you should check crashproofyourlife.com for details.

If you are self-employed, you can contribute up to $35,000 in pretax dollars annually ($40,000 in 2002) to a retirement account. If you do not have a 401(k) plan, you should open an individual retirement account (IRA), which allows you to put away up to $2,000 annually (a sum that will increase steadily to $5,000 over the next few years).

Once you reach the age of fifty-nine and a half, you can, if your plan allows it, begin withdrawing your retirement money and pay taxes on it at that time. At the age of seventy and a half, there are set minimum sums you must withdraw and pay taxes on. If you withdraw money before the age of fifty-nine and a half, you pay taxes immediately, plus, in most circumstances, a hefty 10 percent penalty.

You can also establish a Roth IRA, which allows you to put a specific sum of after-tax dollars into a tax-deferred account if you meet certain income and other requirements. Once you put the money in, *you never pay taxes again on that money*. After it has been in the account for five years, there are no restrictions on withdrawals and, since withdrawals are not reportable income, they do not affect your adjusted gross income, keeping your tax rate low. The disadvantage is that you pay taxes when you are younger, which is when some people have a higher tax rate. For current contribution limits and tables comparing the relative returns of regular IRAs and Roth IRAs, check the crashproofyourlife.com website.

Money that goes into your IRA or 401(k) comes from your investment clearinghouse account. If your employer makes an automatic direct deposit into your 401(k), you should reduce the sum you put in your investment clearinghouse account by the amount of that direct deposit.

Many well-respected financial advisers recommend that you put the maximum permissible sum in your retirement account because the money is tax-deferred. However, if you want to crashproof yourself, you need to adopt a slightly more refined policy. Take this example. A successful, well-educated executive became so smitten with the tax-deferral advantages of his 401(k) that he put all of his investment money into that account. He amassed about $200,000 by the age of forty-one. However, he had no available money. When he experienced a couple of financial setbacks—a partially collapsed roof on his house and some uninsured medical expenses for his son—he had to borrow more than $18,000 just to cover his short-term debts. While some 401(k) plans do have narrowly worded provisions that allow for loans or withdrawals against 401(k) accounts during times of hardship, as a crashproofer, you should not rely upon such provisions.

Crashproofers realize they need to have available cash—no strings attached. The untouchable savings account provides that cash for true emergencies—a loss of home, a financial depression, or a loss of job—but you should also have some liquidity in your investments that will cover the moderate emergencies. When determining whether to contribute to a retirement account or place your investments in an accessible brokerage account, make sure you balance the advantages of tax deferral with those of immediate accessibility. You will better reap the benefits of deferral when you are young, so lean toward putting more money in the retirement account when you are under forty, which is also the time you are less likely to have emergencies that require immediate cash. As you get closer to retirement, increase the amount of money that you have invested in accessible brokerage accounts. Again, while there is no science to the process, a split that puts at least 60 percent of your funds in a retirement account and keeps up to 40 percent accessible when you are under forty, followed by a reversal to 60 percent accessible and 40 percent retirement when you are over forty, would effectively balance the deferral-accessibility issue.

If your employer matches your 401(k) contribution, you should tilt that balance in favor of the 401(k) and take full advantage of the "free money" or stock your employer is willing to give you. If the employer matches your contribution with company stock, be sure you remain well-diversified with your other stock investments. Don't ever rely too heavily upon the stock of one company—even your own—to provide you with your retirement resources.

Spending, Investing, and Allocation Recap

The past two chapters have covered many rules and guidelines about spending and saving. Because of the quantity of information that has been discussed, it is helpful to summarize the crashproofer's approach to dividing up your money among the four corners of the pyramid structure. Here is the nutshell version:

- Learn to live on 70 percent of your after-tax income by buying a home you can afford easily with no wasted space, controlling the auto purchasing process, keeping away from high-end clothing and food outlets, limiting utility expenses to what you really need, and keeping basic entertainment expenses to about 5 percent of your living expenses.
- Eliminate your credit-card debt and other spending vices; then learn to keep your discretionary expenses to no more than 10 percent of your after-tax income.
- Place 10 percent of your after-tax income into an interest-bearing savings account or certificates of deposit until you have built up one year's worth of living expenses.
- Place 10 percent of your after-tax income into an investment clearinghouse account, and increase that sum to 20 percent after you have achieved the savings level of one year's worth of living expenses. Then, allocate your investment money roughly as follows:
  * Prepay your mortgage by one or two payments a year, at a minimum.
  * Get a supply of precious metals equal to 5 percent of your annual living expenses.
  * Allocate the remainder between stocks and bonds, with 1 percent bonds for each year of your age.
  * Divide your bond investments evenly between U.S. government bonds (some inflation-indexed), AAA municipal bonds, and highly rated U.S. corporate bonds. Tilt more toward taxable bonds if you are in a low tax bracket.
  * Build a "bond ladder" of varying maturity dates.
  * Divide your stock investments about 80 percent to 20 percent in favor of domestic over foreign, large caps over small caps, and value over growth. Consider low-expense, no-load mutual funds to achieve some of this diversification, especially in the risky area of foreign stocks. Purchase no supergrowth stocks.
  * Place about 60 percent of your bond and stock holdings in a retirement account if you are forty or younger; reduce that percentage to 40 percent if you are over forty. Tilt that balance as appropriate to take full advantage of matching funds.

It is really quite simple, isn't it? These financial rules represent the ideal crash-proofing structure for the "typical" American. You will, of course, have unique circumstances that may require varying this structure to some extent. That is fine, as long as you carefully plan some sort of similarly reasonable structure and *stick to it*. Then you will go from being your worst financial enemy to your best financial friend.

6

Protecting Your Money from the Evil Around You

At this point in the implementation of your financial crashproofing program, you should feel very secure. You spend your money unpretentiously, but you still have some funds left over to enjoy yourself. You invest your money without believing you have any special insights, but you still enjoy the excitement of playing the market. Things are rolling along quite well.

Maybe not. Someone is lurking in the shadows who wants to take everything away from you. The last piece of your financial crashproofing plan is learning how to thwart those people who want to appropriate your wealth for their benefit.

From the very beginning of the book, the crashproofing laws have been put into an overriding thematic context: you have to work to contain the movement toward disorder that defines the entire universe. In the context of finances, we have discussed how the forces of disorder do not like wealth because wealth represents the capacity to reverse the disorderly direction of the universe. We also discussed how disorder changes its form to accommodate any set of circumstances. It follows, therefore, that if you learn to build solid wealth structures through the responsible handling of your finances, the forces of disorder will simply adopt a new strategy to deprive you of what you have built. That strategy is *slimy people*.

This chapter shall cover two topics: first, how to recognize and avoid people who want to take your money and, second, how to get your money back if someone does in fact take it from you. Many very sophisticated people fall victim to financial frauds; you have to learn to stay away from these frauds. Then, if dishonest people do snare you, you need to be able to strike back and reclaim what is yours.

Learn to Stay Clear of the Financial Parasites

People who want to take your money come in two forms: people whom you do not know at all and people who work to build your trust. Let's discuss each type in a systematic manner that will give you the tools you need in order to recognize and steer clear of such people.

The Unknown Threat

Many people turn their financial futures over to people whom they have never met in person, or perhaps, never met at all. We start, therefore, with a basic concept much like one your parents taught you when you were a child—never trust your money to a stranger. It sounds obvious, but thousands of people still do it. Why? Because the con artists are very good at what they do. In fact, they often play into your belief that you are too smart to fall victim to people like them. There are four types of strangers who will try to take your money: cold callers, pump and dumpers, identity hijackers, and real estate "flippers."

Cold Callers

I feel sorry for young stockbrokers and investment advisers who spend hours on the phone trying to convince strangers to open an account with them. Most of them are honest people who are just trying to get started in the business world. Having now expressed that sympathy, I give you the following advice: tell them you are not interested and hang up. There are thousands of documented cases of pleasant-sounding cold callers convincing people to send them big checks and then just taking the money and running. You simply cannot tell the honest ones from the dishonest ones with just one or two telephone calls.

The dishonest ones are smart. Often they are part of sophisticated organizations that open "boiler rooms" filled with "brokers" who make thousands of calls per week. The boiler room managers train their brokers to manipulate the prospective customers by giving out phony references and claiming membership in fabricated but impressive-sounding trade and professional groups. These brokers may even give you phone numbers for the phony organizations or offer to put you in touch with satisfied customers. The people cited as references are, of course, nothing more than "plants." They are hired by the boiler room operation to lie about the success of the recommended investments. The operations collect a lot of money, close up shop, and then reopen in another city under another name a few weeks later.

If you make it your policy not to let a cold caller get in even one complete sentence before you interrupt, decline, and hang up, you will never fall victim to these clever con artists. That is the crashproofer's approach.

On-Line Con Artists

The boiler room represents the "traditional" or "old economy" scam. It is alive and well, but more technologically advanced forms of investment fraud are gaining steam. The most insidious new means of anonymous investment fraud is the Internet pump-and-dump scheme. Pump-and-dump schemes themselves are not new. What is new is how easy technology has made it to succeed with such a scheme.

A pump-and-dump scheme involves buying a stock, artificially inflating its value, and then selling it before the market realizes that the stock is not worth the price at which it is selling. In the past, large, wealthy criminal enterprises would buy millions of dollars worth of a stock at a low price and then pay brokers kickbacks to spread the word that the stock was about to take off due to a soon-to-be announced merger, a new patent, or a new product that would result in huge profits. Unwary investors would buy the stock, the price would soar, the criminal organization would sell at a high price, the price would fall, and the unwary investors would be left holding the bag.

Times have changed. You no longer need to have millions of dollars and an extensive network of corrupt brokers to effectuate a pump-and-dump scheme.

All you need is a modem. During 2000, the investment world was shaken by two stunning stories of on-line pump-and-dump schemes. A fifteen-year-old "investor," who was also a high school student in New Jersey, made hundreds of thousands of dollars by buying relatively obscure stocks (through a custodial account set up by his parents) and then putting hundreds of messages in different on-line investment chat rooms, making glowing statements about the companies in which he had invested. The young man used many aliases, making it look like everyone was running to buy stock in these companies. Naturally, many unwary investors bought the stocks and the prices soared. The juvenile pump-and-dumper cashed out his investments and became the wealthiest student at his high school. Eventually, other investors realized that all of the great things these "people" were saying about the stocks were the misleading ruminations of a teenager, and the prices fell dramatically. The FBI arrested the young Internet pump-and-dumper, but he only got a slap on the wrists legally (a $285,000 fine) because the laws that apply to on-line pump-and-dumpers, especially minors, are somewhat nebulous.

Similarly, in a unique variation of the pump-and-dump scheme, a twenty-three-year-old community college student recently issued a bogus news release about a company called Emulex, suggesting that the company was in serious trouble. The stock price plummeted until people realized that the news release was false. Investors were left licking their financial wounds to the tune of $110 million.

We have already discussed how crashproofers do not follow hot stock "tips"— even from well-meaning people—because few if any people really have better insight than the market as a whole. The on-line pump-and-dump schemes are particularly clever, however, because they do not involve anyone telling you directly that you should buy a stock. Rather, the schemers simply plant testimonials from satisfied investors in chat rooms or spread false information about the companies' prospects, and they allow the investor him- or herself to make the decision to buy or sell the stock.

The Internet contains valuable information about companies and the financial markets as a whole, and it is a tool you should use in determining how to spread your investment risk. However, you have to stick to websites of established companies and financial press—wsj.com (*Wall Street Journal*), cnnfn .cnn.com. Never buy a stock based upon some posting of unknown origin on a public website or upon the remarks of alleged investors in a chat room. If you do, you are setting yourself up to be the victim of a pump-and-dump scheme.

Identity Hijackers

An identity hijacker is someone who adopts your identity and then engages in financial transactions under your name. Thousands of people fall victim to identity hijackers each year. Identity hijackers steal wallets and purses, search through trash, claim to be a prospective employer, or claim to be a federal agent in order to get your social security number, your bank account numbers, and employment information from the various sources that have this information. With this information in hand, the identity hijacker applies for credit cards (54 percent of the time), opens utility accounts for cellular phones and the like (26 percent of the time), opens checking accounts (16 percent of the time), and obtains car or other loans (11 percent of the time)—all in *your name.* They then write bad checks or fail to pay for their purchases, destroying your credit rating in the process.

While they have not abandoned their old methods entirely, many identity hijackers have new tactics. Identity hijackers are now on-line. They cruise chat rooms and even try to hack into legitimate organizational databases (government databases, employer databases) that contain your personal financial information. Many of them are successful.

A victim of identity hijacking can have a very tough time getting back on his or her feet. By the time the victim realizes someone else is using his or her name, banks and credit-card companies have reported a poor credit history and taken legal action, thereby destroying the victim's credit rating. With current technology, the speed at which information about credit ratings can be spread has increased, making this problem even worse.

There are actions you can take to avoid identity hijackers. First, do not make it easy for them to get your personal data. For example, never routinely discard personal financial information. Always shred it up and discard the pieces in several different wastebaskets. Second, be very careful about giving out your financial information on the phone or on-line just because someone says he or she needs it for market research or to consummate a transaction. For example, when I joined our local community center recently, they asked for my social security number. I asked whether they really needed it. "No," the clerk replied and went on to the next question. Automobile service stations, merchandise retailers, and real estate organizations are notorious for asking for reams of personal information you are under no legal obligation to provide to them. In a similar vein, you should avail yourself of new state programs that allow you to substitute a number other than your social security number on your driver's license. Then if someone steals your wallet, the thief will not get your social security number.

Another action you can take to avoid identity hijackers is to have an unlisted address and phone number. Most identity hijackers need your home address and phone number to fill out various applications for credit cards and loans. They can make up addresses and numbers, but using false information increases the likelihood that they will get caught early in their scheme. Also, only give personal information to those on-line organizations that post a very rigorous security policy. Many websites give you a good level of comfort by linking you to a statement of their security policy and procedures. Finally, keep track of your credit rating. Check the crashproofyourlife.com website for links to sites that will allow you to access information about your credit rating. If you see something unusual, contact law enforcement authorities immediately.

Real Estate Scams

Because people develop a sense of security and attachment to their homes and other real estate investments, it should not surprise you that slimy people will try to siphon away your wealth by tricking you into entering transactions that they claim will improve your real estate value or equity. In a typical situation, a "home improvement" company representative will knock on your door and state that while he was doing work in the neighborhood he noticed your home had windows and doors that were costing you thousands of dollars a year in heating costs. He offers to replace the doors and windows on your home for a few thousand dollars, claiming you will earn your money back in just one or two years of lower heating and air-conditioning bills. He also offers to finance the improvements.

Once he has you convinced, he has you sign up for a loan that has all kinds of points and fees up front, as well as a very high interest rate. Your monthly payment may look low, but you have to pay it for ten or fifteen years; so you end up paying five or six times what the improvements are worth. And—even assuming the work is good, which it usually is not—the savings you realize on your utility bills will not come close to covering the huge amount you pay for the improvements.

It gets worse. Often, after you have signed the loan documents, the company finds new "problems" with your home—inadequate insulation, cracking foundations—and gets you to take out a second loan for the new improvements. That means you have to pay all of the points and fees a second time. The lender structures the transaction so that you are required to take out multiple loans—a variation on the traditional loan-flipping scam.

Shady home mortgage lenders do the same thing. They finance your purchase, but they do not, for example, include taxes in the loan sum, forcing you to come back to them for a second loan when your taxes come due. Then they refuse to just lend you the additional money you need; rather, they offer you a second loan to pay off the first loan and give you the extra money you need to pay taxes. Then you have to pay all of the points and fees a second time. Many lenders also hit you with a 5 percent prepayment penalty that they put into the first loan documents without telling you. By the time the transaction is complete, the mortgage company has effectively appropriated your home for its benefit.

Companies that convince you to take out a home equity loan to reduce your credit-card debt can also engage in shady practices. Typically, the disreputable ones will charge five or six points up front, along with origination fees, documentation fees, and all kinds of other fees, which effectively negate the lower interest rate they offer you. Indeed, there are documented cases where the overall cost to the consumer of consolidating credit-card debt into a home equity loan was actually higher than if the consumer had just continued paying the high credit-card interest rate. You have to demand that the mortgage company provide you an adjusted interest rate that reflects the various points and fees they build into the loan. Make this request in writing, and consider running the answer by a reputable real estate lawyer.

You can take certain actions to avoid home improvement scams. For example, never deal with a mortgage or home improvement company that just knocks on your door. When you are considering improvements (or financing a new home), get multiple bids from companies with established reputations. Check the reputation of the company by consulting with your state attorney general's office or consumer protection department, as well as local nonprofit organizations such as the Better Business Bureau. Also, while I am reluctant to suggest accepting references alone as the basis for deciding to enter into any financial transaction, references in the home improvement area tend to be more reliable than, say, references for stockbrokers or financial advisers (which, as discussed later, I discount heavily). An investment adviser can lie for years before anyone discovers it, but home improvement projects are tangible and visible and they have a clear beginning and a clear ending. If someone is unreliable in the home improvement area, you will find out quickly. For that reason, if someone you know has had a good experience with a home improvement contractor, that reference is probably reliable.

Known Threats

When you think of victims of financial scams, you may envision, as many people do, a white-haired couple in their eighties who have lost some mental capacity and who are pressured into making unwise investments by an aggressive young guy with slick hair and a lot of jewelry. Or, perhaps you think of an inner-city or rural mother trying to work her way out of poverty, but who is taken advantage of by a shady loan shark. There has been a lot of press recently on home improvement scams and mortgage scams, as well as scams related to title loans on cars and paycheck loans, that tend to target the poor and uneducated. Indeed, most people feel that financial scams happen to people who are old, infirm, or financially unsophisticated. They also tend to believe that the perpetrator is rough-looking, aggressive, and a complete stranger.

Think again. In 2000, several very famous movie stars, including Leonardo DiCaprio, Courtney Cox, Lauren Holly, Matt Damon, Cameron Diaz, and others, reportedly lost a combined total of over $10 million by entrusting their money to a corrupt financial adviser who was known for his affinity for champagne and extremely expensive Prada clothing. Similarly, in the mid-1990s, some of the nation's most powerful political elite confessed they had lost many millions of dollars because they, too, had entrusted large sums of money to a con man who had all the trappings of wealth and power—including a wife who was a congresswoman. Also in the mid-1990s, a group of professional hockey players and executives found themselves duped out of $2 million when they invested in a gold mine that turned out to be a scam. In 1997, a group of wealthy and generally well-educated art collectors learned they had paid exorbitant sums for artwork that turned out to be stolen. They had to return the art to its rightful owners, and many of the investors never got any of their money back.

These stories are only the tip of the iceberg. For the past four years running, hundreds of bright people wanting to start an E-business have paid huge fees to "Internet venture capital firms" who promised they would line up millions of dollars in financing for the proposed business venture. These firms then folded up and took the money—often every cent the businessperson had accumulated in his or her entire life.

Most good lawyers can tell several stories like these. In my own experience, I watched two wealthy sisters lose all of their millions of dollars as the result of self-dealing by the man whom they made the trustee of their assets. The man had become a father figure to the young women, yet he took them for everything. He eventually went to prison, but the young women never recovered financially.

I was equally shocked to learn of a man who wrested control of a respected brokerage house from the family that founded it. This man then diverted several million dollars of clients' money into his personal accounts until the whole scheme came crashing down in a tornado of lawsuits, prosecutions, and bankruptcies. Again, some investors were never made whole.

In each of these cases, the scams were very thinly veiled—the con artists perpetrating them had shaky credentials or provided inadequate (or no) documentation for the investments they were hawking. You may wonder how successful people could fall victim to these transparently fraudulent schemes. The scheme is almost always a variation on the same story. In each case, the wealthy and usually sophisticated victims either entrusted their money to someone whom they thought to be a friend, or they relied upon the glowing praise a friend heaped upon the person who eventually stole their money.

When it comes to financial advisers, you cannot rely upon references alone. The good con artists will spend months cultivating the trust of a wealthy investor. Here is the typical pattern for the most grand of these schemes, although thousands of other con artists use similar tactics on a smaller scale. The following story has been cobbled together from a number of true ones. First, the perpetrator moves into the "right" neighborhood and gets an expensive car and clothes. He (or she, although as a factual matter, the vast majority are men) gets the money to lease the home and car by using money stolen from previous victims in other cities or by simply running up huge credit-card and bank loan debts. Then, the perpetrator hangs out at trendy bars and nightspots, trying to lure the victims to his or her house for impressive parties, or he takes potential victims out to expensive restaurants for dinners where the champagne flows freely.

After a few weeks or even months, the perpetrator will call the victim with an "unbelievable" investment opportunity. He will throw around all sorts of complex financial terms to explain why a simple $25,000 investment could double in value in just a matter of a month or so. Because the perpetrator appears to be very successful and has earned the trust of the victim, the victim will give the perpetrator the money. Sure enough, a month later, the perpetrator will call and inform the victim that the investment has exceeded expectations and is now worth $75,000, and he may even tender a check to the victim. At that point the victim begins to tell all of his or her friends about this miracle investment adviser. The perpetrator thereby uses the first victim as a surrogate to snare more victims. In addition, the perpetrator will occasionally make cash payments or "dividends" to the early victims by using money obtained from the more recent victims, but the perpetrator rarely, if ever, sends a formal financial statement to anyone. The scheme continues until the perpetrator abruptly leaves town or the investors catch on to the scheme and turn the perpetrator in to the authorities.

You may not have enough money to be targeted by these lavish-spending con artists, but thousands of middle-income and modestly wealthy people fall victim to scaled-back versions of the same story. For example, an acquaintance with a flimsy investment business takes you to a couple of ball games or takes you out to dinner and then tells you about all the money he has made for his clients over the past few months investing their money in some bizarre scheme—anything from fish hatcheries to foreign currency exchanges. Eventually, you will get the call about the surefire investment you have to make now or never. Do not do it.

The key to realizing you may be the target of a scam is to look for certain common signs. Generally, the person asking for your money displays several of these six telltale characteristics:

1. has no traceable roots in your geographic area
2. spends money on you over a period of several weeks
3. uses acquaintances of yours as references or drops the names of very successful people, claiming they are clients or they will be soon
4. claims you will get vast returns (50 percent or more) in a short period of time (weeks or a few months)
5. discusses complex and far-fetched investments with a lot of jargon designed to make you feel stupid or naive
6. conspicuously displays the trappings of "rentable" wealth

The con artist who is after your money may not exhibit all of these characteristics, but if you start seeing these signs piling up, beware. A crashproofer should take specific steps toward avoiding these traps. Here are a few suggestions.

Avoid Investment Advisers Entirely

Of course, the best way to avoid being trapped by a shady investment adviser is to make all of your own investment decisions and transactions yourself. We have already established that crashproofers do not try to outperform the market; rather, they simply try to spread risk. The rules for spreading risk effectively are not too complex. So once you become comfortable with the investing process, you may not need an adviser. If you open an account with a discount broker or on-line broker, not only will you pay lower transaction costs, but you will also avoid contact with anyone who could trick you out of your money. You must still be sure that your discount or on-line broker is reputable and follows all industry requirements for the insurance of funds and accounts against intentional or negligent mishandling by employees of the brokerage company. However, you can avoid nearly all scams when you do the work yourself.

Pick a Well-Established Investment Advising Company

Many intelligent, successful people still do not feel comfortable doing their own investing, either because they are too technologically challenged to make on-line transactions or because they feel more secure having a professional advise them on their risk-spreading ideas. This is fine. If you choose to use a broker or investment adviser, use one who is affiliated with an established company. If you choose a company that is not publicly traded, remember that smaller investment companies can be subject to rapid changes in ownership and control, sometimes engineered by criminals who want to buy an aura of legitimacy. If you choose a smaller, well-established company, find out who owns and controls it, and use the following methods to carefully research the backgrounds of any new owners.

Research Carefully the Professional History of Your Potential Adviser

Even if you choose an old, very established company such as Smith Barney, Merrill Lynch, Oppenheimer, or Edward D. Jones, you are not out of the woods yet. Sometimes these companies hire a bad egg—indeed, there are many such documented cases. If the broker comes highly recommended, you still need to ask the investment company for the resume of your potential broker or adviser, as well as a listing of any disciplinary actions filed against your adviser by state or federal securities regulators, and the name and caption of any lawsuit in which an unhappy investor sued the adviser. However, just because an adviser had a lawsuit filed against him or her does not mean that the adviser is unreliable. Many frivolous lawsuits have been filed. If, however, you see a *pattern* of legal or regulatory action against an investment adviser, or, worse yet, some of those legal actions have resulted in judgments against the adviser and the company, you should avoid entrusting your money to that person. You can also pay a lawyer a few hundred dollars to do this work for you. It may well be the best money you ever spend.

If you really want to be thorough, tell the broker that you intend to verify that he or she obtained the degrees and licenses listed on the resume. Resume fraud is rampant in the investment industry as it is everywhere else. It is a simple truth that if someone lies on his or her resume, then that person will also lie to get your money and will lie about the status of that money. Checking out the veracity of a resume is an excellent way to determine the integrity of anyone to whom you might entrust your money.

There are also websites that keep records of complaints or disciplinary actions filed against brokers (see, for example, nasdr.com, run by the National Association of Securities Dealers). But these sites tend to require you to already have a fair amount of information about your broker just to do a search, so you will probably need the resume information anyway.

Monitor the Activities of Your Adviser

Once you have found an adviser whom you think you can trust, you must monitor the adviser's activities carefully. First, never give the adviser "discretionary" authority over your accounts. You should give the adviser the authority to engage in a transaction only with your specific, advance consent. If the adviser calls you and tells you he or she bought or sold something for you without your consent, fire that adviser immediately. In such situations, the adviser often defends his or her actions by saying that you couldn't be reached or that the opportunity was just too good to pass up. Do not accept these excuses. If a broker or adviser trades without your consent, the relationship should end immediately and you should report the incident to the company management.

Second, make sure you get regular documentation of your transactions and study that documentation carefully. Read your monthly statement. Determine if the adviser engaged in unauthorized transactions and study the charged fees to ensure they are consistent with what the adviser told you they would be. It is surprising how often untrustworthy advisers fail to send the required documentation of transactions or brazenly include unauthorized transactions and undisclosed fees on the statements they do send to investors.

If you receive money from a trust, make sure the trustee provides you with regular documentation of his or her transactions, and consider having an outside auditor monitor the trustee's activities on a regular basis. If you are the beneficiary of a blind trust—i.e., one in which you relinquish all knowledge and control of your assets to a trustee in order to avoid conflicts of interest (commonly used by politicians, among others)—you can still put language in the trust agreement that requires an outside accountant to audit the activities of the trustee to ensure that the trustee is handling your investments in an honest and responsible manner.

Third, inquire about potential conflicts of interest the adviser may have. If an adviser recommends a particular mutual fund or stock, first ask if he or she owns the same stock and how much. If the adviser does own the investment, it could mean that either he or she honestly believes it is a good one or the adviser may be trying to pump up the investment because it is not doing well. In either event, this is a conflict of interest and you should be aware of the potential for mischief. More important, ask if the mutual fund or company that the adviser is recommending has some sort of a relationship with the adviser or the adviser's company. Brokers should not recommend that an investor buy stock in their own company, nor should they recommend that you buy equity in companies affiliated with the broker's company; and they should not recommend a company in which they have a financial relationship beyond just holding shares in that company.

Fourth, beware of a broker or investment adviser who recommends frequent trades. Brokers make their money on commissions from trades. It is therefore in their interest to have you make as many trades as possible, a practice that generally decreases an investor's returns anyway. Brokers who recommend trades just to generate a lot of fees are engaging in an illegal practice known as "churning." It is a very common practice among disreputable financial professionals, and you have to be on the lookout for it. Always question the broker carefully about his or her intentions when the broker makes frequent trading recommendations.

Read the Prospectus

When you are considering an investment such as a mutual fund or a corporate bond, the investment company will send you a prospectus that discusses—often in excruciating detail—exactly what you are purchasing. While these prospectuses are often very difficult to read, they usually contain a section that specifically discusses the risks associated with the investment.

Crashproofers read the whole prospectus, and they read the risk section twice. The reason you must read the prospectus is that brokers often overstate the potential returns of investments and they understate the risk. The prospectus will usually tell you the truth. That truth allows you to make an informed investment decision, and it also allows you to evaluate the accuracy of the advice your broker has given you.

Moreover, from a legal standpoint, it is very difficult to recover your losses from a shady broker based upon his or her lies that induced you to make an investment if the prospectus the broker gave you tells you the true facts. Courts will often deem the purchaser of an investment to be on notice of anything that is in a prospectus and will discount or even exclude from evidence oral representations made by the broker or investment adviser that run contrary to what is in the prospectus. For example, several years ago, a Midwestern bank issued notes to investors. The bank officials selling the notes allegedly told potential investors that the notes were insured, but the prospectus said they were not insured. The investors lost most of their money. When they sued for the misrepresentations allegedly made by the bank officials, the bank successfully interposed the defense that the prospectus sent to these investors clearly told them their investments were uninsured.

Avoiding an investment scam perpetrated by someone who tries to gain your trust and confidence is usually not too difficult if you follow some very basic steps: pick a reputable investment company, research carefully the individual who will be advising you, monitor his or her activities meticulously, and read scrupulously the written materials relating to the investments that you consider.

Getting Back the Money Someone Has Taken from You

Because the forces of disorder are ever-changing and very clever, there remains a possibility that you will follow the previous recommendations, yet still find yourself the victim of a financial parasite. Even some very careful people— including a few who have adopted the crashproof mind-set—have lost their money to people who outsmarted or outmaneuvered them. While it is unlikely that you, as a crashproofer, will find yourself the victim of a financial scam, you need to know what to do if you do in fact become victimized by a shady investment adviser.

You have three weapons at your disposal: the civil legal system, government regulators, and the court of public opinion. All of these weapons can bring tremendous pressure on or even require the person or entity who cheated you to make restitution.

First I need to emphasize one point that a lot of people do not want to hear. Some people and corporate entities who come to me complaining that they have been bilked, defrauded, or cheated out of money really do not have much of a case for restitution. They have knowingly taken a big financial risk, the risk has materialized, and now they do not want to take responsibility for their actions. Before you try to blame someone else for your financial losses, take a good, hard look in the mirror. If, for example, you invested in an Internet start-up company that sold Lucite-encased, genuine edelweiss flowers equipped with microchips that cause the flowers to sing nineteenth-century German mountain songs and you lost your shirt, you could not sue your broker just because he or she recommended this ridiculous company. Everyone knows that such investments are highly risky. You need to take responsibility for your actions when you deviate from the safe course of conduct and invest in a high-risk venture. Indeed, our legal system has a bad reputation because it is inundated with frivolous claims and lawsuits, and you do a real disservice to the people who really were cheated if you pursue an unmeritorious legal action. With overcrowded dockets and histrionic attorneys running around everywhere, it has become very difficult to pursue a good case because so many bad ones clutter the system. If you screwed up, admit your mistake and move on with your life.

If, on the other hand, you really were cheated out of your money, you should pursue your options vigorously. You should know at the outset that many people who cheat others out of their money move around a lot, change their company names frequently, and even use a variety of personal aliases, so you should have no illusion that it will be easy to recover your stolen money. Nonetheless, a fair number of people do recover lost funds, especially those who pursue their options in a systematic, unemotional, and well-organized manner.

Civil Legal Recourse

Your best chance of recovery is through the civil justice system. The system is, however, a mess. Court dockets are overcrowded, causing judges to often delay trials and fail to address pretrial motions on a timely basis. Slimy con artists often use slimy lawyers who will stop at nothing to win the case—including a deliberate effort to destroy the victim's reputation. Brokerage houses usually require customers to give up access to the court system entirely by putting arbitration clauses in their agreements with customers. If you are to navigate the civil justice system effectively, you need to take some simple steps.

Lay the Groundwork Before You Become a Victim

Most people soliciting your investment money and effectuating your financial transactions are honest and hardworking, so you never want to suggest at the outset that you are going to sue them if they cheat you. Indeed, you should make every effort to establish a positive and constructive relationship with anyone managing your money. However, there are ways you can lay the groundwork, in a subtle and completely nonconfrontational manner, for the successful recovery of your assets should you lose them due to the inappropriate conduct of your money manager.

First, the New York Stock Exchange, the National Association of Securities Dealers, and other trading organizations have "suitability" guidelines for brokers and investment advisers. These guidelines in essence require that a broker recommend only those investments that are within the stated goals and risk thresholds of their clients. Many investment fraud cases proceed on the theory that the broker recommended investments that were much riskier than the client had said he or she wanted. The broker defends on the grounds that the client knew of and wanted to take the risks that ultimately led to the losses in question. It becomes a game of "he said, she said."

You can avoid this finger-pointing. At the beginning of the relationship, you should write a concise and courteous letter to your investment adviser that clearly explains your investment objectives and states how much risk you are willing to take. Take this example. A thirty-five-year-old professional woman decides to implement a crashproofing plan similar to what was recommended in Chapter 5 on pyramid financial structures. She would write a letter to her investment manager stating that her objective is to develop holdings that contain approximately 35 percent bonds and 65 percent stocks, with the balance tipped in favor of domestic, growth, and large-cap stocks. She should update that letter as her investment goals and needs change. That way, if the broker tricks her into making more risky investments, she can immediately produce a piece of paper showing that the broker did not follow her wishes. That letter will then become a key piece of evidence if the legal system must ultimately resolve the dispute.

If you are a very unsophisticated investor, it may be useful to discuss explicitly your lack of sophistication in your letter. Noting your unfamiliarity with investing increases the likelihood that the legal system would determine there existed a "fiduciary" relationship between you and your investment adviser. When someone becomes a fiduciary to you, he or she has a very high legal standard of care in his or her conduct toward you. A person who has a fiduciary relationship with you is required by law to exercise all judgment in a manner that protects your interests above all others. Establishing a fiduciary relationship can, in rare circumstances, even relieve you of responsibility for ill-advised investment decisions to which you consented. While courts frequently determine that no such fiduciary relationships exist between investment advisers and their clients (other than in the case of discretionary accounts), the odds of establishing such a relationship increase when you make it clear that you are operating in an area well outside of your financial expertise. Say so in your letter.

If You Feel You Have Been Defrauded, Take Action Immediately

If you believe someone has cheated you out of money, you must move quickly. If the perpetrator is a small home-improvement company or solo investment adviser, he or she may be preparing to move to another city or to change names. You should consult a lawyer immediately and instruct the attorney to file an action and serve the perpetrator with your petition for legal relief as soon as possible. While I am, in many cases, against the use of private investigators, if the person has already skipped town, you should consider hiring a private investigator to track that person down. When dealing with an individual or a small company, you may even want to hire a private investigator if the perpetrator is still in town so that you can learn where the perpetrator's assets are located and what his real name is. Your lawyer can help you locate a good private investigator who will work quickly.

If the person who defrauded you works for an established company, which diminishes the risk of flight, you or your lawyer should immediately write the company a neatly organized, unemotional letter that lays out the facts and demands a refund of the losses. The brokerage contract that you signed may have a very short period of time in which you must notify the company of your claim. Do not let this time period pass.

Find a Good Lawyer to Assist You, but Remain Informed and in Control of the Situation

It is almost impossible to remedy a fraud on your own. The legal intricacies are just too complicated for a nonlawyer to navigate; you need a good lawyer. To get one, start with references either from friends or the local bar association, which usually keeps a referral list. Then interview potential candidates. Make sure the lawyer has specific experience in getting money back from brokers, home improvement companies, or whatever entity cheated you. Unless you already know the lawyer well, get a resume and his or her agreement that you may verify the items on the resume. Write or call the state bar association to inquire of any disciplinary actions that clients have instituted against the lawyer. If all checks out well, hire the lawyer to help you.

Your work in retaining counsel is not over yet. Understand the fee arrangement. Lawyers can work for flat fees, hourly fees, or fees contingent upon a successful outcome. If there is enough money at stake, you can probably get the lawyer to agree to a contingent fee: he or she gets around one-third of any recovery but no fee if you lose. The contingent fee poses the least financial risk to you.

You should also determine if other investors may have suffered the same fate as you did. If so, you may be able to join their claims with yours or even file a class action on behalf of similarly situated people. This makes the potential cost to the perpetrator much higher, and it increases the likelihood that the lawyer you hire will work for a contingent fee, because a lot more money is at stake.

If the lawyer insists upon an hourly rate, you must get an itemized budget of the process to determine if you can afford the lawyer and if the amount of money at stake is worth the fee you will be paying. You must also learn whether the dispute will be resolved by arbitration or litigation. Arbitration (which is a requirement for the resolution of disputes in most brokerage agreements) means that an expert outside the judicial system will hear your case. Arbitrations are usually quicker and less expensive than court litigation, but some people believe that the arbitrators on the approved lists of the various arbitration associations are pro-broker and anti-victim. If the dispute is of the type that you can get into the civil court system, it will be a longer and more expensive process, but you will likely get a jury trial, which, in some locations, tends to favor the victim. Each type of proceeding has its trade-offs, which your lawyer must explain to you clearly and fully.

Next, retain control over the situation. Remember that you are the lawyer's client. The lawyer works for you. Tell the lawyer you want him or her to consult you before making any significant decision. Read the briefs the lawyer intends to file, ask questions, and make suggestions. Make sure the lawyer tries to stick to the budget and promptly informs you of developments that might impact the budget adversely.

Finally, be reasonable. Many people who feel defrauded make their legal action a personal vendetta against the perpetrator. They turn down reasonable settlement offers because they have visions of punitive damages being assessed against the perpetrator. Sometimes that victim actually envisions "making money" off of the fraud by getting a huge jury verdict. Arbitrators and juries are unpredictable, and litigation is costly—in terms of money, time, and emotion. If you obtain a settlement offer that makes you financially whole or even mostly whole, you should consider it seriously and move on to less stressful activities.

State and Federal Regulatory Authorities

If the fraud is serious enough to warrant the intervention of law enforcement authorities, you can and must bring them into the picture. How do you know if the matter is serious enough to attract the attention of government officials? Generally, you do not. The facts that turn a simple civil dispute into a criminal or civil regulatory matter are legally complex. Whether to contact authorities is something that your lawyer may be the best person to decide, but you are, of course, always free to contact authorities even before you get a lawyer. If you feel you have been the victim of a fraud and want to tell the authorities about it, you should contact your state attorney general first. His or her office will decide whether to bring in federal officials.

The following are some activities that will generally trigger the interest of law enforcement authorities: frauds with many victims, a perpetrator who is selling securities or investments that must be registered with the government but are not, systematic account churning, a perpetrator who provides legally insufficient investment documentation, and a perpetrator who fails to provide investment sale proceeds demanded by the investor. Authorities will generally stay away from cases where investors complain that the adviser simply failed to follow instructions, resulting in financial losses.

Often a criminal action filed by authorities will result in the "staying" or temporary cessation of civil legal action against the perpetrator. That means you may have to wait to get your money back. However, if the perpetrator is convicted, you have an almost guaranteed civil judgment against that person and his or her company after the conviction, so it is worth the wait. The only risk of this course of action is that by the time you get your judgment, the perpetrator and his or her company may no longer have attachable assets because they have squandered or hidden the money they have stolen from unwary investors. This is, unfortunately, a common scenario. Nevertheless, it is always to your benefit to cooperate fully with a government investigation of the person or entity that defrauded you out of your money. It generally increases the likelihood that you will recover lost funds.

The Court of Public Opinion

All reputable companies (and even some disreputable ones that do not plan to fold up anytime soon) hate bad press. So if you feel you have been cheated by a bad employee of a good company, you may have redress in the court of public opinion. Many investors who can present solid, credible evidence that they have been cheated, get a quick and satisfying settlement when they get a news or media organization interested in their plight.

No one likes opening the door and seeing a television crew smiling at them. But you, of course, have many other media options. Most local newspapers have consumer reporters whose job is to root out fraud and corruption in the local area. In order to get them interested in your story, you must present your case to them in a succinct, convincing, and well-documented manner.

First the "don'ts." Media organizations will ignore you if you leave a long, rambling voice mail for one of their reporters. They will (and should) ignore you if you write or call them with a lot of inflammatory rhetoric but no hard facts to back it up. They will ignore you if you take your anger out on them by demanding that they return your calls or pursue the story.

Rather, if you want to put media pressure on a person or organization who cheated you, first write the media organization a letter that reads as professionally as a legal brief. In the first sentence of the letter, identify yourself and the company or person who defrauded you. Then in three or four short paragraphs, state the facts supporting your contention in an unemotional fashion. Attach specific documentation of the wrong you have endured. Finally, close the letter by succinctly stating what has happened to you as a result of the fraud—you lost your house, declared bankruptcy, had your credit rating destroyed, had to move your sick mother to a less desirable nursing home. They will not run a story, even if you have been defrauded out of $100,000, if you have another million in the bank. They want the name of the perpetrator, hard evidence of fraud, and a story of great loss to the victim. If you have those ingredients, write letters to the consumer advocates in your area, and follow up a few days later with a phone call. That process may allow you to short-circuit the entire legal system.

The risk inherent in such a course of action is that the perpetrator will sue you for libel. In order to avoid such a fate, you must be right in your grievance and scrupulously honest in your evidentiary exposition. Even some truly wronged persons have gotten into trouble when they made up a few facts to give added credence to their stories. If you stick to the facts, the risk of a libel judgment is very low. Indeed, libel suits in this type of a situation are usually not successful. Do not, however, be surprised if the company or individual who defrauded you at least threatens to take such action. It is a common, but usually empty, threat.

The Financial Crashproofing Checklist

By this time, you should have a good sense of how to avoid both professional and financial crashes in your life. Here I have distilled all the information about financial crashproofing into a handy checklist. Be sure to check the crashproofyourlife.com website from time to time for some updated tips and ideas on financial crashproofing and what happens to those people who do not do it.

Your Worst Financial Enemy Is *You*

Pyramid Financial Structure

____ I have put into place solid financial structures that allow me to save 20 percent of my after-tax income.

____ I use direct deposit to my various financial accounts to the extent possible.

____ I limit my use of automatic teller cards to reasonable increments of money, and I never make an automatic teller withdrawal on the spur of the moment for an unplanned purchase.

____ I do not use debit cards.

Checking Account

____ I limit my checking account funds to basic necessities such as mortgage payments, car payments, food and clothing expenses, utilities, and modest, routine entertainment costs.

____ I live in a right-sized home with no wasted space or useless extravagances.

____ I have purchased or am working toward purchasing a home with a down payment of at least 25 percent.

____ I use a fixed-rate mortgage.

____ I have carefully researched the model of car I want to purchase, to ensure its long-term reliability.

____ I have considered a modestly used car, after carefully researching the car's service and use history.

____ I control the car purchasing transaction by developing a written specification of my needs, providing that specification to numerous dealers, doing on-line price research, providing that information to the dealers, getting bids from the dealers, and then approaching the low-bidding dealer.

____ I stay away from glitzy malls and purchase the same high-quality clothes at warehouse and outlet stores.

____ I do comparison shopping at local grocery stores to learn which one sells at the consistently lowest prices, with specific attention to markups on generic goods, and the optimum volume for a particular purchase.

____ I limit my utilities to those that I really need, with particular attention to the costs of cable TV, cellular phone, regular phone option features, and on-line services.

Slush Fund

____ I limit my vacation, electronics, and other large discretionary expenditures to 10 percent of my annual after-tax income.

____ I do not smoke, I limit my alcohol intake to occasional social events, and I do not set aside any more money for gambling than I would for a normal night out on the town.

____ I do whatever is necessary to eliminate credit-card debt, including paying cash wherever possible, using only one credit card to avoid the inconvenience of carrying cash, paying more than the minimum due, consolidating debt to the lowest interest rate, negotiating a lower rate with the credit-card company, and if necessary, using a consumer credit bureau to assist me.

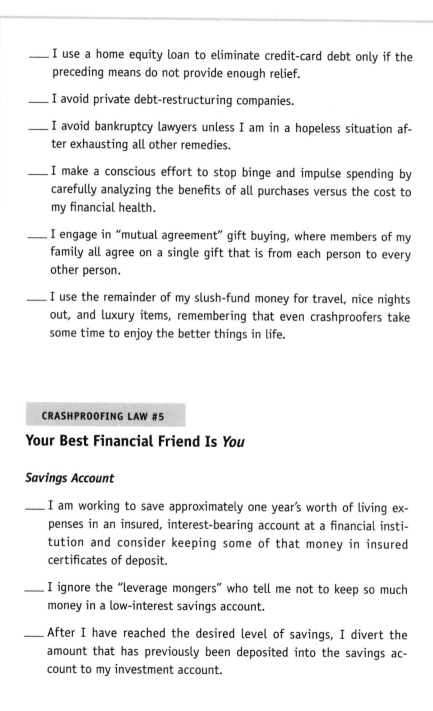

_____ I use a home equity loan to eliminate credit-card debt only if the preceding means do not provide enough relief.

_____ I avoid private debt-restructuring companies.

_____ I avoid bankruptcy lawyers unless I am in a hopeless situation after exhausting all other remedies.

_____ I make a conscious effort to stop binge and impulse spending by carefully analyzing the benefits of all purchases versus the cost to my financial health.

_____ I engage in "mutual agreement" gift buying, where members of my family all agree on a single gift that is from each person to every other person.

_____ I use the remainder of my slush-fund money for travel, nice nights out, and luxury items, remembering that even crashproofers take some time to enjoy the better things in life.

CRASHPROOFING LAW #5

Your Best Financial Friend Is *You*

Savings Account

_____ I am working to save approximately one year's worth of living expenses in an insured, interest-bearing account at a financial institution and consider keeping some of that money in insured certificates of deposit.

_____ I ignore the "leverage mongers" who tell me not to keep so much money in a low-interest savings account.

_____ After I have reached the desired level of savings, I divert the amount that has previously been deposited into the savings account to my investment account.

Investment Account

____ I do not assume that I can outperform efficient markets.

____ I understand the history and risks of the principal categories of investments: real estate, precious metals, government securities, and corporate securities.

____ My investment goal is to spread risk evenly among the various categories of investments.

____ A principal investment goal is to own a piece of real estate, and I accomplish this goal by some prepayment of my mortgage.

____ I own a small reserve of gold or silver.

____ I allocate the remainder of my investment money between stocks and bonds, with approximately 1 percent bonds for each year of my age.

____ I divide my bond investments evenly between U.S. government bonds (some inflation indexed), AAA municipal bonds, and highly rated corporate bonds, with varying periods of maturity.

____ I divide my stock investments about 80 percent to 20 percent in favor of domestic over foreign, large caps over small caps, and value over growth.

____ I consider low-expense, no-load mutual funds to achieve some of this diversification, especially in the risky area of foreign stocks.

____ I place about 60 percent of my stock and bond holdings in a retirement account if I am forty or under and reduce this percentage to 40 percent when I pass the age of forty.

CRASHPROOFING LAW #6

As Soon As You Get It, Someone Will Try to Take It Away

The Unknown Threat

____ I avoid cold callers.

_____ I do not trust what I read about investments in chat rooms or other on-line sources beyond those that are well-established financial sites.

_____ I take the precautions necessary to avoid being the victim of an identity hijacker, including never disposing of financial information in a manner that would allow others to retrieve it, keeping my social security number off of my driver's license, checking the security policy of on-line providers, and refusing to provide unrequired personal information to vendors of supplies and services.

_____ I avoid real estate scams by understanding how people become victims of loan flipping and by relying upon references of trusted friends when I choose a home improvement contractor.

The Known Threat

_____ I do not, however, rely upon references from friends when I choose someone to serve as my financial adviser, and I am not fooled by someone who overtly displays the trappings of wealth and success in an effort to convince me to entrust him or her with my money.

_____ I carefully research the background of someone whom I am considering as a financial adviser, including any disciplinary actions or lawsuits brought against that person.

_____ I monitor the activity of my financial adviser, including never allowing that person to engage in transactions without my consent, reading statements and documentation carefully, learning of any conflicts of interest my adviser may have, and ensuring that my adviser is not recommending trades just to generate commissions.

_____ I read investment prospectuses that are sent to me.

Getting Money Back

_____ I take responsibility for my own financial mistakes.

_____ I periodically send my financial adviser a letter outlining my investment objectives.

____ I take swift action if I feel that my investment adviser has acted inappropriately.

____ I have learned how to locate and use a lawyer in an effective and cost-efficient manner.

____ I report serious fraud to the appropriate government officials.

____ I consider using the media to help me right financial wrongs committed against me.

PART THREE

AVOIDING PERSONAL LIABILITY

With the appropriate professional and financial structures in place, you may start feeling economically invincible. Watch out. While you should be feeling a lot more secure now, do not become overconfident. The forces of disorder have one more trick up their sleeve: ruining your personal life. Indeed, your personal problems can easily destroy the income you generate professionally and the wealth you have built with solid financial structures.

This part of the book will discuss the actions crashproofers must take to protect themselves from financial ruin due to events that occur in their personal lives. You will learn that through a defensive lifestyle, more effective use of insurance, careful estate-planning mechanisms, and open and honest communication with your friends and family on financial issues, you can avoid nearly every conceivable personal economic crash scenario.

As was said at the outset, this book will not cover the emotional repercussions of personal crashes. I'll leave that to the psychologists. However, you do not need a psychologist to know that you will be better prepared to deal with the emotional toll levied by unfortunate events in your personal life if you have effectively addressed their financial implications up front. So this part will complete the crash-proofing process by showing you how to build personal structures that complement your professional and financial structures.

7

Demystifying Insurance

The Perfect Insurance Mix Is Careful Conduct, More Types of Insurance, and Higher Deductibles

Kerry, an advertising executive, is driving a few miles from her home, which is in a wealthy, suburban area outside of a major U.S. city. She has just left the office Christmas party at a local restaurant and bar, and she is talking on her cell phone to her husband about a huge client she recently landed for her agency. The commissions will be substantial, and she plans to take her husband and two kids to Hawaii between Christmas and New Year's Day to celebrate the new account.

Kerry is both a professional and a financial crashproofer. Her career is flying high thanks to her careful, conscientious conduct on the job. Her finances are in great shape, too. She is only thirty-eight years old, but the combined value of the investments she and her husband have accrued is over $550,000—and their accounts are snowballing with interest and dividends. They also have prepaid their mortgage to the point where they have almost $170,000 in home equity. They plan to retire at age fifty-eight.

But disaster strikes almost instantly. The office Christmas party is in an area of town that Kerry does not know well, and as she drives home, she accidentally tries to enter the highway by turning onto an *exit* ramp. A twenty-one-year-old man, who is returning home from work at his father's hardware store, is exiting the highway onto the ramp at the exact time that Kerry enters. The two cars collide.

Kerry walks away from the accident, but the man in the other car dies instantly. The police give Kerry a Breathalyzer test and find that she has 0.06 alcohol level—just below the legal limit. They also note in their report that her cell phone was on when they recovered it from the wreckage of her car. Because Kerry's alcohol level is below the legal limit, the authorities do not prosecute her. Nevertheless, Kerry is devastated and feels tremendous guilt. She learns that the man had just gotten married and his wife is pregnant. She also learns that the man had recently been accepted into a graduate engineering program at the Massachusetts Institute of Technology.

A month later, the wife and parents of the young man file a wrongful death suit against Kerry, claiming that the low level of alcohol, combined with her talking on her cell phone, led her to make a wrong turn that resulted in the man's death. They claim that the family lost over $3 million in income that the man would have earned as an MIT–educated engineer had he not been killed by Kerry.

Kerry has no real defense to this lawsuit. Her one consolation is that she has a reputable automobile liability insurer, which takes over the defense of the action. The insurer advises her to accept a settlement offer of $1 million because the insurance company believes that a jury verdict would be significantly higher in light of the tragic facts. Kerry agrees but soon learns that her insurance policy only covers $300,000 of that sum. She is forced to liquidate all of her assets and take out a home equity loan to cover the difference. When it is all over, her net worth is just less than $25,000.

Kerry's story is an example of what I call the "lightning strike" personal disaster—one instantaneous occurrence that changes her life forever. However, some of the worst personal crashes are what I call the "slow burn"—long and tortuous. Take the case of a man who owned his own appliance business but became ill with a deadly form of diabetes, followed by dementia. As his illness progressed, he had to go into an extended-care medical facility. His wife thought that his health insurance and, eventually, Medicare would pay for the lost income due to her husband's illness. She also thought that his insurance would cover the $68,000 per year that the medical facility charged her, as well as the $22,000 cost for part-time nursing care.

She was wrong. Insurance covered almost none of it. As a result, she had to sell her home to pay for these costs. Soon, she was unable to afford even the small apartment that she rented. She then had to move in with one of her two kids, causing tremendous financial and emotional disruption to that family, which had to build an extra bedroom and bath—at a cost of $75,000—onto their house to accommodate her. In the meantime, the elderly husband lingered on for nine years, completely depleting the proceeds of the sold home. Eventually, the children had to split the cost of the extended-care facility, draining them of much of their own savings. By the time the parents had both died, their kids had spent more than $600,000 of their own money taking care of their parents, which, in turn, greatly compromised their own retirement plans.

This, too, is not an unusual personal-crash scenario, and it will become increasingly common as baby boomers age with inadequate insurance, especially when the economy experiences that inevitable long-term downturn that everyone fears. The lesson to be learned from these two stories is clear: everything you have worked for with your professional and financial crashproofing plans could either disappear instantly or drain away slowly if you do not crashproof your personal life as carefully as you have crashproofed your job and finances.

Most people believe they have protected themselves adequately for the financial repercussions of personal disaster once they have acquired the "big four" types of insurance: homeowner's insurance, life insurance, health insurance, and automobile insurance. However, the normal exclusions in these "basic" insurance policies leave most Americans with wide areas of financial exposure, of which they may be completely unaware. You need a variety of supplemental insurance, combined with a few noninsurance forms of legal protection, to close these potentially devastating loopholes.

The money for insurance should come out of your checking account, as these insurance expenditures are intricately tied to your other checking-account expenses—home and car. Indeed, if you have a mortgage, the cost of basic insurance protection is probably built into your monthly payment anyway.

You can get the additional protection you need at little or no additional cost if you take simple steps to reduce the premiums you already pay on your basic insurance. There are three ways to pay lower premiums: take higher deductibles, research carefully, and reduce the risk that you pose to the insurance company. We'll start with the question of higher deductibles and research—because these requirements apply across the board—and save the issue of reducing risk for the more detailed discussion of each type of insurance later.

Increasing Deductibles

The purpose of insurance is to protect you from serious disaster. Unfortunately, most Americans have insurance that will protect them from small and medium-sized problems but not from the really big crashes. You must adjust your insurance coverage to eliminate coverage for small problems and include coverage for big ones. For example, you do not need insurance for a fender-bender. You can take a few hundred dollars out of your checking account or slush fund to cover minor automobile accidents. Indeed, many people who are in minor car accidents do not even make insurance claims because they fear their rates will increase if they make a claim. That means they are buying insurance they do not use, which is a complete waste of money.

The more intelligent approach is to obtain reduced insurance premiums by taking the highest possible deductible for homeowner's insurance, health insurance, and automobile insurance and then to use the savings you achieve through higher deductibles to purchase the supplemental insurance that will protect you from true catastrophe.

Careful Research

Step two for a personal crashproofer is to carefully compare the cost of insurance at several reputable companies. Confine your search to well-known companies because you can be sure they are keeping the level of cash reserves that the law requires. As with brokers and home contractors, there are many fly-by-night insurance companies that will not be there when you need them. Even as you consider large, reputable companies, do some on-line research in the insurance industry and financial press to determine which companies are the most solid. The crashproofyourlife.com website has some links to sources for this information. You will see that some of the major insurers have paid billions of dollars in claims due to recent natural disasters—especially hurricanes—so their cash reserves, while sufficient to stay within the legal limit, have been deemed questionable by some industry experts. Indeed, some reasonably large insurance companies may not have enough cash to pay all the claims they would likely receive in the event of a big disaster such as a California earthquake or a Florida hurricane. Study your potential insurers carefully. Some twenty insurance companies went under in 1998 and another thirty-five collapsed in 1999.

Start your negotiations by getting bids from three or more reputable companies for insurance with the *lowest* deductible. If you start with the highest deductible, a tricky agent might try to get you to pay the highest rate even with the highest deductible. Once you have the pricing for insurance with the lowest deductible, then fax the insurer back saying that the insurance is a little too expensive and ask what the company rate is for the highest deductible. You will get lower quotes. Once you get those lower quotes, you can choose the lowest rate knowing that you probably got the lowest price. Your savings will allow you the extra cash you need to get the wider coverage discussed later.

Supplementing Your Basic Insurance

When you hear the term *insurance*, you probably think of agents selling policies with lots of fine print. But there is another form of insurance: self-insurance. When you buy a burglar alarm, put in a fire alarm, or decide not to make a cell phone call in your car during rush hour, you are effectively getting a form of insurance against a personal crash. Moreover, by taking these precautions, you may qualify for lower premiums on your formal insurance policies. Consequently, when considering the various types of insurance—home, life, health, and car— it is important to know what you can do to self-insure even before you buy the formal policies.

Then you need to know how to purchase the formal policies from insurance agents or on-line. As with brokers and financial advisers, most insurance agents are reputable citizens who look out for the best interests of their clients. But there are some crooks out there, and there are agents whose conduct falls short of criminal activity but who push high-commission products at the expense of your best interests. Other agents are just too busy to give you effective service or do not even fully understand their own products well enough to give you good advice. Consequently, you need to make it your job to ask the right questions and get clear answers to some key questions about what your insurance does and does not cover.

With these objectives in mind—effective self-insurance and well-understood insurance policies—let's discuss the four major areas where you need to be insured.

Home Protection

With real estate as your financial anchor, you must take all the necessary steps to protect your home and property. Most people do not. Therefore, before discussing homeowner's insurance policies specifically, let's make sure you are taking the necessary steps to protect your home from the major threats that the forces of disorder pose to it. Taking these basic precautions will in many cases have the added benefit of reducing your homeowner's insurance premium.

Protective Location

First, do not buy or build a home where the odds are that it is going to be destroyed. Do not laugh. Millions of people put down roots only to be uprooted soon thereafter. A major network recently ran a story about an island that had been devastated by hurricanes three times in two years. The victims just rebuilt their homes after each hurricane—apparently waiting for the next one. There are plains that flood an average of every five years, and there is ocean-side property that geologists say is almost certain to fall into the sea within the next ten years. Yet this land is just teeming with new homes. It doesn't matter how lucky you feel or how cheap the land is, stay away from a disaster waiting to happen.

I wish I could tell you there is some place you can live where you have no chance of being hit by disaster. There is no such place. The crashproof yourlife.com website has some links to sites that discuss the wide variety of natural disasters that can strike at various locations throughout the country. The best you can do is to stay away from the real problem areas and then learn what your risks are elsewhere. Once you know the risks, do whatever you can to minimize them—including taking the steps we'll discuss later. That process will allow you to get the right types of insurance at a reasonable cost.

Material Issues

Since you can never avoid natural disasters entirely, take all reasonable steps to ensure your home is built to best withstand the disaster or disasters most likely to hit you or to maximize your chance of survival. If you live in Tornado Alley, make sure you have a cellar or basement. If you live on the San Andreas Fault, know the soil type and build accordingly—for example, often a wood-frame home will survive a quake better than a brick or cinderblock home. If you live near an area with frequent wildfires, using specific types of building materials and landscaping will dramatically increase your chances of keeping your home when disaster strikes. There was a man in Laguna, California, whose house was the only one in his neighborhood to survive a wildfire in the 1990s because he had built it out of fire-resistant materials and landscaped the yard to make it hard for fire to spread on his land.

Some insurance companies will give you a break if your home is resistant to disaster. Your local homebuilder's association or trade group can give you free advice concerning disaster-resistant home construction.

Fireproofing

The most common home-related crash is a fire that ignites from within the home (as opposed to a brush fire or a lightning strike that starts a fire outside the home). Approximately two million fires are reported in the United States each year. Fire kills about 4,000 people and injures around 20,000 people per year in the United States alone—more casualties than all other accidental or natural disasters combined. Direct property loss is over $9 billion annually. At least 80 percent of these fire deaths occur in homes.

The leading cause of home fires is careless cooking. The second leading cause is unsafe heating practices. The leading cause of fire *deaths* is smoking. So you need to take more care when cooking, such as never leaving the oven on when you leave the house and monitoring the activities of children in the kitchen very closely. You should have your heating system and fireplace checked by a professional each fall, and you should be extremely careful in your use of space heaters or do not use them at all. And, of course, you should quit smoking.

Then you need to have smoke alarms in the home to detect fire or deadly gas. Test the alarms regularly. Have one, preferably two, working fire extinguishers in the home. Purchase fire-resistant clothes and furniture. Finally, have a fire drill at the house once each year so that your family or others with whom you live know what to do if they find themselves in the middle of a home fire. Your local fire department will probably be happy to advise you on how to conduct that drill and will give you additional tips as well. Take your kids to the fire department to check out the fire engines. Use that as an opportunity for you and your family to discuss home fire safety with the professionals. I have found that fire-fighting professionals in my community and others are eager to assist citizens with all questions concerning fire safety.

Crime Proofing

According to the FBI, over 400,000 robberies occur each year in the United States, with property loss of more than $400 million. You can take a wide variety of steps to reduce your risk of being robbed—on the street or at home. How far you should go to protect yourself is a function of how high the crime rate is in your area and how much money you can afford to spend. Keep in mind that many "good" neighborhoods have a higher crime rate than you would expect because people in the area keep crime statistics quiet for fear of lowering property values. You must learn the true statistics in your area from the local police.

Before you move into an area, learn about the level of police protection and about neighborhood watch programs. For example, many municipalities have a system where all area residents get periodic prerecorded voice mail from the police informing the residents of local crime risks. Then take the personal precautions that will reduce the crime threat to you and your family. Many of them—such as double locks, deadbolts, and security systems—may also lower your insurance premiums. Your insurance agent can discuss those precautions with you.

Nothing substitutes fully for a good home security system. But if you cannot afford one, you can get some protective benefits simply by purchasing a sign or window sticker that *says* you have an alarm system. Some organizations even sell fake key pads you can put in a doorway, which you can see from the outside through your windows, so that a thief scouting your neighborhood for victims will believe you have an alarm system when, in fact, you do not. The point is there are many ways to lower the likelihood of a robbery, some of them very sophisticated and others extremely simple and cost-effective. Do what you can reasonably afford with your checking account or slush-fund money after considering the crime risk in your neighborhood.

Finally, get a safe-deposit box. Put in the box valuable items that you do not use often, including jewelry, coins, and bond certificates. Also put into the box copies of your estate planning documents. In addition, list all of your credit-card numbers, bank account numbers, brokerage account numbers, and various passwords for access to account information on a piece of paper and keep it in your safe-deposit box. You or your family members may need these numbers in the event that someone breaks into your home and steals your credit cards, checkbook, or other personal financial items while you are away.

Just as fire departments are generally very helpful with fireproofing ideas, local police departments usually provide free crime-proofing advice to anyone who calls their public affairs official. These experts can give you surprisingly useful tips. For example, a police officer once told me that floodlights that point outward from my house can actually provide "light cover" to criminals by blinding a neighbor or law enforcement person looking toward the house. He explained that floodlights and motion-activated lights should point "in" at the location where criminals are most likely to enter the home. Every crashproofer should avail himself or herself of this very helpful expertise.

Other Threats

While fires, natural disasters, and robberies represent the greatest threats to your home, you must prepare for other risks as well. We'll run through them briefly here, and you can get more information through links on the crashproof yourlife.com website.

Termites (and other bugs and rodents) can destroy your home, and the damage they cause is not usually covered by a typical homeowner's insurance policy. You need pest protection.

Two silent killers are carbon monoxide gas and radon. Carbon monoxide normally enters the home through faulty heaters. Although carbon monoxide poisoning kills thousands of Americans and sends 10,000 or more to the hospital each year, fewer than 15 percent of American homes have a carbon monoxide detector in them. Radon particles, caused by the breakdown of uranium in the soil around the house, can cause severe lung disease. In order to avoid a crash, therefore, keep a carbon monoxide detector near the bedrooms in your home, and have a radon test done one time to make sure you do not have unsafe levels inside your house. This is very inexpensive and potentially lifesaving advice.

Lead paint and asbestos insulation, although illegal now, are very hazardous and remain common in older homes, apartments, office buildings, and even schools (although most schools have complied with directives to remove the asbestos). With respect to asbestos, when you search for a home, specifically inquire about it. You need to know whether the home contains asbestos because asbestos must be professionally removed, which is very expensive. Lead poisoning can cause a variety of health problems, particularly for children, who can suffer mental impairment from it. You can still find it in older homes of all types, although often the owner will not know about it because it is buried under three layers of latex paint. When I moved into my home, which was built in 1938, I was surprised to learn that the paint on the closet doors in my guest room had two and a half times the legal limit of lead. In most areas, just painting over the lead paint is an acceptable practice. So if you strip a wall of all layers of paint, you must be very attuned to the possibility of lead particles being released into the air, and you must take the necessary precautions to prevent prolonged exposure.

You also need to have some basic supplies in your home to protect you from unforeseen risks, from serious natural disasters to lengthy power outages to simply being snowed in. I am not one of those people who recommend you have guns, ammo, generators, and a lead-lined nuclear shelter ready for the huge international conflict and collapse that some of the doomsday crowd predict. If things get so bad that law and order break down, there is little that any of us will be able to do to prevent our lives from crashing. Someone else will always have a bigger gun. On the other hand, you should have in your household first-aid kits, flashlights, battery-operated radios, fresh batteries, and some canned food and fresh water in case you have to be holed up in your home for a few days. In addition, a fully charged cellular phone provides a real communications safety net in the event of a lengthy power outage or other situation where you become inaccessible to the outside world. Have a scaled-back set of similar supplies in your car.

Formal Homeowner's Insurance Policies

Once you have self-insured by taking steps to protect your home, you will still need a basic homeowner's policy (or renter's policy, which will also be discussed). These policies are riddled with exclusions that allow the company to avoid paying you in many situations where your home is destroyed or vandalized. First, you want what is termed "special form" rather than "general form" homeowner's insurance. General-form insurance covers the losses that insurance policies must cover under the law of your state, but your state's laws may be lenient. Insurance lobbies in state legislatures are strong, so the companies have been successful in keeping general-form policies less than generous in their coverage. Special-form insurance, on the other hand, goes a step further, often covering additional risks (such as water damage from a burst pipe) that general-form policies normally do not cover.

Second, discuss with your agent coverage for the "loss of use" of your home. If a disaster damages your home, you need the insurance company to pay more than the cost of repairing the damage. You need coverage that includes the cost of living somewhere else while you wait for the completion of repairs on your home.

Third, you need to discuss with your agent the trend of home values in your neighborhood. Many people who lose their homes find themselves underinsured due to the often rapid increase in home values in some areas. Good insurance agents will call you and revalue your home from time to time, but do not count on it. Make sure you take the initiative on this issue, as it can be crucial if your most prized investment—your home—has increased in value. Get coverage for the appraised value if possible, although many companies will only cover the replacement value. The replacement value is lower because it does not include the value of the land on which your home stands.

Use the money saved from high deductibles to purchase insurance to cover the exclusions you normally find in homeowner's policies. For example, homeowner's policies do not cover damage from earthquakes. You need a special rider for earthquake coverage. Homeowner's policies do not cover flood damage. You need to purchase flood insurance from the federal government. Homeowner's policies may contain exclusions for damage to specified items inside the walls (furniture, appliances, fixtures) and very low coverage limits (often only a couple hundred dollars) for loss of personal articles such as jewelry, artwork, and collections.

Betterments-and-improvements riders or policies cover damage to fixtures such as bathtubs and fireplaces that may be excluded from your basic homeowner's policy. You do not need this type of insurance if you have normal furniture and fixtures—just use the money in your slush fund to pay for any uncovered losses. In addition, if you have valuable jewelry, coins or stamps, artwork, antiques, or unique furniture, you should consider a "personal articles" rider to your homeowner's policy. In order to get such coverage, you have to send the company an itemized list of each article you want covered and, in some cases, a receipt or appraisal of the value of the item you want to insure. These policies are normally quite inexpensive.

Homeowner's policies can have numerous other exclusions for such damage as the cost of removing fallen trees or damage to gardens. You need to have a full and open discussion with your agent about the exclusions and then determine which loopholes you want to try to close with additional insurance riders. Finally, if you rent, your need "renter's insurance," which normally covers not only the contents of your dwelling but also specified liabilities that you may incur by reason of your living there.

Life Insurance

Another essential part of personal crashproofing is life insurance. Most people fail to provide adequately for their families or themselves in the event of an unexpected death. While it may be unnecessary once you have reached retirement age, life insurance generally forms an essential part of the crashproofing process for those who are not yet retired.

Self-Insuring Your Life

Before discussing life insurance, let's consider life itself. You need to modify your conduct to minimize the chance that you will need life insurance anytime soon. Indeed, if you adopt a healthy lifestyle, your life-insurance premiums will be lower. You can and must, therefore, take steps toward building a lifestyle that will, at least to some extent, self-insure you against premature death.

We have, since page one, adopted a crashproofing strategy that centers upon building structures that resist the forces of disorder that define our universe. What we have not yet discussed, however, is that each one of us already has in place the most miraculous structure of all: ourselves. Life is a structure that is like no other structure in the universe. While it may be smaller than a star, planet, mountain, or building, a living structure is far more complex than any of these larger, more imposing, and monolithic ones. The human brain, for example, contains over 100 billion neurons, which is more cells than there are stars in the Milky Way; and it contains 60 trillion nerve connections. These cells and nerve endings are meticulously arranged to allow you to do things that no other celestial structure can: think, see, hear, taste. The human body contains up to 100 trillion cells, including skin cells that adapt to light and radiation and blood cells that nourish the body. The human body has organs that accomplish pumping, purification, and chemical conversion functions. The body has 206 hard and sturdy bones that form its structural foundation and billions of muscle cells that form around the bones to give you the strength to move your life forward. The typical human heart beats 30 to 40 million times every year and 1.5 to 2.8 billion times during a lifetime. What an amazing structure!

It takes a structure this complex to openly defy the forces of disorder. People build buildings, plan governments, rebuild cities, organize corporations, and otherwise engage in a nearly incessant effort to defy the disorderly forces around them. Indeed, success in life is defined by how well you build the structures that defy the forces of disorder. You need a powerful life structure in order to create the other structures you need in your crashproofing plan.

Because of our beauty, complexity, and capacity to reverse the chaotic direction of the universe, the universal forces of disorder hate living things. Indeed, disorder wants to destroy us. Of course, with time, every life deteriorates and eventually succumbs to disorder. But disorder is very impatient: *it wants you to destroy yourself before time does it for you*. It has several weapons to accomplish this goal.

The forces of disorder want you to weaken your body by being out of shape and overweight, by having high cholesterol and high blood pressure, and by poisoning yourself with cigarettes, alcohol, and drugs. In short, it wants you to harm your body as much and as often as possible.

Disorder also wants your mind to lose its sharpness. It wants to numb your thought processes with inadequate sleep, trash TV, and mind-altering substances. A weak mind feeds the forces of disorder.

And disorder wants to destroy your spirit and your soul by subjecting you to the temptations of prejudice, deceit, and violence. Even fine physical specimens with sharp minds contribute to universal disorder if they apply their strengths and talents to destructive causes. If you want to crashproof your life, you need to supplement your financial, professional, and personal legal structures with structures that maximize the potential of your body, mind, and spirit. It would seem that people would find building structures to protect their own bodies and minds the easiest task of all because their very existence depends upon this task. Yet look around you. Fourteen million Americans have an alcohol abuse problem, another 14 million have used an illegal drug within the past month, and 4.1 million are addicted to drugs. More than 50 million Americans smoke, and approximately 97 million Americans are overweight, including 5 million children. About 19 million Americans suffer from depression. Personal life structures—physical and mental—seem to be very hard to build.

As a result of the pressures and temptations of life, people who work diligently to build professional and financial structures to crashproof their lives often seem to be working equally hard to make sure they do not live long enough to enjoy those structures. You need to avoid this unfortunate paradox. Crashproofers build personal behavioral structures that complement their professional and financial structures. As a nonexpert, I must leave the specifics of diet, exercise, screening for disease, substance abuse, and mental and spiritual health to others. I can say with certainty, however, that you must make physical, mental, and spiritual health part of your crashproofing plan if you are to enjoy professional and financial success for any prolonged period of time.

Life-Insurance Policies

While you can take steps to improve the quality of your life and prolong it, there is always a risk that you will die tomorrow. Several years ago, many people across the country were shocked to learn that a prominent dietitian and a famous long-distance runner had each died suddenly of a heart attack. Both had made careers writing books and speaking about healthy lifestyles, and both died at relatively young ages.

Millions of people who are young, healthy, exercise regularly, and eat carefully will die young. Too often, their families find—at a time of great emotional turmoil—that they do not have enough money to sustain their current lifestyles. In fact, the death of a loved one—often in situations where the surviving spouse was a homemaker or where parents depended upon the person who died for financial support—can drive the rest of the family into poverty. Moreover, thousands of Americans become physically disabled each year, and that can be even more of a drain on family finances than death.

Americans tend to be vastly underinsured. Most professionals have life insurance but they do not have enough or they have the wrong kind. You need the crashproofer's approach to life insurance.

If you are single and unattached but your parents are living, you should still carry some life insurance because a growing number of aging Americans will need additional money during old age. Do not, therefore, feel that you can forgo life insurance just because you have no spouse or children. I recommend that even a young, single person carry at least $100,000 of life insurance with his or her parents being the beneficiaries. If your parents are deceased, make your siblings the beneficiaries. The rates for term insurance for young, nonsmokers is so low that you will experience little to no hardship by doing this favor for your parents, brothers, or sisters.

If you are married, both you and your spouse should have life insurance. The same holds true for same-sex domestic partners, although for ease of reference I will refer to spouses here. It seems callous to talk about money in the context of losing one's spouse, which is one reason that so many people find themselves financially ruined after the loss of a spouse. "I just could not talk about it with her," many an impoverished widower has said. The cold truth is that if both of you have jobs, the family lifestyle will suffer severely if one of you dies without life insurance. Similarly, if one spouse is a homemaker, he or she provides services that experts value at between $50,000 and $75,000 per year. If that spouse dies, the family will have to pay many people a lot of money to make up for the contribution that the deceased homemaker made.

Most people do not have enough life insurance. If you lack substantial income-producing assets, your spouse will need insurance proceeds generally equal to eight to ten times your annual pretax income to continue in that lifestyle after your death. That means a lawyer making $125,000 per year should have over \$1 million in life insurance, and a homemaker should have at least \$400,000. Once you start accumulating investment money, you will not need as much insurance. To calculate the proper amount, multiply your income by eight or ten, and deduct the value of your investment holdings. So if a family has a combined income of \$100,000 and has \$200,000 in investments, the minimum amount of combined life insurance that the family should have is \$800,000 − \$200,000 = \$600,000. Prorate that sum between the spouses based upon their incomes. So if the wife makes \$60,000 and the husband makes \$40,000, the family would carry \$360,000 in life insurance on the wife (\$600,000 × 60 percent) and \$240,000 on the husband (\$600,000 × 40 percent). Any life insurance that the employer provides, of course, applies toward this total, but do not confuse "accidental death" insurance that your employer may provide with "life insurance." Accidental death insurance does not cover death from illness and should not count at all toward your insurance totals.

You need to shop around for insurance and tell the insurance companies that you are doing so. The days when you had the "family agent" who just gave you a quote that you accepted are over. It is the same situation with lawyers, health plans, and car dealers. Competition gets the lowest price. Test the market thoroughly on-line, but do not catch "Net fever." Just because it is on the Internet does not mean that it is cheap or reliable. Often you can get a lower price with in-person visits or phone calls to insurance companies. And with Internet purchasing, you still run the risk of finding yourself the victim of a scam. Almost all insurance agents have ways that they can lower the cost to you without reducing benefits, and often the only way to do it is through direct contact with the agent.

You must address the important issue of term insurance versus whole-life insurance. Term insurance pays a benefit if you die during the term specified in the insurance policy. Whole-life insurance (and closely related products, like universal life insurance) not only pays your estate a benefit if you die but also builds up a "cash value" that you can get while you are alive, after a specified time period. With whole-life policies, the insurance company will apply some of your premiums toward the death benefit and will invest some of your premiums in mutual funds to accumulate the cash value. Insurance agents sometimes describe whole policies as "retirement funds" or "savings plans." It is true that you can use the cash value as a savings vehicle for your retirement, and you can get some advantages from whole-life insurance trusts when it comes time to apply for financial aid for your children's education (or pay estate taxes). But keep in mind that whole-life policies have more fees and greater restrictions on your access to the cash than you would have in a regular savings account. Usually, for example, you must pay a heavy penalty if you stop paying premiums and try to withdraw your money during the first three, four, or five years of the policy.

While insurance companies are making whole-life products more attractive than they used to be, crashproofers generally do not need them and instead stick with term insurance. The reasons are quite basic. First, whole-life policies are expensive. You can get a lot more insurance coverage, especially when you are young, if you buy low-cost term insurance with funds from your checking account. Since the purpose of crashproofing is to avoid catastrophe, your insurance goal should be to have a lot of coverage rather than build up a little extra cash. Second, as was discussed in Part Two, you do not need an insurance company or anyone else to invest your money for you. When you buy whole-life policies, you pay management fees, restrict your access to your own money, and subject yourself to penalties and forfeitures if you attempt to cash in early. With those concerns in mind, the only people who might find that the benefits of whole-life outweigh the costs are people who are not comfortable handling their own finances and unable to manage their own finances for long periods of time—such as military personnel or contractor personnel who are frequently sent on long overseas jobs. In such cases, the convenience of a whole-life policy—having one payroll deduction or direct deposit per month to cover both your insurance and investment needs—might be attractive even to a crashproofer. If you go that route, the money for the premium would come from your investment clearinghouse account.

Health Insurance

No one disputes that the American health insurance system is a mess, and there are a variety of competing plans to fix it. In the meantime, you need to know where it can fail for you. Until recently, the biggest problem was lack of coverage for "preexisting" conditions. People would work at a company and develop an illness; then they would change jobs and find that the health insurer at the new company would not cover expenses associated with the preexisting illness. Recent laws have expanded the "portability" of health insurance and, for the most part, closed the preexisting condition loophole.

However, it is not completely closed. If you are among the 35 percent of Americans who purchase health insurance individually (rather than through a company), you need to be sure that your current health insurer is solvent or you could find yourself caught in the preexisting condition mess even now. Many states have not adopted the cash reserve requirements for health maintenance organizations (HMOs) recommended by the National Association of Insurance Commissioners, although it looks like state legislatures plan to remedy this situation to some extent during the coming years. Nevertheless, from the beginning of 1999 through August of 2000, twenty-nine health insurers collapsed, eleven dissolved voluntarily, and thirty merged into other companies. In 1998, HMOs abandoned 407,000 people. By 2000, the figure was over 900,000. Many of these people found themselves without health insurance because, although other insurers had to offer them coverage, these insurers often quoted very high rates (particularly for people with preexisting conditions), effectively freezing them out of health insurance. Just because you have legal protection, therefore, does not mean that you get coverage.

There are two other major risks associated with health insurance. First, most insurance companies place a lifetime benefit limitation and/or an "incident" limitation on health insurance coverage. The company can stop paying if your total claims exceed a specified sum during your life or as the result of a particular accident or illness. For example, a health insurance policy might say that it will not cover costs over $500,000 for a particular incident or $1 million during your whole life. If you have one serious illness or a lot of small ones, you may receive notice that you have exceeded your limit and the company will stop paying for your health care costs. A crashproofer should consider taking a high deductible on his or her principal health insurance policy and using the premium savings to purchase supplemental insurance that will cover the costs over the basic policy limitations.

Second, health insurance covers only the cost of health care, not lost income due to the long-term disability that often results from a serious accident or illness. The cost of a health problem can be much greater than just medical expenses. When you are incapacitated due to serious illness, you may find yourself unable to work, and you may lose your income. Most Americans have health and life insurance, but they have failed to prepare adequately for the cost of disability. Indeed, while 75 percent of Americans have some sort of life insurance and an even greater percentage have health insurance, only 40 percent have disability insurance. Alarmingly, however, according to the American Society of Actuaries, the odds of a thirty-five-year-old man dying before age sixty-five are 20 percent, while the odds of that same man missing ninety days or more of work due to illness or injury are 25 percent. Americans are not prepared for the greatest health-related economic risk they may face—long-term disability.

Every crashproofer needs a disability insurance policy. Some employers provide such insurance, but often they provide only the minimum policy. If that is the case for you, your employer will cover only a certain percentage of your salary (often 60 percent with a $5,000 per month cap), and you will receive a further reduced benefit once you can still work at any kind of a job. Moreover, the Employee Retirement Income Security Act (ERISA) does not protect your health and disability benefits the way it protects pensions, so your employer can discontinue offering these benefits at any time before you have filed a claim.

Consequently, if your employer provides disability coverage, study the policy carefully. If you do not have coverage for 100 percent of your lost income, you can purchase at a reasonable price supplemental disability insurance from many reputable insurance companies, although the number of companies offering disability insurance is declining. Moreover, if your employer's policy allows a reduction in benefits once you can work at any kind of a job, you should purchase supplemental insurance that contains "same profession" coverage. Then you will receive a full benefit if you cannot work in the same profession that you had before your accident or illness. If, for example, you are an umpire and you lose your sight in an accident, you will not be denied disability benefits just because you could work as a telemarketer.

Automobiles and Umbrellas

As the opening example to this chapter illustrated, when it comes to automobiles and auto insurance, many Americans are exposing themselves to their greatest personal crash risk. By keeping your basic auto insurance premiums low, you can purchase the extra insurance that you need. First, as with other insurance, you need to take the highest deductible possible. Most people do not even report fender-benders to their insurance companies for fear of having their rates raised. If you are not going to report a $400 problem, why do you have a $100 deductible? Change to a $500 deductible and take advantage of the lower premiums.

Self-Insurance on the Road

The best way to keep premiums low, however, is to drive safely. This section will cover four of the leading causes of motor vehicle liability. As you know, the leading cause of driving-related death is alcohol. Do not drive if you have *any* alcohol in your system—even if you believe your alcohol level is below the legal limit. There remains a widespread belief among Americans that as long as you are below the legal limit for intoxication, you can drive without risk. It is true the state cannot prosecute you for drunk driving if your blood alcohol levels are below the typical 0.08 percent limit. However, even with lower blood alcohol levels, you still have motor skills impairment, and you can find yourself the defendant in a civil lawsuit that could wipe you out financially. If you are in an accident, you want to be able to demonstrate that you had no alcohol in your system so that the issue of intoxication is completely out of the picture.

Another leading cause of roadway liability is falling asleep at the wheel. You should never push yourself too hard when you drive long distances. If you start to feel your eyes flutter, you need to pull off the road and get some sleep. Do not succumb to the temptation to push just a little bit longer. A third very common cause of highway accidents is distraction. I have watched people read the paper, put on makeup, and fix their hair while driving. Any one of these is a life-threatening practice. Indeed, the advent of cellular phones has greatly increased the awareness of state and local officials of the risks of distracted driver syndrome. Many municipalities have passed or are considering laws that preclude the use of handheld cellular phones by drivers in automobiles or other vehicles, and these laws will continue to proliferate. Fortunately, automakers now provide headsets and special microphones that obviate the need for holding the phone. Voice-activated dialing is available as well. However, you should not lose sight of the fact that any phone conversation while you are driving will distract you to some extent—even if you have a "hands free" system. If you are going to talk on the phone while in the car, you should, at a minimum, dial numbers only when you are stationary and, preferably, conclude the call before you start driving.

In recent years, there has been a marked increase in reported incidents of "road rage," the fourth leading cause of roadway liability. It is amazing how people who are otherwise courteous and law-abiding go berzerk when they feel someone else has done them an injustice on the road. As with any emotional outburst in the context of performing precise tasks, you run a higher risk of making a serious mistake when you are red-faced and spewing out profanities. Anger release at 60 miles per hour is a bad idea. Indeed, several seemingly decent people have actually committed murders as a result of road rage, and many more have simply lost their sense of care and inadvertently caused the injury or death of other drivers due to an emotional outburst on the road. I remember being quite concerned a couple of years ago when I unknowingly cut off a car being driven by a young lady on a St. Louis–area highway. She swerved all around my car in anger for several minutes, followed me off the highway and into a parking lot, and then exited her car to follow me into a restaurant where I was meeting my uncle for dinner. Finally, as she started moving toward my table, I had to pull out my cell phone and, while looking directly at her, I started dialing as if I were calling the police. She gave me the finger and left. It was a little spooky. A crashproofer must consider the avoidance of roadway emotion as much a part of personal conduct as the avoidance of professional emotion is a part of the workplace conduct (as was discussed in Part One).

The Roadway Umbrella

As a matter of law you must carry automobile insurance that covers damage that you cause to another vehicle (collision insurance) and injury or loss of life that results from a car accident (liability insurance). Most policies and some credit cards will cover any damage or injury that you cause while driving in a rental car, as well. Your own policy will usually cover you if someone else causes an accident while driving your car or if an illegally uninsured driver causes an accident that harms you or your car. Most policies will cover you for damage up to the policy limit even if you are driving while intoxicated, but the company will cancel coverage after just one such incident.

The real risk to crashproofers is that the insurance company normally limits its liability to $200,000 or $300,000. If you accidentally kill a young adult with a lot of potential, as occurred in the case described at the beginning of this chapter, the deceased person's estate will sue you for a lot more than $300,000. The normal measure of damages for negligence in such a case includes the present value of the total income that the deceased person would likely have made during his or her career. If the person had a promising career that would likely have continued thirty years into the future, you could be looking at a jury verdict of $3 million, with insurance covering only one-tenth of that sum.

Indeed, you may find yourself in an even worse situation if you badly injure someone. A badly injured person is an ambulance-chasing attorney's dream, because not only does the defendant have to pay for lost income but he or she has to pay for huge medical bills (and the attorney takes at least a third of the total). I have heard a couple of these nasty lawyers say they would rather have a client who is on a respirator than in a hearse. In such circumstances, verdicts of $5 million and up are not uncommon.

Most insurance companies will not provide automobile liability coverage in excess of $300,000. The only solution is an *umbrella policy*—a relatively inexpensive but highly useful tool to any crashproof-minded person who is building up substantial assets. Umbrella policies cover you for accidents that you may cause to anyone anywhere for any reason. They are generally supplemental in nature; for example, in a car accident situation, the umbrella policy would cover any liability over the $300,000 that the automobile insurance would cover. You can routinely get coverage for up to $3 million, and by filling out a little more paperwork, you can probably get coverage up to $10 million.

The normal exclusions in an umbrella policy include damages caused from such actions as flying an airplane, parachuting or other particularly dangerous activities, and professional malpractice (for which you need a separate malpractice insurance policy). Most policies also exclude damages that you cause by certain acts of intentional misconduct, such as murder or robbery, although one celebrity had a policy that even covered the monetary damages resulting from his commission of intentional criminal acts. So if you are willing to pay a high enough premium, you can probably insure yourself against anything with a special umbrella policy. However, crashproofers generally need not go further than the basic umbrella policy.

Careful conduct with a strong backstop of insurance coverage can prevent you from losing everything you have worked so hard to build in your professional and financial life. If you keep in mind that your own body is the most important physical structure you have, you will naturally conduct yourself in a more self-respectful and careful manner. And if you keep in mind that insurance is perhaps the most important legal structure you have working for you, then you will—unlike most Americans—take the time to evaluate carefully your options and obtain the maximum coverage at a minimum price. Once you have put this process into place, you have moved yet another step closer to crashproofing your life.

8

Working with Your Spouse to Implement Your Crashproofing Plan

Know Your Spouse Financially As Well As You Know Your Spouse in Other Ways

Part One discussed how other people on the job present a crash risk to your professional life—from backstabbing coworkers to arbitrary bosses to executives who plan mergers without a second thought to how many careers they might hurt. Similarly, Part Two covered how other people present a serious crash risk to your finances—from real estate flippers to boiler room brokers to well-healed con artists. It should come as no surprise that you could find your efforts to crashproof your personal life derailed by other people as well.

The risk that others will derail your personal crashproofing plan is even higher than the risk that others will derail your professional and financial activities. The people who are most likely to impact your personal life adversely are those whom you trust the most—your spouse, your parents, your kids, and, in some cases, your friends. This chapter and the next will discuss how to avoid the personal liability others can thrust upon you.

This chapter focuses on the person with whom you spend the most time and when you know the best: your spouse. When spouses work together effectively to build personal financial structures, a synergy develops that allows them to achieve a stronger and more crashproof life together than either could have achieved individually. On the other hand, when spouses work against each other financially, the adverse economic effects can snowball rapidly into a crash of devastating proportions. To encourage the former scenario and discourage the latter one, we need to cover three important marital topics: (1) knowing fully the financial condition of your spouse and his or her family; (2) handling the legal aspects of the marital union and, if necessary, its dissolution, in a professional and businesslike manner; and (3) handling the legal aspects of the marital estate in a manner that best preserves family wealth from the forces of dissipation, including taxation.

The Money Talk

Married people spend a lot of money trying to improve their relationships. They buy books about Mars and Venus, they consult marriage counselors, and they plan romantic getaways—all in an effort to strengthen the bond between them or, in some cases, to repair bonds they have damaged. However, many spouses who spend a lot of time and money on improving romance and togetherness do little, if anything, to improve their financial relationship. "Money doesn't matter," they say. "All you need is love," right?

Wrong. Money does matter. Financial problems are one of the greatest threats to a healthy marriage, yet many married couples do not take even the most basic precautions to make sure they work well together financially. Brides and grooms spend more time picking out their wedding reception centerpieces and rock band than they do planning their financial futures together. Middle-aged couples devote countless hours to picking out countertops for their newly remodeled kitchens, but they do not spend any time discussing how their personal financial habits may be jeopardizing their retirement plans.

It is common for young couples to remain completely ignorant of each other's financial background, goals, and practices, and for long-married spouses to remain ignorant for years of the other spouse's financial problems, such as hidden debt and the precarious financial condition of members of their family who eventually come to them for financial assistance.

Prospective spouses need to have a serious discussion (or two or three) about money. If you are newly married and have not had that discussion or even if you have been married a while and have failed to discuss family finances in an organized manner, you should do it immediately. Indeed, if you have been married twenty-five years and are fighting over money, you may well benefit by "starting over" financially with a money talk. The agenda should cover three topics: your current financial situation, your anticipated financial situation, and your financial priorities. Each topic will be treated here as if it were a discussion among prospective spouses, but the same rules apply even if you have been married for quite some time and have not yet had the appropriate money discussion.

Your Spouse's Current Financial Condition

It is important that you know your prospective spouse's current financial condition because if he or she has a financial problem, it will soon become *your* problem. If your spouse-to-be has major credit-card debt or extensive student loans, you will have to incorporate a means to resolve these problems into your financial plan. Indeed, it is quite common for one spouse to "hide" debts from the other until the bill collectors start calling, which inevitably leads to mutual distrust and the deterioration of the marital relationship. Without knowing each other's debts, you cannot work as partners to develop intelligent financial structures like the ones examined earlier in this book. So the first part of the money discussion must consist of a full and open disclosure of all debts, followed by a plan to reduce them with slush-fund money or any other carefully considered financial mechanism—such as a home equity loan—that suits your particular circumstances.

Hidden debt is not the only issue you may face. It is also a problem if your spouse hides *assets*. In one situation, a marriage suffered terribly when one spouse did not learn of the other spouse's wealth until the couple filed their first joint tax return, at which time they owed a lot of money to the IRS due to capital gains incurred by the wealthy spouse. This did not go over well with the spouse who had been kept in the dark. In another situation, a wife greatly offended her husband several months into the marriage when she informed him that they would have to file separate tax returns because her family did not want him to have any sort of claim on the interest earned by her family money. This caused a great deal of marital strain that lasted several years. In yet another case, five years into a marriage, a wife with greater wealth than her husband set up (at the direction of her parents) a trust that bypassed the husband in the event of the wife's death. Spouses frequently authorize the creation of such trust documents without the other spouse knowing about it, and sometimes these trusts violate state laws that establish presumed marital shares in an estate. Some of these asset-protection maneuvers are of questionable legal value if effectuated without the informed consent of both spouses and serve only to undermine the marriage. Each spouse needs to know about the other's assets, and the two of you must work together to determine how and in what circumstances you will use these assets.

The second part of the money discussion, therefore, must involve the disclosure of assets—including securities, real estate, trust income, jewelry, and collectibles. If one spouse insists the estate be set up so that certain assets remain in the family, the other spouse should try to work out a mutually acceptable arrangement through a prenuptial agreement or trust. As will be discussed later, there are ways to protect the interests of both spouses in such a situation and thereby preserve the mutual respect that forms the basis of a good marriage. The surest way to cause a problem concerning assets is to handle them secretly or spring a legal arrangement on the other spouse without warning.

The final part of the disclosure process involves parents. It may sound like a difficult matter to discuss, but your spouse needs some warning if one or both of your parents is going to run out of money and depend upon you for support. On the other hand, if one or both sets of parents have a lot of money, each spouse should know about it, and you should come to an agreement on how you will dispose of these financial infusions once they occur. Parental financial situations will be discussed later in the book; for now, suffice it to say the money talk needs to cover each spouse's parental financial situation.

Your Financial Plans and Needs

During the money talk, the two of you must also discuss your future financial plans. If you are a young, highly paid Wall Street investment banker but plan to quit your job in two years to travel the country in a trailer, pursuing your dream to become a world-famous painter, your spouse better know about these plans! If you plan to quit your job to raise the kids, you should discuss this matter with your spouse as well, as this decision may have substantial effects—both positive and negative—on your lifestyle. It is essential that you and your prospective spouse discuss not only your current financial condition but also your future financial plans at the earliest possible time and that you keep the lines of communication open as your marriage progresses and your plans change.

Financial Priorities

The last subject for the money talk is financial priorities. You have to decide together how you want to spend and invest your money. First, of course, the two of you should agree upon a financial structure like the pyramid structure discussed in Part Two. As was said earlier, you do not have to follow the pyramid structure exactly as it was laid out in Part Two; rather, it is an example of the type of structure you must implement. You should, if necessary, tailor your plan to fit your own circumstances. The key to crashproofing is to establish a clear structure that will allow you to limit your spending and increase your savings— and *both of you* must make a commitment to follow it. If one of you implements it and the other does not, you really have no financial structure at all.

Within the agreed-upon financial structure, the two of you must decide what your joint priorities will be: how big you want your house to be, what kind of cars you want, what kind of vacations you want to take, what kind of clothes and jewelry you want, and how much you want to allocate for various hobbies and other leisure activities you enjoy. You will have to make trade-offs. Do you want more house and less car? Do you want to buy cheap clothes and expensive antiques? It is all a matter of balancing your priorities within the financial structure you implement.

In making these decisions, you do not have to come up with hard-and-fast rules, but you do need to understand where your spouse stands with respect to each of these areas. Once you have established your relative financial priorities, you will undoubtedly have to do some compromising to allow each of you to achieve as many personal objectives as possible, while recognizing you will not get everything you want. Then, even after you have come to a basic agreement on your financial priorities, you should sit down once or twice each year to reevaluate those priorities. The universe is dynamic and clever, so your plans need to be flexible in order to work over the long term. You can achieve this flexibility with a periodic reevaluation of your financial priorities.

The Legal Aspects of the Marital Union and Its Dissolution

To most of us, marriage most significantly represents a spiritual and physical union. But it also represents a legal and financial union. As soon as you get married, a whole new set of tax and property laws applies to you. In several states, you have "community property": each spouse is deemed to own one-half of all income earned during the marriage, no matter who actually earned it. Property received prior to the marriage or by inheritance or gift remains the property of the individual spouse who received it. Property acquired during the marriage is owned one-half by each spouse. Upon the death of one spouse, only the half belonging to the deceased is included in his or her estate for estate tax purposes, but both halves receive a stepped-up basis for income tax purposes. In some community-property states, however, creditors of either spouse may attach all community property to satisfy a debt.

All states also have a common law that defines (or allows the spouses to define) the type of ownership spouses have in property. These forms of ownership include joint ownership, tenancy in common, and tenancy by the entirety. All of these represent slight variations on the same theme: you and your spouse share the financial structure you build for yourselves during your marriage (with preexisting assets, gifts, and inheritances excluded).

The differences among the types of property ownership relate to complex issues of liability, inheritance, and taxation, which your estate planning attorney can explain to you in detail. But here is a summary. If, for example, you want joint ownership with a right of survivorship, you must put both names on the title to the jointly held property. Then, upon the death of one spouse, the other gets full title to the property with a new tax basis in the property equal to the sum of one-half of the original tax basis and one-half of the market value at the time of the spouse's death. The surviving spouse does not go through probate court to acquire a jointly held asset; rather, the asset passes to the survivor automatically. So, for example, Steve and Edie jointly own 100 shares of stock for which they paid ten dollars per share, and now it is worth twenty dollars per share. Steve dies. Edie immediately gets full title to all 100 shares, with a "blended tax basis" of fifteen dollars per share. Creditors of one spouse may get that spouse's 50 percent share of a jointly held asset to satisfy a debt.

If you are "tenants in common" you each own a stated, undivided percentage of the asset. For example, spouses could each own 50 percent of the family farm as tenants in common. Again, creditors of one spouse can get the 50 percent owned by the debtor spouse. If one spouse dies, the person named in his or her will as the heir to the common tenancy property gets the 50 percent interest of the deceased spouse with the tax basis stepped up for that 50 percent interest. The transferring of such an interest upon death *does* require probate, however. Unlike joint tenants, tenants in common may own unequal fractional shares of property, such as 60 percent for one tenant and 40 percent for another.

Finally, with a tenancy by the entirety—generally available only to married couples in noncommunity-property states—you each own an equal interest in *all* the property, which automatically passes to the surviving spouse upon the death of the other. Both signatures are required to dispose of the property, and creditors of only one spouse cannot get any portion of the asset. Surviving spouses also get the one-half step up in the tax basis described previously.

While these nuances can be important in some circumstances, any one of these systems usually leads to a just result for a surviving spouse. However, there remains one problem with this legal structure. The system, which provides for the orderly disposition of property upon the death of one spouse, is designed for a successful marriage, not an unsuccessful one. If your marriage does not last, this system of ownership may well present a financial crash risk to you.

When there is a divorce, someone has to divide up the property, and it often gets very ugly. At the outset, you should realize that property division in a divorce is always a no-win financial proposition. When the two of you live together, you need only one home and one set of personal property—from furniture to silverware. When you split up, each of you still needs all of the property, but you must divide it up. Your individual expenses will thus, by definition, increase at a time when your combined income remains the same.

Worse still, when spouses split up, they tend to use property as a symbol of their need for emotional victory over the other spouse. Consequently, the couple will fight viciously for real property, furniture, a vehicle, or jewelry—often spending more in legal fees than the items in dispute are worth. For example, when I was a very young lawyer, I worked on a divorce case in which each spouse spent more than $5,000 in legal fees fighting for an old tractor that was valued at $1,200. This is financially very counterproductive. Many spouses (and their broken families) experience financial disaster concurrent with the emotional turmoil of divorce.

There are only two ways to minimize (and no way to eliminate) the negative financial repercussions of divorce: prenuptial agreements and postnuptial cooperation.

Prenuptial Agreements

Prenuptial agreements are premarital contracts that state how spouses will divide assets in the event of divorce. They are highly controversial because they change by contract the normal division of assets provided for under state law.

The controversy arises because a marriage is supposed to be a legal union until death, with both partners as equals. In effect, the prenuptial agreement says that the marriage may not last until death and that it is not an equal partnership. Acknowledging either of these facts can create marital risk, so insisting on a prenuptial agreement may actually *contribute* to your problems rather than solve them. On the other hand, with over 40 percent of marriages ending in divorce, you may want to give yourself some financial protection should the worst occur. The critical question for crashproofers is, when are the risks great enough that you should insist on a prenuptial agreement despite the problems inherent in such an agreement?

The answer is *not very often*. Prenuptial agreements are only appropriate if there are dramatic differences between where you and your prospective spouse are in life. If you both have similar socioeconomic backgrounds and are close in age (say, within ten years), you almost certainly do not need a prenuptial agreement. The vast majority of the marriages in this country fall into this category. If, on the other hand, one spouse is much older and wealthier than the other or there are children by previous marriages, there may be legitimate reasons for such an agreement. First, from what I have seen, it is not uncommon for an older, wealthier spouse to have underlying suspicions about the motivation of the younger spouse for marrying him or her. If the younger spouse willingly agrees to a prenuptial agreement, it can actually strengthen their relationship. Second, even if the older spouse fully trusts the motivation of the younger one, the older spouse may have grown children from a previous marriage who could become very resentful of the younger spouse, perceiving the younger spouse as a gold digger. Again, a prenuptial agreement can promote family harmony in that kind of a situation.

Equally important, even a validly conceived prenuptial agreement promotes nothing but problems and discord if it is not negotiated and executed properly. First, both parties must have independent legal representation in the negotiation of the agreement. Courts will often declare prenuptial agreements invalid if one side forces such an agreement on a spouse who is unrepresented, especially if the spouse who gave up marital rights takes the position in divorce proceedings that he or she did not fully understand the terms of the agreement or what rights he or she gave up. Second, the party with the greater assets must provide a fair arrangement for the spouse who is giving up marital rights. The prenuptial agreement may well strengthen the marriage if the wealthier party provides a specific guarantee of payment that would allow the less wealthy spouse to live comfortably in the event of a divorce. In sum, consider a prenuptial agreement only if you and your prospective spouse have wide disparities in age or income, make sure each side is fairly represented by counsel, and negotiate an agreement that looks out for the interests of both parties. This will turn the process into a positive development for everyone concerned.

Postnuptial Cooperation

Why would a person spend $5,000 in legal fees to acquire a $1,200 tractor? In a similar vein, why would a man contest an increase in child-support payments, fail to show up at the court hearing on the issue, and then appeal an adverse result? Or why would a person risk prosecution by transferring assets to secret accounts prior to a divorce proceeding? All of these things have happened.

The answer is simple: to destroy the economic security of an ex-spouse. Often, divorcing spouses engage in what I call *financial cannibalism*. They have grown so bitter about their failed marriage that they play a game of attrition—trying to drain the resources of the other. If you are in the unfortunate process of dissolving your marriage, you must consider a couple of factors. Because of the resulting duplication of living expenses, you will suffer financially even if the two of you cooperate fully in the divorce proceedings. Consequently, any vindictive activity that causes you to waste money on legal fees and court battles only contributes to an already bad financial situation. In such a situation, no one "wins"—not you, not your ex-spouse. Also, the laws are fairly well-established in stating what you get and what your spouse gets as a result of the divorce, so no amount of legal wrangling in the world should make too much difference in terms of who gets what. Child-support payments, for example, are set by statute; real estate ownership is governed in large part by state law.

It is therefore in everyone's interest to cooperate during the divorce process. If there are serious nonfinancial issues such as child custody, you must try to separate those issues from the other, purely financial aspects of the divorce. Otherwise you both could be asking for a financial crash. If you are fighting over the kids, avoid face-to-face contact to the extent possible by speaking through your lawyers; ask your lawyer what he or she thinks is reasonable in terms of a financial settlement, and do not fight for too much more than that. The quicker you put this situation behind you, the better your chances are of recovering and getting your crashproofing program back on track. You simply cannot consider financial cannibalism to be one of your options.

The Marital Estate

Everyone should have an estate plan, including single people. A properly planned estate allows for the orderly disposition of assets upon your death or the proper administration of your assets if you are incapacitated. However, when it comes to crashproofing, the time that you must have an estate plan is when you get married. Indeed, if you are married and do not have a will, a durable power of attorney, and in some cases, appropriate trusts, you are setting your spouse and other loved ones up for a potentially major crash at a time when you will not be there to help them. Some of the most unfortunate situations I have ever witnessed as a lawyer involved spouses, ex-spouses, siblings, children, and stepchildren fighting like vultures over the assets of a deceased person who had failed to provide an adequate estate plan. In other cases, families have been torn apart when a loved one became permanently incapacitated without leaving instructions on when the family should end life-supporting medical care. In still other cases, taxes ate up so much of an estate that heirs did not receive even close to the financial cushion they had counted on for their retirement. You must take steps to avoid these potentially tragic situations. Therefore, this section will discuss the essential elements of an estate plan: wills, living wills and durable powers of attorney, and trusts and other liability-shielding legal structures.

Entire multivolume treatises have been written on estate planning and tax avoidance, so it is always worth the money to engage the services of a reputable estate-planning attorney to assist you with your estate planning. Your attorney will be able to discuss with you a variety of planning options, including some that are not discussed here. To the extent that the attorney's advice relates to taxation issues, you can usually take a tax deduction for some of the fees you pay the attorney, which increases the affordability of your estate-planning activity.

That said, you and your spouse should already have an understanding of the essential elements of an estate plan before you go into discussions with your estate-planning professional. Such an understanding will prevent you from feeling as though you are in over your head when you consult a professional. Learning the basics will also save you some money because your estate-planning professional will not have to spend a lot of your time and money by starting from ground zero.

Where There's a Will

The most basic element of your estate plan is your will—a legal document that states how to divide your assets upon your death. Seventy percent of Americans die without a will. I know many lawyers who do not have one. People do not have wills because they do not want to face the fact they are going to die someday, because they believe they will have some advance warning before they die, because they feel they do not have enough assets to warrant a will, or because they assume their spouse or kids will get everything anyway.

These are lame, head-in-the-sand excuses. Everyone needs a will. If you die without one (which is called dying "intestate"), your estate, no matter how large or small, will get tied up in your local probate court for a lot longer than it would if you had executed a valid will. Your heirs will then have to spend extra money to resolve your affairs, and they may have to wait a long time to get money or other assets from your estate that they may need right away. While jointly held assets, life insurance, and retirement-plan funds will pass to your spouse automatically, the disposition of other assets will be decided by the laws of the state where you live, and that state's laws may not reflect your wishes. Eventually, the judge will appoint an administrator to handle your affairs and make any distribution of assets, but the process can be very frustrating.

Worse still, the court may appoint an administrator whom you did not like or trust when you were alive. While state law will determine the ultimate disposition of your assets that pass through probate, the court-appointed administrator can have enough input into the process to hurt the people you cared the most about during your life. Indeed, even a well-intentioned administrator cannot make up for the lack of a will. Significantly, without provisions for minor children, the children's shares would be held in a court-administered custodianship and, in most cases, would go right to the child at age eighteen. In addition, the probate judge would be forced to decide who should serve as guardian for your minor children without your input.

Proper estate planning provides an important structure to ensure that those whom you love, particularly your surviving spouse and children, will benefit from what you built during your lifetime. Indeed, if there is one fact we have stressed thus far it is that crashproofers value structure. There is no time when structure is more important than at the time of a death. Upon death, the deceased person is not there to fix things that go wrong, and the emotions of the survivors are high. Such emotion tends to be antistructural. A validly executed will, therefore, becomes the cornerstone of the legal structure that prevents a sad situation from spinning out of control. Millions of people have died without wills, resulting in serious financial problems and legal battles among their distraught survivors. You need to put together a legally valid, witnessed, and signed will that clearly delineates whom you want to be your executor (the name given to an administrator appointed in a will). Then you need to instruct that executor, within the bounds of the law and with great specificity, who gets what.

When there are changes in your life—divorce, birth of a child, or death of family members—you need to update your will with a formally executed document called a "codicil." Indeed, even some very conscientious people who took the time to execute wills have caused great financial and emotional heartache for their loved ones when they failed to update their wills to reflect new life situations.

Living Will and Durable Power of Attorney

A living will is a legal document in which you state that health-care providers may (or may not) take heroic measures to save your life in the event that you become incapacitated with no chance of recovery. A related document, a durable power of attorney for health care, designates a person to make health-care decisions for you in the event of your incapacity. The durable power of attorney for health-care decisions is legally effective even when you are expected to recover from your illness, while the living will applies only to situations where you are not expected to recover. The principal benefit, however, of both living wills and durable powers of attorney for health care is that they avoid the emotional turmoil and destruction of family relationships that can occur if there is a split within the family as to whether to keep you on life support. The living will states your desires during terminal illness, and the durable power of attorney for health care gives someone the authority to pull the plug, if that is what you want them to do.

I cannot tell you how important it is to have these documents in place. Recently, in a Midwestern city, the wife and the mother of a young man on life support battled it out in court on the issue of whether to stop the life-support machinery that was keeping the man alive. After weeks and weeks of legal wrangling, fanned by the press, the wife, who wanted the life support stopped, won the court battle and had the hospital stop the life support. However, the fight ruined the wife's relationship with her in-laws; the parents of the deceased man actually called his wife a murderer in public. It was a terrible tragedy, and similar tragedies have played out many times throughout the country over the past several years. You can do your best to avoid such a situation by executing a living will and durable power of attorney for health care.

Moreover, if you execute a living will that states no one may take heroic measures to save your life, you may also be helping your family to avoid a financial crash. Health insurance does not cover every form of treatment that may be necessary to keep you alive, and you may exceed a benefit limitation if you are on life support for an extended period of time. If your spiritual beliefs require that doctors make all efforts to keep you alive, so be it. If not, however, you may prevent a financial crash for your loved ones by executing a living will stating that no one should take heroic steps to save you when there is no hope of recovery. You should take comfort in knowing that living wills have provisions in them that require the medical community to be sure you will not recover before allowing anyone to pull the plug.

You can and should also execute a separate durable power of attorney that is not confined to health-care decisions. This document allows someone, whom you designate, to act on your behalf for your benefit at any time with respect to any matter. Normally, the person whom you designate would only use this power to conduct your affairs when you are incapacitated, although many people fail to realize that a durable power of attorney is valid even when you are in fine health. If you do not want your designee to be able to act for you when you are healthy, you have the option of executing a "springing" durable power of attorney that becomes effective only when you are incapacitated. You are deemed incapacitated when your physician certifies in writing that you are unable to handle your affairs on your own. You should note that your physician may deem you temporarily incapacitated even in situations where he or she expects you to recover fully. In such a case, the person you designate will handle your affairs until you have recovered enough to inform that person that you can now resume control.

It is essential to your crashproofing activities that someone be designated to carry on your business when you cannot do so, because if you do nothing, the disorderly direction of the universe will take over for you. When you execute a durable power of attorney, you must designate someone whom you know well and trust completely to act for you. That person should also be very familiar with business and real estate transactions because he or she will have the power to buy and sell property, invest assets, deal with financial and brokerage institutions, borrow money, execute legal documents, handle the affairs of your minor children, bring or defend lawsuits, exercise stock voting rights, file tax returns, arrange health care, obtain insurance coverage, make gifts, and transfer assets to trusts. With a durable power of attorney in place and the right person designated to handle your affairs, the financial structures you have built will remain intact no matter what happens to you.

I also recommend that you authorize your spouse, assuming he or she is financially literate, to make both the health-care and financial decisions for you when you are incapacitated. You two agreed to remain married until death do you part, and that commitment means your spouse should make the important decisions at times when death is a real possibility.

Revocable Living Trust

The revocable living trust is a legal device that allows you to control your assets during your lifetime and then, upon your death, to leave them to your designated beneficiaries or keep them in trust for anyone whom you choose, subject to state law. A living trust accomplishes many of the same objectives that a will does, but the trust has one great advantage over a will: you can have the trustee dispose of your living trust assets without going through the costly, time-consuming probate process. If you have a complicated estate, a living trust may save your heirs a lot of time and money. Remember, however, that if you want assets to go into the trust, you must be sure you put the title to those assets in the name of the trust—otherwise you have wasted your time and money setting it up.

You should note that many slick lawyers have vastly oversold the advantages of living trusts in recent years by suggesting that these trusts help you avoid estate taxes. This is not true. Revocable living trusts provide no tax benefits. Indeed, if you have a simple estate and already have a valid will, spending the money to purchase a living trust might not be cost-effective. Assets that you held jointly with your spouse (like your home) transfer by operation of law directly to your surviving spouse without probate, regardless of whether you have a trust. Similarly, if your insurance policy names your spouse as beneficiary, the proceeds from that policy will go directly to your spouse without probate. Consequently, if most of your assets are jointly held and you still decide to get a living trust, you may spend several hundred or even a few thousand dollars for a document that provides you with only marginal legal benefits.

Other Trusts and Corporations

As has been discussed, revocable trusts do not usually provide tax benefits. If, on the other hand, you want to avoid (or defer) tax liability, you can set up a variety of other trusts that are *irrevocable*, meaning once you set them up, you cannot, under most circumstances, change them. In short, the rule is that if you want to reduce your tax bill, *you must give up some degree of control and ownership of your assets.* There are spousal trusts, insurance trusts, spendthrift trusts, and a variety of other instruments where you (known as the settlor) turn your assets over to someone else (known as a trustee) for the benefit of a third party (known as the beneficiary), and you receive in return a tax benefit for having given up some degree of ownership and control of your assets. Which types of trusts you may wish to consider will depend entirely upon your individual situation—the type of assets you have, their value, and what you want to do with them. So if you are considering an irrevocable trust, get the assistance of an estate-planning professional.

If the estate tax is eliminated, as many predict it will be, some of the estate tax reasons for creating such trusts will evaporate. Indeed, the tax relief legislation passed by Congress and signed by the president in 2001 steadily increases the sum that is exempt from estate taxes—from $675,000 in 2001 to $3.5 million in 2009 (after which it is anybody's guess as to what will happen). The increased exemption will obviate the need for irrevocable trusts for many people in the coming years.

Even so, you may still use charitable trusts to avoid *income* tax, and if you do it right, you do not have to lose all control over the property that you place in trust. For example, if you donate money or valuable items such as artwork, stamps, or coins to your own charitable trust, you may still be able to use and enjoy the items to some extent while taking an income-tax deduction for their value. A friend of mine formed an educational trust that makes his coin collection available to schools and other groups. He gets a large income-tax deduction every time he donates coins to the trust. The trustee allows him to manage the showing of the coins, so he still gets to enjoy them. The catch, however, is that he no longer owns them, so he cannot sell them for his own benefit and his heirs will not get them when he dies.

Some rather sly people also set up trusts in an attempt to avoid their creditors. For example, you can form an "Alaska trust" whereby you turn your assets over to a trustee, who puts some restrictions on your ability to use the money. That gives you at least an argument that your creditors cannot get the money because it is not really "yours." These trusts are risky propositions that you should effectuate only upon the advice of a reputable trusts and estates lawyer. As a general matter, I discourage crashproofers from liability-avoiding gimmicks like Alaska trusts because they often backfire. If these structures are not set up correctly, you may be accused of a "fraudulent conveyance"—i.e., a transfer of assets in violation of the law to avoid paying money you legally owe—and then you can be in real trouble. If you follow the crashproofing advice in this book, you will not need dangerous legal ploys to get you out of financial problems. Why? Because you will not have any financial problems.

The only exception to the general rule against creating such liability-avoiding structures is incorporation. I am in favor of incorporation in limited circumstances. If you or your spouse operates a small business from your home or somewhere else—whether it be making jewelry, woodworking, or serving as an electronics consultant—it may be a good idea to form a corporation that legally separates the business activity from the marital estate. Unlike the Alaska trust, it is well-established that a corporation is a legal, effective, and desirable liability-limiting legal structure. A corporate structure will shield you from personal liability for the debts and liabilities of the corporation. The reason states have allowed people to create corporations is to limit the liability of those who decide to engage in commerce that is beneficial to the community.

Many marital estates have been wiped out when a spouse was hit with a judgment in a big lawsuit arising out of a small business that had not been incorporated. You want to avoid this disaster as much as you want to avoid the financial problems that can occur in other aspects of the marital relationship. In order to shield your marital assets from legal liability that one spouse may incur in his or her personal business activities, the spouse conducting the business should form one of a variety of corporate structures that, as a legal matter, conduct the business in question. You can get a lawyer to form the corporation for you (which I recommend, as it is not expensive and will result in a reliable product), or you can do it yourself with legal forms that you can buy at book or stationery stores. For a small business venture, you will want a limited liability company (LLC) or an "S" corporation, which will allow you to avoid some of the taxes that traditional corporations have to pay. However, the corporation must have a truly independent board of directors, a bank account with adequate capital to run the business, and all of the corporate formalities required by law. If the corporation is simply a piece of paper that functions as your personal "alter ego"—as the courts say—you will get no legal protection from it.

To sum up this chapter, crashproofers learn about their spouse's financial conditions and priorities; they take advantage of the well-established, legitimate legal structures that allow spouses to keep their financial holdings intact in the event of death, divorce, or incapacity; and they take care to separate their business activities from their marital estate. It is hard to think about the potential dire times in which you or your loved ones will need the protections afforded by these structures, but everyone involved will find a silver lining in times of misfortune if you and your spouse have planned effectively for such times. Everyone faces them at some time, so you need to be ready.

9

Limiting the Financial Threat Posed by Children, Parents, Relatives, and Neighbors

Love Thy Neighbor, but Do Not Support Him or Her Financially

We are coming to the end of the crashproofing process. To get there, we must discuss one last group of people who threaten your financial security: parents, children, relatives, and neighbors. It may seem a little awkward to consider people whom you love or like as potential financial threats. But they are, and you need to prepare yourself for the possible financial assault they will mount—an assault that usually drips with emotions ranging from desperation to guilt to anger. If you carefully plan your financial relationships with your children, parents, relatives, and neighbors, you will find that you can improve your emotional relationships with them while you crashproof your life.

Children and Crashproofing

It is a good thing kids are cute because if they were not, they would have no place in our crashproofing structure. A child born to a middle-class family in the United States in 2000 will cost his or her parents almost $160,000 in today's dollars through the age of seventeen. Then, if the child is halfway intelligent, the real expenses begin. The cost of sending a child to an in-state public college exceeds $10,000 per year today, and those prices are increasing dramatically. It is expected that a child born in 2000 who ultimately goes to a public college will incur costs in excess of $100,000. Meanwhile, sending a child to a private college today costs up to $35,000 per year, and those costs are expected to *double* over the next ten years. You can expect to spend from $250,000 to $300,000 to get today's toddler through a typical private college when the time comes. Worse still, more and more children land right back at home for a few years after college while they "get on their feet," resulting in a further financial burden on the parents.

You already know what you can do to minimize the $160,000 up-front cost of having a child. Part Two discussed how to reduce your expenses for food, clothing, and gifts, which should help you trim the costs of child-rearing, although there is no escaping the fact that you will spend a lot on your children while they are young. With your crashproofed financial plan in place, however, you should be able to make it through those first seventeen years without too much risk.

The best opportunity to save money, and to do so in a manner that will *improve* your relationship with your child, comes in those two later periods—college and postcollege. Let's go through the options you have in those critical areas.

College Options

You should start preparing to pay for your kids' college before they reach the age of one. Many parents with young children ignore the college issue because they plan to be making enough money to afford college for their children when the time comes. This is the faith fallacy rearing its ugly head once again. These parents assume—on blind faith alone—they will be making a lot more money when their kids grow up. You are tempting the forces of disorder in a big way if you assume you will be making enough to afford college for your children. Crashproofers do not work this way. They hope for, but never assume, a better financial future. Do not let the faith fallacy lure you into inaction while your kids are young.

Some approaches to saving for college, while financially sound, are still unsatisfactory to a crashproofer. For example, a parent in a western U.S. city told me he had pretty much "solved" the college problem when his kids were quite young. He simply informed his children that they would be going only to a public, in-state college near home. That way the tuition would be low, and the kids could continue to live at home, saving the family a lot of money. This approach has, in fact, been advocated in popular self-help books. These books endorse the idea of limiting your childrens' college options in order to save money.

I can prove with real-life cases that this approach is a bad one. For example, this father had a daughter who had a gift for foreign languages. She studied her college options carefully and decided she wanted to go to a private college on the East Coast that had a world-renowned foreign languages department. This private school had many graduates who had gone on to become successful diplomats, translators, and interpreters—all lines of work that the daughter was considering. The nearby public college, although academically solid, was not well-known for its foreign languages department. Nevertheless, the father insisted that his daughter go to the nearby public school. In the end, he created a major rift with his daughter by refusing to consider the private school with the strong foreign languages department. And although she went on to do reasonably well in the work world, she always felt her father had limited her opportunity for great success.

Her father's approach to financial crashproofing reminds me of the philosophy in those books that tell you you can become a millionaire only if you live like a pauper. We know that is not true. This book has already established that you can afford to have some fun while you build your economic security. Similarly, you need not and should not sacrifice the dreams of your children in order to maintain a strong personal financial structure. Even more compelling, when you provide your child with the best education possible, you are making an investment in that child's emotional and financial future. You increase the chances that you will have a happy, financially secure child in the long run. Conversely, by limiting an intellectually stimulated child's opportunities, you only increase the chances that the child will stray from the good path that he or she is on and possibly even depend upon you for support in the long run.

In order to give your children the education they deserve, while concurrently avoiding financial catastrophe, you must base your college planning structure on three premises: (1) the earlier you start saving for college, the less painful it will be, (2) federal and state government programs provide you with many tax incentives that make saving money for college easier than ever before, and (3) the prices colleges quote publicly are only the "sticker price," which you can reduce substantially by taking advantage of grants, scholarships, and work programs. By adopting strategies based upon these principles, you will never need to limit your child's dreams.

Early Action

If you plan to write a check from your investment clearinghouse account to cover your child's education in a private college, you will have to put away more than $7,500 per year to accumulate the necessary amount. That's just for one child, leaving nothing for your own retirement. If you are earning enough money to save this much and have plenty leftover for yourself, good for you. However, most married couples cannot save that much and still keep enough money for their retirement. If you cannot afford to simply write a check for your child's education, you need to develop an alternative family education plan. This plan must use a combination of accumulated wealth, current income, contributions from the child, and special grants and scholarships.

Soon after the birth of each child, you must determine how much money you need from each of these categories and plan accordingly. First, determine how much savings you are likely to have for each child's education. Take, for example, the family with the combined income of $92,000 that we used as our baseline in Part Two. That family takes home $72,000 after taxes and saves a total of $14,400 per year in its investment clearinghouse and savings accounts. The family has two children. The parents determine that in order to maintain their lifestyle at retirement, they must put away at least $10,000 per year for themselves until their kids are through college; after that, the entire $14,400 can go toward their retirement. That plan, they calculate, will leave them with between $1 million and $2 million in cash at their retirement. Combined with Social Security and a pension, they should be just fine.

With $10,000 put away for retirement, this plan, therefore, leaves the parents with about $2,200 per year that they can save for each child's education ($14,400 total savings, minus the $10,000 that the parents need, divided by two children). At this savings level, and depending upon market fluctuations, if the parents start saving from the year of the birth of each child, they will have, with interest, $50,000 to $75,000 per kid by the time the college bills arrive. If the kids go to a public school, this savings will cover the majority of the college costs, and the parents could probably make up the difference from current income— due to less expenses at home because of the departure of the kids, combined with some slush-fund money. No problem.

If, on the other hand, the kids would better benefit from a more expensive private school, the $50,000 to $75,000 may only cover two semesters. Supplemented by some of the parents' current income, the parents may get each kid through three or four semesters on their own. They obviously need a supplemental college financial plan.

If you are in this boat, the first element of that supplemental plan is to let each child know at a young age—nine or ten years old—how you plan to get him or her through college and what contribution you expect him or her to make. First, while you should never preclude your child from attending an expensive private college, you must also quash the perception that the child has to go to a private college. Many high schoolers believe that in order to be cool they have to find a private college that will accept them. Many parents spend exorbitant sums to send their kids to some academically average private institution in Southern California or Florida, where the kids surf and party day and night and learning is an afterthought. Your child should know from an early age that you will not pay for a private college unless that college offers a unique educational opportunity and the child earns the right to go there. Make sure your child understands that most public colleges provide an excellent basic liberal arts or engineering education, and many have unique and special programs that may be perfectly suited to the child's talents. At the same time, let the child know you will never limit his or her opportunities, so if the child has a talent that would be better served by a private institution you will find a way to get him or her through it.

Next, make sure the child knows that private schools are expensive and that he or she will have to make a contribution to the cost. Tell the child he or she has three options and may choose any one of them or a combination: savings, work, or a loan. Make sure the child understands that the money he or she is saving is an "investment" in the future and that the money that he or she contributes will supplement the large contribution that you, the parents, are making. Instilling in the child at an early age the need for a financial contribution will contribute to healthy savings and work habits on the part of the child, and it will prevent the child from resenting you later on. To do so, open a college account in the child's name and work out a plan whereby some of the money that the child gets for everything from holiday gifts to summer jobs goes into this account. Have the child set savings goals that are consistent with your financial plan. You may even agree to "match" contributions the child makes to this account. If the child ends up going to a public school and you, the parents, can afford the entire cost yourselves, then the child's savings becomes a windfall to the child—a solid financial base for when he or she enters the work world after college.

Also let your child know that if the combination of your savings and the child's savings does not cover the costs, he or she may have to get a job during the academic year, summer breaks, or both. Many colleges offer jobs to students in their areas of interest. For example, I am a coin collector, and I had no trouble getting a job as an assistant to the curator of the coin collection at my college. Similarly, professors frequently hire student assistants for research in areas related to their majors. Many universities pay very high wages to student workers to help subsidize the students' educations—even for menial jobs like cafeteria help. Again, as long as your child knows from an early age that you expect him or her to take advantage of such opportunities, he or she will not resent you for it. Most enjoy their college jobs.

Finally, your child needs to know that if the other methods do not work, he or she may need to take out a student loan. This should, of course, be a last resort. Too many kids start out in the work world with too much debt, so I encourage you to use the previously described savings and employment avenues, as well as scholarship and grant mechanisms (which will be described later), before you go the student loan route. Nonetheless, the stark financial reality is that you may have to cover some of the costs with loans. Some children greatly resent their parents for making them take out student loans. Again, early action is the key. If the child understands how the loan fits into the entire college financial picture, he or she will be much less likely to resent having to go this route—especially if you have covered most of the costs with accumulated wealth, job income, or grants and the loan is merely a supplemental device. The recommended reading at the end of the book, as well as the crashproofyourlife.com website, have links with detailed information on student loans and the other college payment options this chapter discusses.

Federal and State Savings Programs

In order to minimize the amount that your child must contribute to his or her college education, you should consider taking advantage of the many federal and state programs that provide incentives for college savings. These programs rely upon three savings mechanisms, all tied to the Internal Revenue Code: tax credits, tax deferral, and tax rates. The programs effectively give you money by allowing you to avoid taxes, wait to pay them, or pay them at a lower rate. The following is an overview of the programs, but because the plans are changing rapidly, you should check the links on the crashproofyourlife.com website to get the most current information.

You have three general categories of options that will help you stretch your college dollar. The oldest is the Uniform Gifts to Minors Act (UGMA). UGMA allows you to set up an investment account in the name of your child or otherwise give assets to your child without setting up a formal trust. A specified amount of the income generated by such an account is taxed at your child's tax rate rather than yours. The only problem with UGMA is the money that has accumulated in the account typically becomes your child's money when the child reaches the age of eighteen or twenty-one depending on the applicable state law, and you no longer have any legal say in how the child spends that money. You want the money to go toward college; the kid might decide that a Land Rover looks more appealing. If you plan to use UGMA, you better instill the purpose of that money into the child at an early age, or the account could cause real problems between you and your child.

You can also take advantage of federal credits and tax-deferral mechanisms, including Hope scholarships, the Lifetime Learning credit, and education IRAs. Depending upon your income level, these programs allow you tax credits and deferral for relatively small sums of money per year, but the value of credits and deferral of even small sums can really add up over time. As noted earlier, because these programs seem to be ever-changing, I will not list specifics here. For example, the tax cut package signed into law in 2001 expanded some of these benefits for a specified period of time, after which Congress will revisit the issue. The crashproofyourlife.com website has links to sites that explain clearly how to go about taking advantage of federal college incentive programs and indicate the dollar and income limitations that apply to them.

In addition, you have the tax advantages provided by state prepaid tuition plans and college savings plans, as provided for by Section 529 of the Internal Revenue Code. Under a prepaid tuition plan, you set up an account in which the money for an in-state college grows tax free until the child withdraws it, at which time the taxes are paid at the child's rate. In addition, there is usually a state income tax deduction for contributions to that state's plan. If the child opts to go out of state, however, there may be a substantial penalty.

A better option for most people is a state-run college savings plan because these plans do not limit the child's college choices—the child can go in-state or out-of-state, public or private—but you still have the advantage of the tax-free growth of the funds. With either type of "529" plan, the money can be transferred to a different beneficiary if the person for whom the account was set up decides not to go to college. If the beneficiary does not use the funds for certain specific reasons (death, disability, or receipt of a scholarship) then the funds can be withdrawn without penalty. However, if you decide to use the money for that Land Rover you've been wanting, there will be a penalty. The severity of the penalty varies by state. In some states it is quite significant (the growth in the portfolio, for example). In others, the penalty is more reasonable (10 percent of the growth, for example), such that, given the tax-free nature of the account, your "loss" from the penalty may not be too significant.

Under "529" plans, you set up an account in a manner dictated by the state whose program looks most appealing to you, and you or anyone else can make contributions in the form of regular payments or lump sums. A professional money manager invests the contributions that you make to the plan. Generally the dollar limits on the annual contributions exceed the federal gift tax exemptions—that is, a relative can give more money tax-free to such an account than he or she could with an outright gift. In some cases, you can treat a contribution as having been made over several years to avoid gift-tax liability. In addition, the state may give you a state tax exemption for contributions up to a certain sum; and, as originally structured, you enjoy accumulations of funds with both federal and state taxes deferred until the time you withdraw the money to pay for college, at which time the money is normally subject to federal tax at the student's rate. Interestingly, under the tax laws passed in 2001, you can actually withdraw specified funds *free of federal tax* until the year 2011, at which time the situation will revert back to the tax-deferred status. You can get more-detailed information on these plans from the crashproofyourlife.com website, which has links to savingforcollege.com and other important college savings sites.

These programs are becoming increasingly popular. For example, during the first four months after New York opened its plan, some 25,000 investors opened accounts with a total value of over $90 million. If you open such an account, you should encourage grandparents, aunts, and uncles to contribute to these accounts, rather than just giving your kids cash gifts. It is a financial plus for everyone and a valuable crashproofing tool.

These legal structures are the principal means to use the Internal Revenue Code to stretch your college dollar, and I encourage you to study these options carefully and take advantage of them fully. A crashproofer does not throw away free money, and that is effectively what these programs are. If you are still looking for help after taking advantage of these options, consult a tax professional to discuss how you can use such mechanisms as insurance trusts, treasury securities, zero coupon bonds, loans against retirement accounts, hiring your kids, and other clever ways to ease the college burden. The options discussed previously, however, are still the most attractive and should serve most people well enough that they need not go further.

Grants, Scholarships, and Financial Aid

Yale, one of the most expensive colleges in the country, has a motto: no one has ever missed a Yale education due to lack of funds. Many other colleges have a similar policy. If you are smart enough to get in, they will find a way for you to go there. Therefore, before you even consider limiting your children's college options due to financial considerations, remember that the prices colleges quote for tuition, room, and board are the sticker prices. Most people do not pay the sticker price. There are many ways to get the cost of college down, and some people are just too lazy to learn how to do it. You start, of course, by studying the financial aid policies of the colleges that offer the best educational opportunities for your children. Get an idea of how much aid a family with your income and assets can expect. Most colleges and universities have charts to help you determine the maximum amount for which you can qualify. You will note, however, that it becomes increasingly difficult to obtain financial aid once your family income crosses the $50,000 per year mark. It may also be difficult to obtain aid if the family has a significant sum of invested assets (either in the parent's name or in a college savings plan for the child). So you may have to look elsewhere. Fortunately, you still have many options.

Consider applying for academic and athletic scholarships. Some schools—including some prominent Ivy League schools—do not offer these. Their financial aid is based strictly upon need. However, hundreds of excellent institutions do offer merit scholarships for those students who demonstrate outstanding talent. Even if your child is not at the top of his or her class academically, colleges offer a variety of scholarships that focus upon a unique skill or talent. You should encourage your child not only to be well-rounded but also to develop an area of great skill or expertise—be it as a violinist, a field hockey player, or a science whiz. I know a young woman who is on a full scholarship at a good college because she is an excellent squash player. Talents come in all shapes and sizes, and one of your jobs as a parent is to learn the skills at which your child excels and to encourage your child to develop those skills. It could be worth tens of thousands of dollars to both you and your child, even if it does not become that child's ultimate profession.

If you do not find money at the college or university your child wants to attend, numerous private foundations offer grants to qualified students. You have probably heard of the Fulbright or Rhodes scholarships, but there are thousands of others that are not as well known. Sometimes they are reserved for persons of particular economic or cultural backgrounds, and in other instances they require the student to excel at a particular cultural skill—music, art, writing. But a majority of parents do not adequately research these often-surprising options. I know a woman who helped put herself through law school with the grant money she got from a beauty contest! You never know where your college money will come from until you research the thousands of potential sources out there. The crashproofyourlife.com website and the recommended reading at the end of this book have information on many organizations that can get you started in the right direction.

I must conclude this section with a word of warning. Many companies advertise or even "guarantee" that, if you pay them a hefty fee, they will get you grant money. The Federal Trade Commission found, for example, that just eight of these companies have bilked 170,000 people of some $22 million dollars. No one can guarantee you will get a grant or scholarship. Because so many of these companies are unreliable, I encourage you to do the research yourself, on-line or with the references listed at the end of this book. Also, beware of companies that tell you they have "nonpublic" information about grant money. Organizations that give grants want nothing more than to tell the public about it. No one keeps their money secret, so an organization that claims to have nonpublic information about grants is most likely being untruthful. Finally, you may get a letter or fax claiming you or your child has received some sort of award from a "national foundation" to receive some sort of grant or award you never sought. Most of the time, these organizations, too, are just out to get some sort of fee from you, and you are likely to get nothing in return.

Honest organizations that hand out free money to college students take painstaking care to ensure their money goes to the right people. You get a grant by writing or E-mailing a reputable charitable institution, asking for an application. You fill out the application, and maybe your child even submits to an interview or provides a sample (video, writing, etc.) showing his or her talent. Then the organization weighs each application carefully and makes its decision. Any group that purports to shortcut this arduous process is probably a sham.

Failure Dependence and Crashproofing

Young children naturally depend upon their parents for just about everything. This is part of the very process of life, and parents cherish the years their kids live at home learning about the world. However, crash risks arise when grown children, who should be out on their own, continue to depend financially upon their parents.

Grown children depending upon their parents is not natural, although it is becoming remarkably common. I have read article after article about grown children who live with their parents. As strange as it may seem, this situation constitutes yet another face of the disorderly, and often destructive, direction of the universe because it tends to deplete the financial resources of the parents and the emotional resources of both the parents and the kids. Like most destructive forces, the more your kids depend upon you for money, lodging, and other tangible financial support, the less likely it is that they will build their own financial structures. It is a downward spiral that I call failure dependence. With each failure, the grown son or daughter depends upon you a little more. You, as parents, have to build your own structures to prevent this situation from happening. We'll first discuss how to avoid having children who remain dependent upon you into their adulthood. Then we will cover aging parents.

Being a cold trial lawyer, I like the way mother birds just drop their babies out of the nest after a little while and force them to fly and fend for themselves. However, I am also a parent, so I realize it is not that easy to instill independence in human children. Rather, you need to set some clear but flexible ground rules that balance the love you feel for your children with the need for your children to be on their own.

Moving back in is the first crash risk, and millions of kids do it. If your son or daughter wants to move back in with you after college, you need to establish that the child will stay for a fixed, limited duration. The duration does not need to be tied to a date on a calendar, but it does need to tie into an event in the progress of the child's quest for independence. For example, I know parents who told their son who had just graduated from law school, "We would be happy to have you move back in with us until you have passed the bar exam." The implication was clear: we will help you get on your feet, but we will not support you indefinitely. Allowing your child to live with you during a particularly intense period during his or her life, such as postcollege job interviews, building a new house, or going through a divorce, is an excellent idea. Limiting the duration of the stay is what keeps support from degenerating into failure dependence.

You, as parents, should not hesitate to provide some financial support to your children at critical times. For example, if an unexpected reduction in workforce costs your child his or her job, you should help him or her bridge the financial gap between careers, as long as he or she is actively seeking new work.

You should also be willing to reward a child in good times, but be reasonable. Parents should not support their children financially in lifestyles that the children's own accomplishments do not warrant. If your child has worked hard to build a successful career and could use a little help on a down payment for a house, that is no problem, as long as you can afford it. However, do not try to put him or her in a house or neighborhood far more costly than his or her own successes would allow. If your grandchildren have excelled in school, helping a little with college costs is very appropriate. By rewarding an accomplishment in a measured manner, you are encouraging independence, not causing failure dependence.

Most important, you should gently instill in your children the overriding principles of crashproofing when they are very young. By taking them to open their own bank accounts, encouraging them to have summer jobs, and making sure they keep their rooms as well-organized as you keep your office, you are building a foundation of future independence for your children. Include them in the crashproofing process that you set up for yourself, and they will fly from the nest with grace.

Conversely, if you, the reader, are the kid rather than the parent, you, too, should keep in mind the need to break the financial dependence upon your parents at the earliest possible time. If, for example, you are just graduating from college or graduate school, you should make sure you do not become dependent upon your parents for lodging for a lengthy period of time. If you become dependent, you will develop a false sense of financial security (and turn off dates as well). It is the wrong way to get started in the world.

You should not put your parents in the awkward position of having to turn you down when you ask them for money. I have never known of a case where a kid who depended upon parents for money—even where very wealthy parents provided extensive funds to the kid—lived a satisfying and successful life. From my law practice, I know several stories of kids experiencing divorce or depression and even engaging in serious criminal activity—all of whom had wealthy parents who gave them too much. In one situation the unemployed son of wealthy and overly generous parents became so bored with his lavish lifestyle that he decided to start smuggling cocaine and illegal weapons to and from South America. He did not need the money. Rather, he said he did it because he was bored and needed a thrill in his life. He is now doing twenty years in prison with no possibility of parole. This is the downward spiral of failure dependence, and you, as a child going into the work world, must resist its temptations.

Parents and Crashproofing

Susan and Royce were a successful couple by almost every measure. He was a financial analyst and she was a part-time manager at her father's grocery store. They had three well-rounded children and lived in a great neighborhood. They also had the essential crashproofing structures in place, although in a somewhat different format than has been laid out in this book. Correction: they had all of the essential crashproofing structures in place, save one.

Susan's father was diagnosed with Alzheimer's disease at the age of fifty-seven. The disease progressed rapidly, and the family closed the grocery store. They put the father in a nursing home that specialized in Alzheimer's patients. The basic cost of the nursing home was $45,000 per year. His unreimbursed prescription-drug costs were another $10,000 per year. Miscellaneous expenses related to dental and eye care ran a few thousand more. When it was all said and done, the cost of caring for Susan's father ran over $60,000 per year.

About a week after the family had taken the difficult step of institutionalizing the once-proud patriarch of the family, Royce asked Susan a tough question: "Can your mom afford to pay for your dad's expenses?" Susan gave the answer that so many children of sick parents give: "I don't know." She soon found out the hard way.

Parents—the very people who brought us into the world and gave us their best years—now constitute one of the greatest crash risks in our lives. In 1970, the average life expectancy for an American was sixty-eight years—sixty-four for men and seventy-one for women. In 2000, the average life expectancy was seventy-seven years—seventy-four for men and eighty for women. These life expectancies will increase in the years to come. Just by virtue of their longer life spans, older Americans will suffer an increasing number of illnesses that cost a lot of money to treat and require special care. Many of these costs are not and will not be covered by Medicare or insurance. In many cases, the costs will fall on the children.

In 1998, the last year for which I could find statistics, Americans spent $2 billion per month caring for their aging parents. As the baby boom generation moves into old age, the percentage of older Americans in the population will continue to increase. The math is simple. An increasingly smaller percentage of people will have to care for an increasingly larger percentage of people. While our politicians have made Social Security and Medicare reform a priority, you—as a crashproofer—simply cannot adopt the faith fallacy and assume everything will be fine ten or twenty years down the road. You must plan for the old age of your parents.

You must make plans even if your parents seem healthy and wealthy. Consumptive lifestyles have led to a large group of seemingly well-off seniors who have not saved enough money for their futures. Your parents may "outlive their money"—a phrase you will hear more and more over the next few years.

Indeed, outliving money even happens to people who make a lot of money. I remember, for example, visiting the parents of a college friend of mine. My friend's parents lived in a palatial home and belonged to a top country club. Her father was a partner in a major New England business, and her mother spent most of her time organizing high-profile charitable events. One day my friend, who was quite intelligent but not very informed in business matters, approached me with a question: "What is Chapter 13?" I told her the phrase refers to a type of bankruptcy. She had overheard her parents in a very tense conversation about "maybe going the Chapter 13 route." Over the next few days, my friend was totally surprised to learn that her parents, while enjoying a high income, had more money going out of the household to support their lifestyle than they had coming into the household. As she came to realize her family's true situation, she recalled that since her childhood, she had heard her father on the phone talking about loans, and her father got calls at dinner time that apparently related to large debts the family had. Her father had always told her these were people who wanted to hurt him because he was so successful. It sounds almost ridiculous that this intelligent person did not figure out what was going on with her parents, but it is not an uncommon occurrence. Children want to believe their parents represent security, and they will deceive themselves into believing so—even into their adulthood.

Children have not only a right to know but also a duty to learn their parents' true financial condition. I recommend a three-step approach to ensuring that parents do not become a significant financial burden on their children: (1) a grown son or daughter must sit down with his or her parents to discuss the parents' financial situation at least ten years, and preferably fifteen years, before they retire; (2) if there is a potential problem, the child must disclose it to his or her spouse; and (3) all of the parties—parents, children, and spouses—must work together to develop a long-term financial plan that allows the parents a comfortable retirement with minimal adverse impact on the children.

Four Categories of Parents

Preparing for your parents' old age is a delicate process that you must undertake with care and understanding. Your goal should be to ensure a comfortable retirement for them, fully maintaining their dignity and sense of independence. The first rule of crashproofing concerning care for aging parents is you must show compassion for the people responsible for bringing you into the world.

When you sit down with your parents to discuss their financial situation, do it without your spouse present. Tell your parents you will need to disclose some of the information to your spouse so you and your spouse can effectively plan your own financial futures. You must also assure your parents that your spouse will not disclose the information to *his or her parents*. Your parents are less likely to be concerned about personal financial information going to a younger generation than they are about it going to others of their own generation.

Discuss with your parents in general terms that many older people, even hardworking and successful people, will outlive their money in the years to come and ultimately rely upon their children to support them. For that reason, you need to know where they stand financially—at a time when they are relatively young and completely self-sufficient—so you can work together to ensure that the situation never changes for the worse.

With this or a similar groundwork laid, your parents should then disclose to you the following: the value of their accrued assets, including their home equity, investments, accessible savings, life insurance policies, and retirement accounts; the amount of any guaranteed fixed income they will receive, such as military pensions, corporate pensions, and social security; and all of their liabilities, including first and second mortgages, business loans, financed cars and appliances, costs of caring for *their parents*, and tax debts.

Take this information and calculate what their likely net income will be when they retire. While how to best calculate this depends to some extent upon how your parents have organized their finances, here is the basic template. Add up their invested liquid assets (stocks, bonds, retirement funds), and assume a conservative increase in the value of those investments until retirement (say 5 to 7 percent per year). That will give you a conservative estimate of their likely total liquid assets at retirement. Now subtract the liabilities, if any, that will be outstanding at the time of retirement.

Then take the total amount of investment equity you expect them to have at retirement and multiply that sum by the rate the government pays on treasury securities—say 7 percent—which would represent a safe income level from the retirement money. Add to that number the expected Social Security and pension benefits, and you will have a pretty good idea of how much reliable income your parents will have in their old age. Never assume your parents will get an inheritance from their parents or other relatives; too often it does not pan out. Then determine how much income the surviving spouse will have after one of them dies, by adding in the interest on proceeds of life insurance they may have.

So, for example, if you project your parents' investments at retirement will consist of $225,000 in an investment account and $125,000 in a retirement account, your father will have a military pension of $800 per month, and your parents expect, according to government tables (linked on the crashproofyourlife.com website) $1,400 per month in Social Security, their combined retirement income will be about $50,000 per year, or just over $4,000 per month. If they have taken out $100,000 insurance policies on each other's lives, the monthly interest income would increase to a few hundred dollars per month for the surviving spouse after one of them dies.

Because this income comes from interest and dividends on investments as well as vested pension money, they could have this sum for the rest of their lives without ever digging into their investment principal. As will soon be discussed, some parents will need to spend their investment principal, and, of course, the rules regarding IRAs require that your parents make certain specified minimum withdrawals. But for planning purposes we'll start with the assumption that they will live only off of the interest.

Next, you have to compare their likely retirement income to what their income is today. To do so, take the list of their liabilities and determine whether any of them will be paid off by the time your parents retire. Then compare the amount your parents make now in earned income, minus the short-term liabilities, with the amount they will have in retirement. When subtracting liabilities from income, make sure you are comparing either pretax dollars or posttax dollars; you have to do an apples-to-apples comparison. For example, if your parents have a combined current earned income—excluding investment income—of $72,000 per year, but they pay $500 per month on a tax deductible, home equity loan that will be paid off at the time of their retirement, they have an effective current income of approximately $66,000 per year ($72,000 annual income minus $6,000 in loan payments). Compared to the $50,000 per year that they will have at retirement, there is a significant shortfall. Most aging parents will find that they will have such a shortfall, and the goal is to figure out how to handle it.

Once you have made these calculations, put your parents into one of four categories:

1. They will have a lifestyle throughout their retirement that is about equal to their preretirement lifestyle.
2. They will be able to maintain their lifestyle throughout retirement if they increase their preretirement savings at an achievable rate.
3. They will be capable of maintaining their current lifestyle for only a limited time during retirement by depleting their investment principal.
4. They will be unable to maintain their current lifestyle for any extended period of retirement.

Category-One Parents

If the numbers prove that your parents are financially secure, you should thank them for discussing the situation with you, tell your spouse you have nothing to worry about, and move on with your lives. You are very lucky indeed. You may wish to discuss with your parents the possibility of their making gifts to college tuition savings programs for your children or gifts that can avoid estate taxes (to the extent that the government has not phased out such taxes). Do not, however, allow your financially secure parents to spoil your children. You do not need wealthy grandparents encouraging the type of failure dependence that was discussed earlier.

Category-Two Parents

If Mom and Dad are in category two—capable of achieving lifetime security but not there yet—discuss with them how close they are to being where they need to be, and work with them to determine the alternatives they have to get to financial security. Unless they are extremely extravagant, your parents should not stop taking vacations nor hold off on plans to remodel the kitchen, but you should go through some of the cost-reduction ideas that were discussed in Part Two—less impulse spending on you, your children, and other relatives; smart travel planning; and the reduction or elimination of expensive vices. Make sure they have set specific savings goals for themselves, and help them monitor their own crashproofing plan. If they just add the same kind of financial discipline to their lives that you have added to yours, the whole family will be in good financial shape for the future.

Category-Three Parents

I have not done a formal survey, but anecdotal experience suggests that a large percentage of the baby boomers—people from their mid-forties into their mid-fifties—risk finding themselves in category three when they retire. Their parents may be in that category now. Their current financial trajectory indicates that although they will enjoy their present lifestyle for several years into their retirement, eventually they will dig into their investment principal. Absent a good pension, their lifestyle will slowly deteriorate, starting five to ten years into retirement. If one of them lives into very old age, he or she risks outliving all of the money they have saved. If one or both of them must go into a home for the elderly or experience medical costs that insurance does not cover, they risk a severe financial crash.

If you are still in your thirties or forties, you can avoid being in this category by merely following the crashproofing advice already provided by this book. If, however, you have aging parents who are in category three, then you may have to take more drastic measures. In addition to doing what category-two parents must do—reduction of impulse spending, more intelligent leisure spending, and so on—consider the following possibilities.

First, your parents may wish to purchase long-term-care insurance, or you may wish to purchase it for them. Medicare does not in most circumstances cover long-term-care costs. Long-term-care policies cover the costs of a nursing home or other special-care facility when the doctor determines that such care is a "medical necessity"—which means, depending upon the policy, that the policyholder is unable to perform by him- or herself certain basic life functions and/or has a designated degree of mental impairment. Some plans will allow you to substitute home nursing care for a nursing home, which is often preferable to many partners of ill people. Premiums for seniors generally range from $2,000 to $10,000 per year, depending on the age and health of the beneficiary.

These policies are, however, fraught with risk, especially when the parents rather than the kids are paying the premiums. For example, the premiums increase as the beneficiaries age, often resulting in a situation where the beneficiary can no longer afford the policy right when he or she may soon need long-term care. Insurance companies make a lot of money on the sad fact that policies get canceled just as people get old enough to use them. Therefore, even if the parents are going to pay the premiums initially, the children of aging parents need to plan to pick up some or all of the premium costs if the parents live into very old age. Equally important, your parents might be losing their mental capacity when they decide they need the long-term care, and they may not be able to meet the notice requirements and other paperwork that are a precondition to coverage, which could then result in a loss of benefits. Even if you buy the policy, you must stay involved, especially when the time comes for your parents to use the policy. Also, these policies sometimes have major exclusions, such as for Alzheimer's disease or for providing even marginally inaccurate information in the application for insurance. Other policies have a fixed benefit that is not adjusted for inflation. It is essential that you assist your parents in applying for long-term-care insurance and that you get policies without unreasonable exclusions or limitations. You, as the children, need to read the policy and make sure your parents get the coverage to which they are entitled when the time comes. Check the crashproofyourlife.com website for articles and information that will allow your parents to purchase the right policy.

Here are some other alternatives for category-three parents. If your parents find themselves retired but not yet eligible for Medicare, they should seriously consider "bridge insurance" that will cover their health-care costs until they are eligible for Medicare. They should also consider various forms of supplemental insurance that cover costs that Medicare does not cover, such as co-payments for treatment or prescription drugs. Again, if your parents are in category three, you may have to pay for some or all of these premiums as your parents age. At least the costs will be fixed and predictable, which will prevent you from being hit with huge expenditures when illness strikes.

Another option for mitigating and controlling the diminishing financial assets of aging category-three parents is a *reverse mortgage*. If your parents are age sixty-two or older and own their own home, they can effectively sell their home back to the bank. The bank will pay your parents a monthly sum (or in some cases a lump sum), which will reduce their equity in their home. When they die, move, or sell the home, the bank gets the amount of equity that your parents have given up by virtue of the reverse mortgage. Contrary to popular belief, the bank cannot kick your parents out of the home when they run out of equity. While a reverse mortgage reduces the estate that your parents will leave, it represents a very dignified way to keep your parents self-sufficient while they are alive. The terms of such mortgages are very thoroughly governed by law. However, some scammers out there will take a fee for helping you find a reverse mortgage lender. You do not need this "help." Check the recommended reading at the end of the book for more information on reverse mortgages, or contact an office of the United States Department of Housing and Urban Development.

Category-Four Parents

Many people will find that their parents are likely to outlive their money entirely and probably before reaching old age. Without help, they will be left to live on Social Security and state or federal programs such as Medicaid, usually with a lifestyle substantially below what they enjoyed when they were part of the workforce.

There are basically two approaches to resolving this situation. The first, which is often recommended by those who look at the situation in a cold, purely financial sense, is to plan for the poverty of your parents. Some children, spurred on by financial advisers, urge their parents to give the children what money and material possessions the parents have so that the parents then qualify for state or federal assistance programs. I have heard intelligent people recommend exactly that course of action. The rationale is that if the parents give away what they have so that they qualify for aid, then the kids can use the assets they received from their parents to make their parents' lives a little more enjoyable. This is a risky proposition. Federal law prohibits people from qualifying for aid if they have given away their assets within a specified time preceding their application for aid. You have to orchestrate this "controlled poverty" very carefully, or you might find yourself in trouble with law enforcement authorities.

Aside, however, from the questionable legality of such a course of action, I strongly discourage it for other reasons. Primarily, it would be demeaning to your parents. You would be forcing them to give you everything they have so that they can qualify for *welfare*. What kind of a son or daughter is that? You should, instead, consider an important alternative. You must decide if one or both of your parents will live with you when their money runs out. Such a situation can be a real strain on both the parent-child relationship and the relationship between you and your spouse, but you can minimize this risk with early planning. If your parents and your spouse know this will be a likely scenario, you will be able to plan effectively for its arrival.

Consequently, you must make sure your parents and spouse know as early as possible that one or both of the parents might have to move in with you at some time down the road. Psychological preparation is half of the battle. Then, put that time period off as long as possible through the various money-extending devices discussed previously. Supplement these methods with, for example, paying one of your parents to take care of your kids rather than using a day-care center. This might give them enough money to live several more years in their own home. In other words, find ways to keep money in the family.

Prepare for the arrival of a parent; for example, make sure there is a separate "guest" bedroom and bath in your house either when you buy it or when you make home improvements. Many houses now offer guest quarters that you can easily convert into a parent's home when the time comes.

Finally, when the parent does move in with you, establish, if possible, a relationship whereby the parent feels that he or she is earning the right to live with you. Let the parent baby-sit, cook meals, clean, and make other substantive contributions to the family that ease others' burdens. While you should not turn Mom or Dad into some kind of a serf, by working out with your parent what he or she wants to do to help in the house—in advance and with respect—your parent will feel appreciated, not abused.

Friends and Neighbors

While I show a great deal of compassion for parents and some compassion for kids, my compassion-meter goes way down when it comes to distant relatives, friends, acquaintances, and neighbors. I cringe when I hear stories of financially desperate third cousins, who never implemented any crashproofing structures in their own lives, coming to their successful relatives for money.

Of course, some people outside of your immediate family may warrant and deserve your financial assistance, but such situations are rare. If, for example, someone has been a loyal employee for many years or has otherwise been an important and positive influence in your life, you should treat that person more like a close family member than a friend. For example, I know of one family that paid $8,000 in back taxes for a domestic servant who had served the family well for twenty-five years before retiring and getting into some financial trouble. Similarly, what police officer could not support a trust fund set up for the children of a fellow officer killed in the line of duty? Helping a close and dear friend or being one of many contributors to the victims of a terrible tragedy that hits close to home is part of the basic duty of charity that we all have.

These situations are, however, the exceptions. You ultimately have to judge just when and where to draw the line, but you need to remember some basic facts. First, as you become successful in building your financial security, people will come to you for money. Second, most people who will come to you for money will not deserve it. They have made irresponsible decisions in their lives, and they will not want to take responsibility for them. Third, they will manipulate you just as they have manipulated others for their entire lives. For example, they will ask for a "loan." These loans to distant relatives and acquaintances will not be paid back. These people will come to you because every other option has closed—employer, bank, their own parents, and their own kids. Fourth, there is usually a pretty good reason why the other options have closed: the people who will want you to lend them money are unreliable, irresponsible losers. They have blown their money and their jobs with alcohol, crime, irresponsible spending, or some combination of the three. If you get involved with them, they will drag you down with them, just like the office loser. Fifth, the moment you crack and give them even just a little money, you will have a leech for life on your hands.

Some of these people use less-direct tactics than an outright plea for money. They will ask you to "invest" in some harebrained business scheme they developed while watching afternoon soap operas. Again, these business schemes are usually just another way to get money out of you. If they cannot get a bank or a close relative to support their business ventures, then there is no reason that you should do it.

Am I totally coldhearted? No, but there are better approaches to handling desperate acquaintances and opportunistic relatives than just handing them cash. You need to balance compassion with the need to keep financial distance from these people. If, for example, you have outsiders who are angling for money from you and you care about them to any degree, I recommend a "carrot-stick" approach. Let them know from the beginning, and in no uncertain terms, that you will not support them financially. You will give them no money, period. You will not let that person move in with you either. I could tell countless disaster stories of people who let non–family members move in with them to "get back on their feet." Six months later, these people were still sitting—very much not on their feet. You must say no to money and lodging. That is obviously the "stick" part of the "carrot-stick" approach. And, as if you are dealing with a child, you must hold to your position without even the slightest amount of moderation, no matter how pathetic and manipulative their pleas may become.

The carrot is to offer to help them with the problems that got them into their mess in the first place. If the person has a drug or alcohol problem, research the treatment options in your area and encourage the person to get help with specific suggestions—whom to contact, where to go. If he or she has bills piling up due to irresponsible spending, give the person the number for the local consumer credit bureau. If the person cannot find a job, help him or her find the nearest job placement center. Offer to help him or her with writing a resume or even volunteer to baby-sit his or her kids while the person has a job interview. In short, you can show your concern by your compassionate actions without becoming a financial support system for someone who does not warrant such support. It is an unfortunate fact of crashproofing that you cannot provide a financial support system to everyone who needs it without jeopardizing your own security. With careful management of the situation, however, you can still execute your duties as a friend by assisting in nonfinancial ways people who have fallen on hard times. You may even give them a crashproofing lesson or two.

The Personal Liability Checklist

Now that we have covered the essential rules for protecting against personal liability, here is a brief checklist you can use throughout the last leg of your crashproofing endeavor.

The Perfect Insurance Mix Is Careful Conduct, More Types of Insurance, and Higher Deductibles

Home Protection

_____ I keep my homeowner's insurance deductible high to free up money for more types of protection.

_____ I live in a location where the risk of natural disaster is relatively low.

_____ I have taken steps to fireproof my home as recommended by my local fire department.

_____ I have taken steps to crime-proof my home as recommended by my local police department.

_____ I have a safe-deposit box.

_____ I have taken steps to reduce other risks to my home, including insects, radon, carbon monoxide, lead paint, and asbestos.

_____ I have basic supplies of food, water, radios, batteries, etc. in my home and car so that I could withstand a period of isolation for several days.

_____ I have a "special form" homeowner's insurance policy, with appropriate riders for natural disasters, fixtures, and personal articles.

_____ I have researched the solvency of my home insurance company.

Life Protection

___ I reduce the chance of premature death by taking care of my body—eliminating destructive vices, exercising, and watching my diet.

___ Both my spouse and I have life insurance policies.

___ I have life insurance equal to at least eight times my salary minus my accrued assets.

___ I have term insurance rather than whole-life or related policies.

___ I have researched the solvency of my life insurance company.

Health Protection

___ I use a high deductible to pay for supplemental insurance that covers the costs over the lifetime of and incident limitations in my basic health insurance policy.

___ If my regular policy does not include disability, I have supplemental insurance for disability that covers my salary if I am unable to work in my own field of employment.

___ I have thoroughly researched the solvency of my health insurance company.

Automobile Protection

___ I have developed safe driving habits—avoiding driving while under the influence of alcohol, while sleep deprived, or while distracted.

___ I have learned to control road rage.

___ I have an umbrella policy that will cover me for liability in excess of the limits in my basic policy.

___ I have thoroughly researched the solvency of my auto insurance company.

CRASHPROOFING LAW #8

Know Your Spouse Financially As Well As You Know Your Spouse in Other Ways

The Money Talk

___ I have talked with my spouse about our current financial situation, our anticipated financial situation, and our financial priorities.

___ I do not hide debt from my spouse.

___ I do not hide assets from my spouse.

___ I have disclosed to my spouse any changes in career that I plan that could affect the family finances.

___ I have or do not need a prenuptial agreement.

___ If divorcing, I do not engage in financial cannibalism.

The Estate

___ My spouse and I have a will. Even if I am unmarried, I have a will.

___ I have a living will and/or a durable power of attorney.

___ I have considered a revocable living trust.

___ I have considered other trusts as means to limit tax liability.

___ I have considered corporate structures to protect my side business.

CRASHPROOFING LAW #9

Love Thy Neighbor, but Do Not Support Him or Her Financially

Children and Crashproofing

___ I have discussed with my children how I expect them to contribute to college: savings, working, loans.

____ I have considered a gift under the Uniform Gifts to Minors Act but understand that this money will become the child's when he or she reaches the age of eighteen.

____ I have taken advantage of federal tax credits and deductions for education.

____ I have thoroughly investigated opening an account in a Section 529 state college-savings program.

____ I have thoroughly investigated the financial aid offered by the colleges my children are considering.

____ I have researched scholarship and grant opportunities and encouraged my children to develop the skills that would qualify them for such aid.

____ I understand and avoid grant and scholarship scams.

____ I have taken the steps necessary to avoid failure dependence by my children.

Parents and Crashproofing

____ I have had a money talk with my parents and determined how likely they are to outlive their money.

____ If my parents are very well-off, I have discussed with them the possibility of educational gifts to my children and charitable gifts to avoid taxes.

____ If my parents run some risk of outliving their money, I have worked with them to develop a crashproofing plan like mine.

____ If my parents run a substantial risk of outliving their money, I have investigated reverse mortgages and long-term-care insurance for them.

____ If my parents are very likely to run out of money, I have prepared my home and family for our job in taking care of them in their old age.

Friends and Neighbors

___ Unless they have made a major contribution to my life, I do not support acquaintances and distant relatives financially.

___ I do not allow acquaintances and distant relatives to move in with me and my family.

___ I do provide nonfinancial support to acquaintances and distant relatives, including referring them to treatment centers, job placement outlets, and consumer credit counseling organizations.

Conclusion

The Introduction to this book established the most fundamental rule of crash-proofing: structure contains disorder. Part One developed the structures that will help you crashproof your career. These structures ranged from the careful drafting of E-mail to the development of successful working relationships with coworkers. Part Two established the structures that will allow you to take the income from your job and grow it into a stable financial system, including risk-balanced investing, the elimination of debt, and the avoidance of financial scams. Part Three showed you how to protect all that you have built in your professional and financial life by establishing personal structures that limit your financial liability to outsiders. We covered such topics as insurance, crime-proofing, and how to deal with family and friends who want financial support from you.

You may feel overwhelmed now. You may be asking yourself: how am I going to do all these things? You may even feel like a loser because you have done so little crashproofing in your life. Let me try to make you feel better.

The most important part of crashproofing is to establish a crashproof mind-set. You need to think about how you can reduce the risk in your life all the time such that crashproofing becomes part of your very being. If you have read this book and consulted the recommended reading where necessary, and if you pay an occasional visit to the crashproofyourlife.com website, you will almost instinctively start to conduct yourself in the risk-averse manner that defines crashproofing. You'll stop yourself before you send a stupid E-mail. You will pick up an expensive electronic device at the store and then say to yourself, "No, I don't need this," and put it back on the shelf. You won't have to think about crashproofing, you will just do it naturally. Adopting the crashproof mind-set is more than half of the battle, and it will come to you without too much difficulty.

Then, of course, you have to take some specific steps. This process will be more arduous, but it need not be painful. You should print, copy, or download the three crashproofing checklists contained in this book and on the website. Go through the lists and check off the items you already do now. You may not do many of them, but at least it is a start. Then identify items on the list that may not be relevant or appropriate for your life, cross them off, and *replace them with more applicable goals*. The lists are generic. Most of the lists will apply to most readers but none will apply to all readers. Tailor your lists to your situation, but never eliminate something because it is just too hard to do, and always replace something you have crossed off with a different structure that applies to your life. For example, if your employer provides matching funds in a 401(k) retirement program, you might decide to put a little more money into your retirement structure than was recommended in Part Two because to do otherwise would be throwing away free money. This plan makes sense for you—put it in writing.

Once you have an appropriately tailored list and you have checked off the structures you have already implemented, you need to start building the structures you do not have yet. The list will look intimidating. Do not lose heart. Crashproofing will always be a work in process. Plan to implement the process in many steps over the course of months or even years. To do so, you must prioritize your crashproofing goals. Do not just pick the easy ones first. Rather, pick the ones that mean the most to you. If you have a lot of credit-card debt and you know such debt will be a real hindrance to any of your other financial plans, make the elimination of that debt with slush-fund money your top crashproofing priority. On the other hand, if you have no credit-card debt, but you have six children, you may want to set up your Section 529 college-savings plan first. By the same token, if your engineer husband has a tree-cutting business on the side, your first step may be to incorporate his business because the personal liability to which such a business could expose you could wipe you out financially.

Once you have some of the big risks eliminated, you will feel your crashproofing plan building momentum. Identify your next priorities and move forward. If you need a little break, do some of the easy things, and then get back to the more serious efforts. I predict that once you get into the crashproofing process, it will not be a burden at all—it will be exhilarating. You will watch as a wall of protection builds around your life. As that wall becomes higher and stronger, you will start to feel the peace of mind and strength of soul you have always sought. You will know that, no matter what the dangerous, devious world may throw at you, you will still be standing.

Notes

Introduction

All the stories I have related in the book, including those in the Introduction, come from true stories from my law practice, the law practices of colleagues, or public sources. If the cases received widespread publicity, I have cited some of the public sources so readers may investigate the cases further. In cases where the information is generally nonpublic, I have not given facts that would allow readers to identify the specific people involved. In most instances, I have made minor changes to the facts—to product lines, names, cities, and so on—in order to protect the privacy of these individuals. In no case have I made statements that would waive the attorney-client privilege for any individual or entity.

The example about the executive who sent the offensive E-mail about beer being better than women is based upon a well-publicized story involving Chevron Co. in 1999. See, for example, "New Survey Reveals over Half of Employees Receive Offensive, Adult-Oriented Messages via Corporate E-mail," *Business Wire* (March 22, 1999); see also "The Phantom Menace," *CFO Magazine for Senior Financial Executives* 15, no. 6 (June 1999): 89–90.

For more information on results of the inappropriate use of E-mail and the Internet at Dow Chemical Co., *New York Times*, Xerox, and other companies, see, for example, "Some Firms Are Now Using Computer Investigators to Uncover Employee Wrongdoing," *Los Angeles Times*, 29 October 2000, sec. 1A, p. 1; "Keeping a Virtual Eye on Employees," *Occupational Health and Safety* 69, no. 11 (November 2000): 24–28; "Expert Available to Discuss Workplace Privacy Issues and Solutions to Inappropriate Use of Business Computers," *Business Wire*, 1 November 2000; "Employee Internet Abuse Software Allows Companies to Capture Picture of Computer Screens," *Charleston Gazette*, 6 November 2000, sec. 1D. Note that the Dow firings came in two waves, so the individual stories understate the total number of employees fired as a result of inappropriate use of their office computers.

The story about the retirees losing their savings is based upon allegations made in a case that occurred in southern Illinois in the early and mid-1990s. These allegations were and are disputed, although the case did result in criminal convictions of bank officials. For more details on this and other cases of alleged bank securities fraud against unwary investors, see "Keep Your Cash Safe," *Money* (February 1991): 68.

The last story notes that almost 500,000 others were laid off or downsized during the year the subject lost his job. The published statistics on how many Americans have lost their jobs due to company downsizing or other reasons during the past ten years seem to vary somewhat from source to source. I relied upon the following. Congressional hearings in 1998 indicate that 473,000 lost their jobs in 1997 (when the related story occurred) and 434,000 lost their jobs in 1996. See "Prepared Testimony of John R. Reinert, D.M." before the Committee on the Judiciary of the United States Senate (Federal News Service, 25 February 1998). See also "Downsizing Fills up the Spoon-Fed Class," *Newsday*, 12 May 1996, p. A42, indicating that 600,000 lost their jobs in 1995. *U.S. News & World Report* indicates that the numbers were closer to 700,000 in 1998 and 1999. See "Charting Your Own Course," (November 6, 2000): 56.

For a professional physicist's (rather than a lawyer's) explanation of the disorderly direction of the universe, see Timothy Ferris, *The Whole Shebang* (Simon & Schuster, 1997), pp. 91–95.

Chapter 1

I conducted the survey of corporate employees, referred to in the early part of Chapter 1, during the course of my lawsuit-avoidance training programs in 2000. The audiences ranged from executives of individual corporations to trade groups to small-business owners. In general, I did not ask any individual audience more than three of the ten questions, so the figure of 99 percent of employees answering yes to at least one of the ten questions is a statistical extrapolation rather than an actual result. In addition, the questions relating to sexual conduct on the job and illegal activity on the job were worded such that I asked if respondents "knew of" anyone who had committed these acts rather than if they had committed these acts themselves. Attendees generally did not feel comfortable being asked whether they themselves had committed these acts because often supervisors were sitting next to subordinates and the supervisors potentially could see the answers being written down. When doing the statistical extrapolation, therefore, I assumed only 5 percent of employees would say yes to having committed these acts, even though much higher percentages of people acknowledged that they "know of" people who committed them.

The source for the statistic that 73 percent of "large companies" monitor the on-line activities of their employees comes from a survey cited in the article, "No Joking Matter to Employers," *Seattle Times*, 26 September 2000, p. E2. In addition, the American Society for Industrial Security states that 73 percent of employees say their employers have the right to monitor their on-line activities. See *Security Management* 44, no. 8 (August 1, 2000): 16. Other surveys, however, suggest that a lower, but nonetheless substantial, percentage of employers monitor the on-line activities of their employees, although these surveys cover the employer community as a whole rather than just large companies. For example, a different article in the *Seattle Times*, citing a survey it conducted with other organizations, indicates that "at least" 45 percent of employers monitor on-line communications or telephone calls. See "The Internet Effect," *Seattle Times*, 24 September 2000, p. A1; see also "Agency's Staff Cited for Abusing E-mail," *Florida Times-Union*, 30 April 2000, p. B3. A survey by the American Management Association concluded that 67.3 percent of all employers monitor one or more forms of their employees' electronic communications, with 38 percent monitoring telephone use, 54 percent monitoring Internet connections, and 27 percent monitoring E-mail. See "Keeping Watch," *Computer Reseller News*, 2 October 2000.

The statistic that the average Fortune 500 company has over four hundred lawsuits going on at any given time comes from my first book, *Protect Yourself from Business Lawsuits (and Lawyers Like Me)* (Scribner, 1998). The source for the lawsuit statistics in that book was the *Price Waterhouse Law Department Spending Survey* (1996). The information was reprinted with the permission of what was, at that time, Price Waterhouse LLP, Law Department Consulting Group, New York, New York.

For the full text of the Microsoft antitrust trial court decision referenced in this chapter, see *United States of America v. Microsoft Corporation*, 84 F. Supp. 2d 9 (D.D.C. 2000). For the appellate decision, see 253 F.3d 34 (D.C. Cir. 2001). For articles concerning the use of E-mail during that trial, including the E-mail cited in the book, see, for example, "Microsoft Adds Allies as Former Presidential Lawyers, Attorneys General," *Associated Press*, 31 January 2000; "The Eroded Self," *New York Times*, 30 April 2000, sec. 6, p. 46, col. 1; "E-mail:

The Smoking Gun of the Future," *The National Law Journal*, 11 December 2000, p. B9; "Prosecution Rests in the Microsoft Trial," *Ft. Worth Star-Telegram*, 14 January 1999, Business section, p. 3.

The source for the insensitive E-mail about "fat people" is *Vadino v. American Home Products Corp.*, as quoted in "Ex-Wyeth-Ayerst Official Admits Diet Drug Warning Was Inaccurate," *The Pharmaceutical Litigation Reporter* 15, no. 4 (September 1999): 13.

Results of studies on resume fraud may be found in "Background Checks Help Safeguard Companies," *Capital Times*, 9 October 1996, p. 1C; "On the Job: It's No Lie—Resume Padding Can Mean Lawsuits, Firings," *Nashville Banner*, 21 August 1996, p. D1, citing research by the Society of Human Resource Management; "Know the Risks of Resume Hype," *Kansas City Star*, 16 March 1997, p. D1, citing research by Goodrich & Sherwood Associates.

For some interesting reading on specific examples of high-profile resume fraud, including those cited in the book, see "Problem Pasts: Now There Are 2," *Chicago Tribune*, 10 May 1988, Business section, p. 3 (law firm fired much respected partner because he had never finished law school and never passed the bar exam); "Law Firm Partner Never Applied to Bar," *New York Times*, 11 January 1997, sec. 1, p. 29, col. 4 (partner did pass bar exam but never applied for a license); "3 Mayoral Candidates Swing Away," *Baltimore Sun*, 8 September 1999, tel. 1A (mayoral candidate lied about degree from Loyola College); "Jones Says He Opposes Half-Cent Increase in Sales Tax," *St. Louis Post-Dispatch*, 16 February 1989, p. 8A (mayoral candidate, eventually convicted of an unrelated felony, lied about having a college degree); "GOP Spending in 42nd District Topped $1.3 Million," *Los Angeles Times*, 24 July 1988, part 9, p. 1, col. 1 (congressional candidate lied about having a degree from Wayne State University); "DeKalb Attorney to Fill 16th Circuit Judgeship," *Chicago Tribune*, Metro section, p. 3 (circuit judge admitted he lied about receiving the Medal of Honor); "Man Who Claimed to Be War Hero Must Aid Veterans," *Atlanta Constitution*, 5 December 1996, p. 05D (retired truck driver prosecuted as a "Medal of Honor impostor"); "Brazen Sales Tactic Could Mean Prison for 'General'," *Orange County Register*, 23 September 1995, Metro section, p. B04 (man claimed to be an ex-army general and Medal of Honor winner in order to get a contract with Pepsico on behalf of his employer).

The sources for the statement that listening devices have been placed in commercial aircraft include, "Hotel Security and Other Travel Myths," *Industry Week*, (March 20, 1995): 57; "Don't Overlook Security . . ." *Vancouver Sun*, 29 October 1997, p. D2.

The sources for the statements on people's practices during meetings are a variety of published articles. See, for example, "The Juggling Act," from the *Training & Development* magazine of the American Society for Training and Development, 54, no. 9 (September 1, 2000): 67.

The figures comparing the percentage of Americans who fear giving speeches versus the percentage of Americans who fear death were taken from a Bruskin-Goldring Research poll, the results of which were published in the *Chicago Tribune*, 29 August 1999, Jobs section, p. 1, zone C. The Executive Speaker Co. makes the same comparison but cites different percentages, stating that 41 percent of Americans fear public speaking and only 19 percent fear death. See "Timing and Fear," *Executive Speaker* 20, no. 12 (December 1999): 3.

A recent, well-received book on overcoming the fear of public speaking is Janet E. Esposito's *In the Spotlight: Overcome Your Fear of Public Speaking and Performing* (Strong Books, 2000). See also Max D. Isaacson, *How to Conquer the Fear of Public Speaking and Other Coronary Threats* (Farnsworth Publishing Co., 1984).

The source of the statistics on unethical conduct at work is a survey of 2,390 people conducted by Global Consulting and KPMG, released publicly in June 2000. See "Work Dilemma—See No Evil or Speak No Evil," *Orlando Sentinel*, 14 June 2000, p. E4.

For more details on Andrew Carnegie and his business practices, see Joseph Frazier Wall's *Andrew Carnegie* (University of Pittsburgh Press, 1989).

The federal laws prohibiting insider trading referenced in this chapter are Section 10(b) of the Securities and Exchange Act of 1934, 15 U.S.C. Sec. 78j(b) and Rule 10b-5, 17 C.F.R. Sec. 240.10b-5; and Section 17(a) of the Securities Act of 1933, 15 U.S.C. Sec. 77q(a). See also the Insider Trading Sanctions Act of 1984, 15 U.S.C. Sec. 78(u)-1; as well as the Insider Trading and Securities Fraud Enforcement Act of 1998, 15 U.S.C. Sec. 78t-1.

The standard for when outsiders who receive inside information, known as "tippees," may become liable for insider trading is a complex one, defined by a series of federal court cases. The leading cases are *Dirks v. Securities Exchange Commission*, 463 U.S. 646, 103 S.Ct. 3255 (1983) and *Chiarella v. United States*, 445 U.S. 222, 100 S.Ct. 1108 (1980).

The source for my description of the facts of the insider-trading case involving an IBM secretary is "Tax Views: Insider Trading Law Suffers Severe Setbacks," *The Lawyers Weekly* 19, no. 14 (August 20, 1999).

For more information on the strategies for suppressing competition adopted by John D. Rockefeller, as referenced in this chapter, see Ron Chernow, *Titan: The Life of John D. Rockefeller, Sr.* (Vintage Books, 1999).

The full citations for the federal antitrust laws are the Sherman Antitrust Act, 15 U.S.C. Secs. 1, 2, 3 and the Clayton Act, 15 U.S.C. Sec. 14.

The results of the survey on theft of proprietary data conducted by the American Society for Industrial Security and PricewaterhouseCoopers were made public in the summer of 2000. See, for example, "Security Troubles Growing for High-Tech Companies," *Milwaukee Journal Sentinel*, 7 August 2000, p. 05D; "High-Tech World Is Rife with Low-Tech Spying," *Associated Press*, 1 July 2000.

The story of the Missouri lawyer who repeatedly billed thirty-one hours for individual days of work comes from "Aide Accuses Attorney for Overbilling State Fund," *St. Louis Post-Dispatch*, 7 April 1994, p. 10A. The defendant actually billed the client eighty hours for one day and thirty-one hours for each of five days. The story about the New York consulting firm that billed several companies full price for what was essentially the same diversity study was widely reported. For a good article on the subject, see "Consultant's Diversity Advice Was Anything but Diverse," *Tampa Tribune*, 23 March 1997, Business and Finance section, p. 3. For more information on the story about the attorney inflating expense accounts, see "Station Casinos Appeals Revocation of Missouri Gaming License," *Associated Press*, 6 October 2000.

For information concerning the ValuJet matter and the falsification of safety records generally, see "News Briefs," *Air Safety Week* 14, no. 49 (December 11, 2000).

The article to which I refer in my discussion of overorganizing your files is "Look No More . . .," *St. Louis Post-Dispatch*, 4 January 1999, Business Plus section, p. 10.

Chapter 2

The only state in the union that does not adopt the "employment-at-will" standard is Montana. The Montana Wrongful Discharge Act gives specified categories of employees in Montana additional rights if they are fired without good cause. For more details, see "WDA's Passage Means Death of Employment at Will," *Montana Employment Law Letter* 4, no. 6 (July 1999). In addition, statutes and court cases in California, Arizona, and a few other states have eroded the employment-at-will doctrine to some extent.

The statistics on workplace romance come from a survey of 1,118 employees conducted by Vault.com. and reprinted in "Cupid at the Water Cooler," *New York Times*, 6 February 2000, sec. 3, p. 11, col. 1. The statistics on sex at the office come from informal surveys I have done during my lawsuit-avoidance seminars. See the first note for Chapter 1.

Chapter 3

The figure that 90 percent of Americans hate their jobs is perhaps suspect, which is why I said "up to 90 percent." The statistic comes from an unattributed "business expert" in "Are You Suffering the Symptoms of Burnout?" *The Los Angeles Business Journal* 22, no. 34 (August 21, 2000): 46. Other sources, however, confirm this number, citing a 1995 study by Yankelovich Partners of Norwalk, Connecticut, which concluded that 87 percent of Americans hate their jobs. See, for example, "Many Giving Up High Incomes for Life in the Slow Lane," *Atlanta Journal and Constitution*, 6 November 1995, p. 11E. However, still other experts say the figure is much lower. See, for example, Barbara Bailey Reinhold, *Toxic Work* (Plume, 1997), which states that only 10 percent truly hate their jobs, although it also notes that most others experience extensive dissatisfaction. The Federal Bureau of Labor Statistics stated in 1994 that 30 percent of Americans hate their jobs. Your guess is as good as mine.

The statistics concerning the percentage of Americans who fear losing their jobs are somewhat more consistent than those concerning the percentage of Americans who hate their jobs. See "Fewer Money Worries," *American Demographics* (October 1997): 35 (30 percent fear losing their jobs); "As CEOs Get Rich, the Rest of Us Run in Place," *The Record*, 20 October 1997, p. A13 (citing a Harris Poll indicating that 22 percent fear losing their jobs within the next year); see also "A Pulse That Lingers," *New York Times*, 22 July 1997, sec. A, p. 1, col. 5 (citing studies from the mid-1990s indicating that 34 to 47 percent of Americans feared losing their jobs during key years of the economic boom). The figure cited in the book that 51 percent fear that they might be merged out of a job comes from "Money on Your Mind," *Journal of Commerce*, 27 October 1997, p. 4A.

The statistics concerning the failure rate of businesses come from "Thank Goodness the Dotcom Bubble Is Pricked," *The Evening Standard* (London), 4 April 2000, p. 13 (stating that 75–90 percent of Internet start-ups will fail or be acquired). The U.S. Commerce Department indicates that 80 percent of new businesses close in the first five years and 80 percent of the survivors close in the next five years. See *The Gazette*, 18 January 2000, Business Advisor column. For more detailed information state by state on business failures, see the *Statistical Abstract of the United States* published annually by the U.S. Department of Commerce and the Bureau of the Census, Washington, D.C.

The source for the number of jobs that workers will have during their careers is "Charting Your Own Course," *U.S. News & World Report*, November 6, 2000: 56 ("The average employee has 12 to 15 jobs over the course of a career," citing the Walker Information Global Network and the Hudson Institute, which covered workers both inside and outside the United States but focused on the United States); see also "Retention," *HR Focus*, (November 2000) p. 1, for a more detailed discussion of this study.

Chapter 4

For more information on the real pyramids mentioned in the introduction to this chapter, I recommend Moustafa Gadalla's *Pyramid Handbook* (Tehuti Research Foundation, 2000).

I cite the dipping of the typical American's savings rate to negative territory toward the end of 2000. This was reported, among many other places, in the *New York Times* in an editorial titled "The Recession We Need," 4 January 2001, sec. A, p. 27, col. 2. Figures on the Japanese savings rate vary, but all sources indicate a very high rate. See, for example, "Analysis: Japanese Government Flogs a Dead Horse," *United Press International*, 14 November 2000, citing a 13 percent savings rate among the Japanese. See also "Are the Risks of Foreign Investing Worth It?" *Santa Fe New Mexican*, 7 February 2000, Business section, p. A8, citing a 25 percent savings rate among the Japanese.

For stories about the effects of the Texas real estate crash referenced in this section of the book, see "Land Commissioner Says '80s' Real Estate Crash Ruined Finances," *Dallas Morning News*, 22 December 1992, p. 19B; "Real Estate Quarterly: Where Are They Now?" *Dallas Business Journal* 14, no. 43 (June 21, 1991): sec. 1, p. 15.

For information on the relationship among debt, divorce, and emotional and spiritual problems, see "Dealing with Financial Woes Brings Stress for Some Couples," *Arkansas Democrat-Gazette*, 3 January 2000, p. B3 ("Eighty percent of divorce records in the United States cite financial stress as a factor contributing to the break up"); "The Power of Prayer: Many Americans Seek Guidance in Financial Affairs," *Arizona Republic*, 3 August 1999, p. E1 ("about 70 percent of divorces are about money"). See also Teresa A. Sullivan, Elizabeth Warren, and Jay Lawrence Westbrook, *The Fragile Middle Class: Americans in Debt* (Yale University Press, 2000).

For detailed information on making sure you do not suffer financial problems as a result of the home-buying process, see Ilyce R. Glink, *100 Questions Every First-Time Home Buyer Should Ask* (Times Books, 2000).

With respect to learning the service history of a car you are considering buying, the websites I used for my research were cardetective.com and carfax.com.

The story about comparison food shopping related in this chapter comes from "Penny-Pincher Says: 'Be as Smart as the Stores Are,'" *Salt Lake Tribune*, 18 October 1998, p. E1. See also Jil Abegg, *Eat Well, Stay Well, Spend Less* (SunRise Publishing, 1998).

The statistic that generic drugs can be 30 to 55 percent cheaper than name brands comes from "Duke MD, Statistician Touts Name Brand Drugs," *Triangle Business Journal* 13, no. 12 (November 21, 1997), p. 3. See also "Merck Expands Generic Operation," *Associated Press*, 12 April 1993, stating that the Generic Drug Industry Association claims that generics are usually 30 to 40 percent cheaper than name brands but can be up to 80 percent cheaper. The difference in price between name-brand drugs and generic drugs tends to increase the longer a drug has been on the market.

My research revealed over three hundred news stories and articles about ways to reduce the costs of utilities and the percentage of cost savings you can expect to achieve by employing energy-saving devices and strategies in your home. Here are a couple of good examples, "Southface Energy Institute Executive Director Offers Energy-Saving Tips," *CNN Morning News*, 5 January 2001; "Blue Dot Experts Offer Cost-Cutting Tips to Stem Rise in Heating Bills," *Business Wire*, 2 January 2001.

The calculations concerning the costs of vices like cigarettes and alcohol are as follows. The yearly cost of cigarettes is $2,190 (two packs per day at $3 per pack for 365 days per year). Assuming the smoker started smoking at age seventeen and will retire at age sixty-five (if he or she lives that long), the period of expenditure is forty-eight years. Assuming the price of cigarettes remains constant and the smoker could have averaged a 9 percent annual return on that after-tax money in a Roth IRA (although by the standards in effect at the time I wrote this note, the limit would be $2,000 annually), the total amount available to the smoker at retirement if he or she had invested rather than smoked the money would be $1,498,574.10. The retirement cost of drinking alcohol assumes $3 per day average expenditure—a couple of beers per day or one bottle of wine at a restaurant per week ($21)—for a total alcohol expenditure of $1,095 per year. Using the same financial assumptions but starting at the drinking age of twenty-one instead of age seventeen, the total value of the account at retirement would be $527,266.24. The combined total for alcohol and cigarettes would, therefore, exceed $2 million for one person. Even assuming that the typical couple only cut alcohol consumption in half, if you add a spouse, add the interest a typical person pays on his or her $6,000 in credit-card debt, and assume gambling expenditures in the nature of half of alcohol expenditures, it follows conclusively that a typical smoking couple could easily accrue an additional $2 million, possibly much more, in retirement money if they cut down on their vices as recommended in this book.

The figure that the average American family carries $6,000 in credit-card debt is widely publicized in all forms of media. See, for example, "Saving Your Way into Debt," *New York Times*, 15 October 2000, sec. 6, p. 106, col. 1. But see "The Way We Spend Now," *New York Times*, 15 October 2000, sec. 6, p. 55, col. 1, with the same paper stating on the same day in a different article that the figure has gone up to $7,564.

The statement that the average American will spend $800 on Christmas presents comes from a Maritz Marketing Research survey, released in "No Joy in Retail-ville," *PR Newswire*, 21 November 2000, which states that the total is $830. Other sources cite a variety of different statistics, but they tend to average out at about $800. See, for example, "For Various Reasons, Some People Reduce or Eliminate Holiday Shopping," *The Register Guard*, 26 December 2000, citing a Deloitte & Touche survey stating that the average American spends $836. *USA Today*, 13 December 2000, p. 1A, reports a figure of $797. However, in "Keep the Receipt" (December 26, 2000: 95), *Time* magazine puts the number at $1,161. At the other end of the spectrum, CNN reported on November 23, 2000, that the average family spends only $500 on holiday gifts. See, "Holiday Cheer for Retailers," CNN Ahead of the Curve, November 23, 2000.

At the time I wrote this book, some of the best websites for getting good travel deals were sidestep.com, expedia.com, travelocity.com, priceline.com, and just about any airline website.

Chapter 5

The source for the statistic that 50 percent of Americans have brokerage accounts is CNBC Business Center, October 9, 2000.

With respect to my discussion of the efficient market, the leading book will always be Burton G. Malkiel's *A Random Walk Down Wall Street* (W.W. Norton, 1973; rev. 1999). The historical description and quotations come from several excellent, easy-to-understand articles about the efficient market: Warwick Lightfoot, "Investment: Playing Darts with Monkeys," *Sunday Business*, 9 July 2000; Stephen J. Brown, William N. Goetzmann, and Alok Kumar, "The Dow Theory," *Journal of Finance* 53, no. 4 (August 1998): 1311; Gary Taubes, "Wall Street Smarts," *Discover* 19, no. 10 (October 1998): 104; Dick Youngblood, "An Amusing Way to Pick Stocks . . .," *Star Tribune*, 21 January 1998, p. 2D. Many modern investment books discuss the efficient-market theory—some seeming to adopt it and others rejecting it. Compare, for example, John C. Bogle, *Winning the Loser's Game* (McGraw-Hill, 1998), which at pages 18–19 and 47–48 indicates a belief in the accuracy of the efficient-market theory, and John Merrill, *Outperforming the Market* (McGraw-Hill, 1998), which at pages 197–199 emphatically rejects the efficient-market theory.

For an excellent and amusing article about the *Wall Street Journal* and other "monkey" tests of the efficient market, see "How to Beat the Pros . . .," *National Post* (Canada), 1 September 2000, p. 78.

The results of the study by professors Terry Odean and Brad Barber, University of California, Davis, concerning the negative effects of frequent trading were published in numerous sources across the country, including, "The Mania of Momentum and the Cost of Trading," *New York Times*, 21 November 1999, sec. 3, p. 1, col. 1; "'Pretend' Investing Can Teach Bad Habits," *USA Today*, 1 August 2000, p. 3B; "Day Trading Is Harmful to Your Net Worth," *Kiplinger's Personal Finance Magazine* 53, no. 10 (October 1999): 36.

The discussion of the term *fee simple absolute* and the other interests in land that a person could have had in medieval England comes from my law school education. It is succinctly restated in *Blacks Law Dictionary*, 7th edition (West Publishing, 1999), pp. 630–631. *Blacks* states that fee simple absolute is "the broadest property interest allowed by law" and, citing Peter Butt's *Land Law*, 2nd. ed. (1988) at 35, further states, ". . . to a layman of the 14th century the term would have been perfectly intelligible, for it refers to the elementary social relationship of feudalism . . . the largest estate known to the law . . . and the most absolute in respect to the rights which it confers."

For an article about the dangers of cash management companies referred to in this chapter, see "Want to Shorten Mortgage Period? Try to do it yourself; beware of those lenders touting 'accelerated' payment plans. You already may have the option," *Orange County Register*, 15 October 2000, p. K04.

For stories that discuss the price of gold in the 1970s and 1980s, see "Etonian with Midas Touch," *Sunday Times*, 16 October 1994; "Gold Taking on New Luster in '90s," *Fresno Bee*, 2 July 1995, p. C2. For a recent book full of novel ideas on the investment opportunities in precious metals, see Philip Gotthelf, *The New Precious Metals Market: How the Changes in Fundamentals Are Creating Extraordinary Profit Opportunities* (McGraw-Hill, 1998).

Much of the information on economic history in this chapter comes from my personal knowledge and experience as a coin and paper money collector and a writer on subjects of numismatics and economic history. For good sources on the history of coinage and currency, see, for example, N. J. Stillman, *Coinage of the Greeks* (Obol Intl., 1975); David Vagl, *Coinage and History of the Roman Empire* (Fitzroy Dearborn, 2000); Eric P. Newman, *The Early Paper Money of America*, 4th ed. (Krause, 1997); A. Barton Hepburn, *History of the Currency of the United States*, (Augustus M. Kelley Publishers, 1970).

With respect to the discussion of John Law, I should note that others had used paper money before he came along, most notably the Chinese and the Swedes. However, it would be accurate to say that the Law notes represented the first attempt in a major Western economy to issue an extensive number of notes for circulation based upon the economic potential of a government. For more information about both the Law experiment and the South Sea Bubble, see "8 Fat Swine for a Tulip: A Brief History of Bursts," *International Herald Tribune*, 10 October 1998, p. 19; "The 10,000 Dow; Some Experts Warn Bubble Will Burst," *Atlanta Journal and Constitution*, 16 March 1999, p. 01E. There is also a book about John Law, which is out of print and which I was unable to obtain, *John Law: The Father of Paper Money*.

The United States went off of the gold standard for domestic transactions in 1933. It did not go off of the gold standard for international transactions until 1971. For a good article on the gold standard in the United States, see Paul Hallwood, Ronald McDonald, and Ian W. Marsh, "An Assessment of the Causes of the Abandonment of the Gold Standard by the U.S. in 1933," *Southern Economic Law Journal* 67, no. 2 (October 1, 2000), p. 448.

With respect to my discussion of the various forms of U.S. government securities, as well as other basic matters of financial literacy, I recommend, among the dozens of books out there, Andrew Tobias, *The Only Investment Guide You'll Ever Need* (Harcourt Brace, 1996; rev. 1999). The website I used for information on government securities, as well as the current level of the national debt, was the Bureau of the Public Debt online, publicdebt.treas.gov/bpd/bpdhome.htm.

For some rather alarming articles on the potential for default by issuers of municipal bonds, read any of the following: "Wall Street, California; Odd Lots; Contrary to Popular Wisdom, Muni Bonds Can Yield Pain . . .," *Los Angeles Times*, 3 February 1998, sec. D, p. 7; "Default from Grace," *Los Angeles Times*, 28 January 1997, sec. D, p. 8; "Bond Defaults Skyrocket in 1997," *California Public Finance* 7, no. 47 (December 8, 1997): p. 1; "When Government Fails: The Orange County Bankruptcy," *Public Budgeting and Finance* 19, no. 1 (spring 1999), p. 115–117.

I state in the section on corporate securities that many investors have been devastated when the companies in which they invested disclosed accounting errors or irregularities. 2000 was a banner year for such unfortunate incidents. Perhaps the most widely reported case was the Cedant securities fraud case, which began in 1998 as the result of the disclosure of accounting irregularities and which ended in the summer of 2000. That case resulted in a $2.8 billion settlement to investors and a payment of $335 million by the accounting firm that had failed to catch the problems. See "Cedant Lawyers Get $262 Million; $3.1 Billion Pact Sets Record for Securities Fraud," *The New York Law Journal*, (August 22, 2000): p. 1. For other examples of the devastation caused by accounting irregularities, see "Class Action Commenced Against Quintus Corporation . . .," *PR Newswire*, 15 December 2000; "Lernout & Hauspie Fights for Survival," *AP Online*, 1 December 2000; "Rent-Way Suspects Small Group of Employees Tampered with Their Books to Artificially Boost Earnings," *CNN Business Center*, 31 October 2000.

The statement that a money-market fund lost 40 percent of its value due to the fund manager's decision to invest in risky securities was relayed to me by an attendee at one of my risk-avoidance seminars in Washington State. I have no independent verification of this story other than the person who was embarrassed to admit it. I did find a story about a couple of investment managers at The Woodlands financial group who took their clients' funds, telling them that they would invest in money-market instruments but in fact invested the money in unstable foreign securities. See "Business News," *Associated Press*, 8 November 2000.

The information on annuities and variable annuities comes from the website Annuities Online (annuitiesonline.com), which contains information compiled by Lipper, Inc.

For a discussion of the litigation involving charitable annuities to the Lutheran Church, see "A Flock Divided: When a Church Made Some Bad Bets, Donors Say They Were Fleeced," *Wall Street Journal*, 21 November 2000, sec. A, p. 1, col. 1. The actual investment instrument in that case was called a "charitable remainder uni-trust" rather than a charitable gift annuity, but it functions essentially the same way, and the story strongly supports the basic premise that handing your money over to others to give you a variable rate of annual return is a risky proposition.

The information on allocating investments to obtain low cross-correlation comes from discussions with my partners at Bryan Cave LLP, as well as materials and information provided to me by H. Chandler Taylor of the Moneta Group, St. Louis, Missouri.

With respect to information concerning retirement savings, in addition to the general investing sources cited earlier, I found the MSN Money Central and E*Trade websites (moneycentral.msn.com and etrade.com) particularly useful. They have common questions and answers about retirement planning, including the issue of whether to use a Roth IRA or a traditional one, as well as helpful financial tables and links to yet other sites.

The dollar limits and restrictions on various tax-deferred retirement options are ever-changing and the reader should ensure that he or she has the right, current figures when making retirement savings decisions.

Chapter 6

For more on the pump-and-dump schemes in this chapter, see "S.E.C. Says Teenager Had After-School Hobby: Online Stock Fraud," *New York Times*, 21 September 2000, sec. A, p. 1, col. 2; "Minor Achievement; Adults Manipulate the Market, So It's No Surprise That Teens Would, Too," *Washington Post*, 1 October 2000, p. B02; see also *Investor's Business Daily*, 2 January 2001, sec. A, p. 2 (discussing the Emulex scheme).

The federal government has now stepped in to try to reduce identity hijacking. It has established a toll-free number, 1-877-ID-THEFT; it has a website with valuable information for consumers on identity hijacking, consumer.gov./idtheft; and it has a booklet for victims titled *ID Theft: When Bad Things Happen to Your Good Name*, available from the Federal Trade Commission, Washington, D.C. The statistics contained in the book concerning identity hijackers comes from the statement to Congress of Jodie Bernstein, Director, Bureau of Consumer Protection, Federal Trade Commission, July 12, 2000, reprinted by the Federal News Service.

For more information on predatory home loan practices, see "Room at the Bottom," *Community Banker* 9, no. 7 (July 1, 2000): p. 20.

For further discussion of the investment scam involving various movie stars referenced in this chapter, see "Canned Scam," *People* magazine, (November 20, 2000): p. 173. The scam involving the husband of a congresswoman was widely reported across the country. See, for example, "Nation Briefs," *Chicago Sun Times*, 8 November 1996, p. 26. For an interesting story on the mining scam that ensnared National Hockey League players and executives, see "Fool's Gold . . ." *Calgary Herald*, 23 May 1997, p. C2.

Chapter 7

The information on the solvency of insurance companies—and a good site to research as you investigate potential insurers—is from insure.com, which publishes a wide variety of information on the solvency and reputations of insurance companies, including up-to-date information from Standard & Poors rating service. See, for example, "Insolvency Graveyard: The Insurance Companies That Didn't Make It in 1999," by Mark Cybulski of insure.com.

Undoubtedly, the best source of information concerning natural disasters and how you can prepare for them is the website for the American Red Cross. See redcross.org/disaster/safety/index.html. The site covers earthquakes, fires, tornadoes, floods, and just about any other disaster that can hit you. I highly recommend that you spend a couple of hours perusing this excellent site.

I obtained my information on flood insurance backed by the National Flood Insurance Program from a website sponsored jointly by the AARP and The Hartford Insurance Company, floodcoverage.com/.

The story of the man in Laguna, California, who built his home to withstand wildfires and whose home was therefore the only one standing after a wildfire in the early 1990s, was related by Michael Armstrong in his testimony before the Senate Committee on the Environment and Public Works on June 4, 1997.

As with most statistics, the figures for how many fires occur in the United States, the number of deaths, and the amount of property damage vary from source to source. I have put in the numbers that appear to be most reliable based upon extensive research. The best information comes from the National Fire Protection Association (nfpa.org/) and the U.S. Fire Administration (usfa.fema.gov/). See also, for example, "Gateway Health Plan Introduces Prevention Program to Reduce Fires, Burns and Scalds, *PR Newswire*, October 24, 2000 (citing officials at the Gateway Health Plan for the proposition that fires kill 4,000 and injure 20,000 each year in the United States); "Is Your Home a Fireplace?" *Pittsburgh Post-Gazette*, 11 September 1994, p. W7, (quoting the National Fire Protection Association as stating that 3,720 people died of residential fires in the previous year); "Fire Safety," *Take It Personally*, CNNfn, 17 March 1999 (citing the National Fire Protection Association as saying that 4,000 people die annually, with smoking as the leading cause). The figures that over 80 percent of deaths due to fire occur in the home and that direct property loss is over $9 billion are also widely reported. See, for example, "Keep a Cool Head to Escape Home Fires," *Milwaukee Journal Sentinel*, 7 January 2001, p. 07F; "Fire Drill," *Chicago Tribune*, 5 January 2001, p. 15, zone C. See also "The Importance of a Fire Escape Plan," *Associated Press*, 25 December 2000; "Fire Danger in Home Increases in Winter," *Times-Picayune*, 15 October 2000, River Parishes section, p. 1 (citing statistics from the U.S. Fire Administration). Finally, the U.S. Fire Administration also provides information on the causes of home fires. See, for example, "Furnace Explosion," *Des Moines Register*, 8 October 2000, Metro Iowa section, p. 2.

The figure of 400,000 robberies in the United States with property loss in excess of $400 million was reported in "Crime Rises in Houston Despite National Decline," *Houston Chronicle*, 16 October 2000, sec. A, p. 1.

In addition to calling local police departments for tips on crime prevention, several police departments have good websites that provide such information. While researching this book, I consulted, for example, the San Antonio Police Crime Prevention Services, ci.sat.tx.us/sapd/CRIME.HTM.

The figure that up to 4,000 people die each year from carbon monoxide poisoning was reported in "Keeping Deadly Gas out of Home," *New York Times*, 21 May 2000, sec. 11, p. 5, col. 1. Others cite a lower number. See, for the low-end statistic, "Keeping Them Healthy," *Redbook* 194, no. 2 (February 1, 2000): 138, stating that 500 to 600 die each year in the United States from carbon monoxide poisoning. For two good articles on the subject, see "Carbon-Monoxide Poisoning Can Be Avoided," January 2000, published by the U.S. Department of the Army and available through the Federal Document Clearinghouse, Inc., and Joseph Varon, M.D., and Paul E. Marik, "Carbon Monoxide Poisoning," *The Internet Journal of Emergency & Intensive Care Medicine*, ISSN 1092-4051, updated July 10, 1997, ispub.com/journals/IJEICM/Vvol1N2/CO.htm.

For my discussion of radon gas, asbestos, and other environmental hazards in the home, I consulted numerous sources but found the following two to be the most helpful: "A Home Buyer's Guide to Environmental Hazard," *The Consumer Law Page*, published by Alexander, Hawes & Audet, LLP, consumerlawpage.com/brochure/home-haz.shtml; and "Radon: You Can't Ignore the Facts," posted by National Safety Products, Inc., testproducts.com/radon1.html.

Because the numerous facts and figures about the human body quoted in this chapter are merely for introductory purposes, I simply accepted the numbers stated in various popular news stories published around the country, and I did not consult technical medical journals. The numbers that are cited in the book have been widely reported in dozens of articles in the popular press and are available for review on request.

For basic information on insurance policies, I consulted MSN Money Central, moneycentral.msn.com/insure/home.asp?redir=1. I would also like to thank Mr. Steven Wood of State Farm Insurance, St. Louis, Missouri, for the information he provided me concerning the various forms of insurance policies. The reader should not construe his support as either an endorsement or a rejection of my analysis of which policies are best for crashproofers.

The statistics on health insurance company failures come from "Is Your Health Insurance Secure?" *St. Louis Post-Dispatch*, 28 August 2000, BP7, citing a national study.

My source for the discussion of the percentage of Americans with life insurance as opposed to the percentage with disability insurance comes from "In Case of Illness . . ." *Wall Street Journal Sunday*, reprinted in *St. Louis Post-Dispatch*, 8 October 2000, p. E5.

The full citation for the Employee Retirement Income Security Act (ERISA) is 29 U.S.C. Sec. 1001 *et seq.*

Chapter 8

For information concerning the relationship between finances and divorce, see the fourth note for Chapter 4, *infra*.

My sources for the discussion of the various types of property ownership are my legal education in property law, discussions with my partners at Bryan Cave LLP, and a very straightforward article in *Forbes* magazine titled "When Should a Couple Hold Property in Joint Names, and When Not?" (June 14, 1999): p. 260.

The statistic that 70 percent of Americans die without a will comes from Brian H. Breuel, *Staying Wealthy: Strategies for Protecting Your Assets* (Bloomberg Press, 1998). See also "Lawyers on Disk: Consumers Can Draft Legal Documents with New Software," *ABA Journal*, 76 A.B.A.J., 18, July 1990 (also citing the 70 percent figure); "Who Needs a Will? Just About Everyone," *New York Times*, 1 May 1993, sec. 1, p. 37, col. 3 (citing 60 percent as the figure).

For details on the story in this chapter about the wife and mother who battled over whether to remove a man from life support, see "Man on Life Support Received Care Until Death, Lawyer Says," *St. Louis Post-Dispatch*, 12 October 2000, p. B1. For a virtually identical case, see "Family Fights Life or Death Battle over Accident Victim's Fate . . .," *Ottowa Citizen*, 5 January 2001, p. A7.

Information on the various estate-planning mechanisms such as revocable living trusts, durable powers of attorney, and so on comes from my partners at Bryan Cave LLP. There are also several good websites on these topics. I found, for example, the Deloitte & Touche estate-planning website, dtonline.com/estate/cover.htm, to be very readable and informative.

Chapter 9

The estimate of the cost of raising a child to age seventeen comes from a Consumer Expenditure Survey conducted by the U.S. Department of Labor from 1990 to 1992, which MSN Money Central then revised to reflect 1998 dollars. The table appeared at moneycentral.msn.com/articles/family/kids/tlkidscost.asp. A Canadian survey comes up with similar statistics. See ccsd.ca/factsheets/fsrzch98.htm.

The estimate of the cost of sending a child born today to college comes from numerous sources, including, "Clinton Again Warns Senate Not to Pass GOP Tax Cut Plan," *The White House Bulletin*, 29 July 1999; "College Savings Accounts Offer New Options, *The Arizona Republic*, 21 March 1999, p. AZ6, (citing $100,000 for state schools and $400,000 for private schools for a child born in 1998).

The information on state college tuition-savings programs comes from "A Crash Course on Saving for College," *Wall Street Journal Sunday*, as reprinted in the *St. Louis Post-Dispatch*, 12 March 2000, p. E4. At the time I wrote this book, the website savingforcollege.com/ provided excellent information about Section 529 plans and links to each state's web page on the subject, and another good website on grants and scholarships was About.com.

The statistics for average life expectancy are widely publicized. See, for example, the previously cited *The Statistical Abstract of the United States*.

The source for the statistic that children spend $2 billion per day caring for aging parents is "The Challenge of Caring; Boomers Divide Lives Between Kids, Parents," *The Daily News of Los Angeles*, 12 March 2000, p. N1.

My sources for information on long-term care insurance included the Long Term Care Insurance National Advisory Council, longtermcareinsurance.org, and an article titled "Avoiding Fraud When Buying Long-Term Care Insurance," Richard Alexander, editor, consumerlawpage.com/article/insure.shtml.

A good source for information concerning reverse mortgages is the American Association of Retired Persons, Home Equity Information Center, aarp.org/hecc/basicfct.html.

Recommended Reading

The following is a list, by chapter, of reading I recommend for those who want to take the crashproofing process one step further. In a few cases, the authors of the cited books express philosophies that are somewhat different from those recommended in *Crashproof Your Life*, but I believe that learning multiple perspectives on the economic choices confronting you is always a good idea.

Chapter One

Doyle, Michael, and David Straus. How to Make Meetings Work (Berkley Publishing Group, 1993).

Eisenberg, Ronni, and Kate Kelly. Organize Your Office! Simple Routines for Managing Your Workspace (Hyperion, 1999).

Esposito, Janet E. In the Spotlight: Overcome Your Fear of Public Speaking and Performing (Strong Books, 2000).

Isaacson, Max D. How to Conquer the Fear of Public Speaking and Other Coronary Threats (Farnsworth Publishing Co., 1984).

LeBon, Paul, and Sara Karam. Escape from Voicemail Hell/Boost Your Productivity by Making Voicemail Work for You (ParLeau Publishing, 1999).

Nolan, John A., III. Confidential: Uncover Your Competition's Top Business Secrets Legally and Quickly—and Protect Your Own (HarperBusiness, 1999).

Parr, Russell L. Intellectual Property Infringement Damages: A Litigation Support Handbook (John Wiley & Sons, 1999).

Rosenberg, Arthur D. The Resume Handbook: How to Write Outstanding Resumes and Cover Letters for Every Situation (Adams Media Corporation, 1996).

Schweich, Thomas. Protect Yourself from Business Lawsuits: An Employee's Guide to Avoiding Workplace Liability (Fireside, 2000).

Shertzer, Margaret D. The Elements of Business Grammar (Pearson Higher Education, 1996).

Strunk, William, Jr., E. B. White, Charles Osgood, and Roger Angel. Elements of Style. 4th ed. (Allyn & Bacon, 2000).

Walters, Stan B. The Truth About Lying: How to Spot a Lie and Protect Yourself from Deception (Sourcebooks Trade, 2000).

Whitcomb, Susan Britton. Resume Magic (Jist Works, 1998).

Chapter Two

Agonito, Rosmary. *Dirty Little Secrets: Sex in the Workplace* (New Futures Publications, 2000).

Petrocelli, William, and Barbara Kate Repa. *Sexual Harassment on the Job: What It Is and How to Stop It* (Nolo Press, 1998).

Webb, Susan L. *Sexual Harassment, Shades of Gray: Guidelines for Managers, Supervisors & Employees* (Pacific Resource Development Group, 1999).

Chapter Three

Bowlby, Brenda, Paul Jarvis, and Ellen E. Mole. *Employment Contracts: An Employers Guide* (Butterworth Pub. Ltd., 1991).

Edwards, Paul, and Sara Edwards. *Finding Your Perfect Work: The New Career Guide to Making a Living, Creating a Life* (J. P. Tarcher, 1996).

Fein, Richard. *101 Dynamite Questions to Ask at Your Job Interview* (Impact, 1996).

Chapter Four

Abegg, Jil. *Eat Well, Stay Well, Spend Less* (Sunrise Publishing, 1998).

Consumer Reports Used Car Buying Guide (Consumer Reports Books, 2001).

Dayton, Howard L. *Getting Out of Debt* (Tyndale House, 1986).

Glink, Ilyce R. *100 Questions Every First-Time Home Buyer Should Ask* (Times Books, 2000).

Leon, Burke, and Stephanie Leon. *The Insider's Guide to Buying a New or Used Car* (Betterway, 1997).

Marquis, Derek A., and Calvin Grondahl. *Till Debt Due Us Part* (D.C. Publishers, 1993).

Sullivan, Teresa A., Elizabeth Warren, and Jay Lawrence Westbrook. *The Fragile Middle Class: Americans in Debt* (Yale University Press, 2000).

Sutton, Remar. *Don't Get Taken Every Time: The Insider's Guide to Buying or Leasing Your Next Car or Truck* (Penguin USA, 1997).

Chapter Five

Bogle, John C. *Winning the Loser's Game* (McGraw-Hill, 1998).

Gotthelf, Philip. *The New Precious Metals Market: How the Changes in Fundamentals Are Creating Extraordinary Profit Opportunities* (McGraw-Hill, 1998).

Hepburn, A. Barton. *History of the Currency of the United States* (Augustus M. Kelley Publishers, 1970).

Malkiel, Burton Gordon. *A Random Walk Down Wall Street.* 7th ed. (W.W. Norton & Co., 2000).

Merrill, John. *Outperforming the Market* (McGraw Hill, 1998).

Morris, Kenneth, Virginia B. Morris, and Alan M. Siegel. *The Wall Street Journal Guide to Understanding Money & Investing* (Fireside, 1999).

Newman, Eric P. *The Early Paper Money of America* (Krause, 1997).

Strauss, Spencer, and Martin J. Stone. *The Unofficial Guide to Real Estate Investing* (Hungry Minds, 1999). (Author's note: While this book has a lot of valuable information about real estate investing, it advocates practices that are in some respects riskier than those advocated in this book.)

Tobias, Andrew. *The Only Investment Guide You'll Ever Need* (Harcourt Brace, 1999).

Chapter Six

ID Theft: When Bad Things Happen to Your Good Name. A booklet published by the Federal Trade Commission, Washington, D.C.

Chapter Seven

Scott, David L. *Guide to Buying Insurance* (Globe Pequot Press, 1994).

Silver Lake Editors. *How to Insure Your Home* (Silver Lake Publishing, 1996). (Author's note: The Silver Lake Editors have a series of books on purchasing insurance of all types.)

Chapter Eight

Bruel, Brian H. *Staying Wealthy: Strategies for Protecting Your Assets* (Bloomberg Press, 1998).

Clifford, Denis, and Cora Jordan. *Plan Your Estate: Absolutely Everything You Need to Know to Protect Your Loved Ones.* 5th ed. (Nolo Press, 2000).

Dublin, Arlene G. *Prenups for Lovers: A Romantic Guide to Prenuptial Agreements* (Villard Books, 2001).

Mercer, Diana, and Marsha Kline Pruett. *Your Divorce Advisor: A Lawyer and a Psychologist Guide You Through the Legal and Emotional Landscape of Divorce* (Fireside, 2001).

Reiser, David R. *Wealthbuilding: Investment Strategies for Retirement and Estate Planning* (John Wiley & Sons, 2000).

Chapter Nine

Abromovitz, Les. *Long Term Care Insurance Made Simple* (Health Information Press, 1999).

Martz, Geoff, and Kalman A. Chany. *Paying for College Without Going Broke* (Princeton Review, 2000).

Scholen, Ken. *Reverse Mortgages for Beginners: A Consumer Guide to Every Home Owner's Retirement Nest Egg* (Nchec Press, 1998).

Index

U.S. savings bonds, 157
Untouchable savings account,
    134–37
Utilities, reducing number of,
    119–20, 276

Vacations, 129–30
ValuJet, 40, 274
Variable annuities, 164–66, 279
Violence, in E-mails, 11
Voice mails, 18–19
    privacy and, 6
Volume purchasing, 119

Wills, 234–36
    living trusts and, 238
    living wills, 236–37
    power of attorney and, 237
Workplace romances. *See* Attractions
Workplaces, emotion in, 15
Written communications. *See also*
    Oral communications

career crashes and, 7
checklist for, 92
E-mail, 7–14
letters, 15–17
resumes, 14–15
Wrongful acts, 27–29
    anticompetitive actions, 32
    antitrust conspiracies, 32–33
    bill padding, 36–37
    competitive bidding and,
        33–34
    dishonesty, 36
    falsifying records, 39–40
    inflating expenses, 38
    insider trading, 30–32
    lying about illness or lateness, 39
    misuse of Internet, 28–29
    misuse of software licenses,
        29–30
    reallocation of hours, 37–38
    theft, 28
    trade secrets and, 34–35